For my clients

Asian American Psychology and Psychotherapy

Intergenerational Trauma, Betrayal, and Liberation

Shin Shin Tang, PhD

ROWMAN & LITTLEFIELD
Lanham • Boulder • New York • London

Published by Rowman & Littlefield
An imprint of The Rowman & Littlefield Publishing Group, Inc.
4501 Forbes Boulevard, Suite 200, Lanham, Maryland 20706
www.rowman.com

86-90 Paul Street, London EC2A 4NE

British Library Cataloguing in Publication Information Available

Library of Congress Cataloging-in-Publication Data

Names: Tang, Shin Shin, 1970- author.
Title: Asian American psychology and psychotherapy : intergenerational trauma, betrayal, and liberation / Shin Shin Tang.
Description: Lanham : Rowman & Littlefield, [2024] | Includes bibliographical references and index. | Summary: "This book addresses the double-bind Asian diaspora in the West commonly find themselves in—that of having to cope with high rates of maltreatment within the family, as well as racism and other forms of discrimination from without"— Provided by publisher.
Identifiers: LCCN 2023011635 (print) | LCCN 2023011636 (ebook) | ISBN 9781538167205 (cloth) | ISBN 9781538167212 (paperback) | ISBN 9781538167229 (epub)
Subjects: LCSH: Asian Americans—Psychology. | Asian Americans—Mental health. | Asian Americans—Counseling of. | Decolonization.
Classification: LCC RC451.5.A75 T36 2024 (print) | LCC RC451.5.A75 (ebook) | DDC 362.2089/95073—dc23/eng/20230501
LC record available at https://lccn.loc.gov/2023011635
LC ebook record available at https://lccn.loc.gov/2023011636

PRAISE FOR *ASIAN AMERICAN PSYCHOLOGY AND PSYCHOTHERAPY: INTERGENERATIONAL TRAUMA, BETRAYAL, AND LIBERATION*

"This is a crucial book that teaches and guides us to appreciate the fullness, complexity, and nuance of Asian Americans' experiences from historical, intersectional, holistic, relational, and liberatory perspectives. Dr. Shin Shin Tang offers us a clear and critical analysis of the dominant psychotherapy paradigms while offering a new praxis to decolonize and humanize the therapy space for Asian American clients." —**Yunkyoung Garrison, PhD, licensed psychologist; former** *Asian American Psychologists* **newsletter editor**

"In *Asian American Psychology and Psychotherapy*, Dr. Shin Shin Tang provides a critical, compassionate, and unflinching view of Asian Americans as both diverse and complexly human. Alongside identifying various forms of betrayal, violence, and oppression, Dr. Tang shares tangible, trauma-informed, and culturally congruent information that clinicians, educators, students, researchers, and others can use to co-create liberation—both within and in solidarity with the Asian American community." —**Jennifer M. Gómez, assistant professor, Boston University; chair, Research Advisory Committee, Center for Institutional Courage; and author of** *The Cultural Betrayal of Black Women and Girls: A Black Feminist Approach to Healing from Sexual Abuse*

"Dr. Tang has written a courageous and insightful book that integrates a critical analysis of widely cited research findings, professional and personal experience, and nuanced self-reflection. I highly recommend this book to students in psychology, educators, clinicians, researchers, and anyone interested in learning more about therapy with Asian Americans, especially for those interested in social justice issues.

"This is not a manual book on providing therapy to a specific population—far from it. This is a book that contains both wisdom and compassion—one I wish had been available to me as an Asian American graduate student in Clinical Psychology so many years ago!

"No other book offers so much insight into how to provide culturally sensitive therapy to Asian American clients. This is a heartfelt, well-researched, and practical book for therapists and anyone who provides mental health care to Asian American clients." —**Jessica Murakami, PhD, clinical psychologist, Oregon State Hospital**

"This book takes a concise, specific dive into Asian culture as it relates to generational and historic trauma, recent hate crimes and violence, and culture betrayal trauma. As more Asian Americans seek support, current and aspiring therapists need to be up-to-date on the recent research on this topic and understand how current and past traumas can coincide and impact each person in a variety of ways. Expanding awareness on these subjects will largely contribute to improving best practices for treatment and support of communities in the Asian diaspora. Highly recommended for higher education students, anyone teaching multicultural diversity courses or trauma, and helping professionals." —**Kendra Simpson, Rio Salado College**

"Shin Shin Tang's work contributes to the current conversation by focusing on trauma in a population that is not often addressed in the trauma literature and on aspects of working therapeutically with Asian Americans that moves beyond exemplification (that is, model minority trope) and exotification. I really appreciate this approach to addressing trauma and recovery, as it steps away from prescriptivism and, while focused on Asian diaspora, places Asian diaspora in a cultural context. I also appreciate the use of trauma and crosscultural counseling theories as organizing framework. The addition of historical and contemporary stories, case examples, and clinical vignettes further anchors this work's place among key texts on Asian American psychology." —**Donna C. Owens, Lesley University**

"This book is a courageous gift to the profession of psychology. It is important not just for clinicians but for everyone, as it calls attention to deeply established and harmful methods of helping and carves a practical path toward more inclusive and compassionate practices. In each chapter, Dr. Tang brings a collective lens to trauma and psychotherapy, highlighting voices and viewpoints that have been obscured by the dominant cultural narrative. As she examines the psychology of Asian trauma, she beautifully weaves her personal experience as a Chinese American woman with solid scholarship and clinical insight. It is exquisitely written and comes directly from the heart, bringing us closer to a psychology of liberation."
—**Lori Allen, licensed psychologist; director, Oregon Mind Body Institute**

"Shin Shin Tang highlights the struggles encountered by Asians and Asian Americans seeking therapy in the United States, underscoring the need to decolonize Western psychology, particularly in light of the burgeoning contemporary awareness of the intersectionality of racism and intergenerational trauma that afflicts these groups. It is refreshing, and long overdue, to see emphasis placed on examining the historical and cultural contexts in trauma therapy and recovery. These contextual understandings are imperative in treating Asians and Asian Americans, especially given America's complicated imperial, colonial, and military-industrial relationships with Asian countries over the past two hundred years; these international relationships find their domestic mirror in America's long history of Orientalism and racialized Othering of Asian American communities." —**Jeannine Chandler, New York University**

"Seamlessly contemporary and historical, *Asian American Psychology and Psychotherapy* provides a sociocultural analysis of intergenerational trauma, racism, and the impact of abuse and adverse childhood experiences on Asian Americans. With guidance for practitioners and educators, the book includes paths to practical and urgently needed actions alongside relevant social scientific analysis. To understand the Asian diaspora and the experience of Asian Americans and Asian Canadians, read this book."
—**Sadie R. Pendaz-Foster, PhD, Inver Hills Community College**

"Informative, insightful, critical, and deeply personal. Shin Shin Tang masterfully integrates research and individual experiences to provide a broader perspective for those trying to navigate Asian American psychology and guidance for providers seeking to further integrate cultural understanding in their practices."
—**Jedidiah Chun, LMFT, co-founder, Asian Mental Health Collective**

Brief Contents

Contents

Acknowledgments

I feel a mixture of wonder and gratitude as I reflect on the many people who have played a role in bringing this book to fruition. Many I had never even met before, yet they graciously offered their time, advice, and, sometimes, their most personal stories.

The editorial team at Rowman & Littlefield, Mark Kerr, Courtney Packard, and Sarah Rinehart, embraced institutional courage in taking on this project since trauma within Asian American communities remains both a controversial and underrecognized topic. I also thank the production team for the dedication and care with which they handled the manuscript, including Jenna Dutton and Melissa Hayes. Additionally, many people kindly offered advice and encouragement for this first-time author, including Drs. Yolanda Tai Becker, Grace Bullock, Don Goldsmith, Rachel Goldsmith, Deb Merksin, Denichiro Otsuga, and Ken Pope. Dr. Claire Guidinger provided instrumental support in the form of literature reviews. Dr. Oksana Yakushko was an early supporter of my book proposal. She also shared valuable resources on epistemic violence and psychology's long involvement with eugenics, while Dr. Jennifer M. Gómez offered her seminal research on cultural betrayal trauma, all of which was vital to the content of this book.

I am also indebted to the following people who read chapter drafts and provided invaluable feedback, including Drs. Lori Allen, Pamela Birrell, Jennifer Freyd, Audrey Medina, Melissa Platt, Asha Stephen, and Robyn-Wong Lee, as well as to Antoinette MacMillen, who edited several chapters. My gratitude extends to the twenty-one peer reviewers, including those below, who took the time to share their expertise and provide detailed, constructive suggestions on the book's proposal, especially during the stressful time of the pandemic. I would like you to know that I incorporated nearly all of the advice you offered:

Jeannine Chandler, *New York University*
Loan Dao, *Saint Mary's College of California*
Suzanne Degges-White, *Northern Illinois University*
Lea Dougherty, *Marywood University*
Danielle Glassmeyer, *Bradley University*
Larry Hashima, *California State University Long Beach*
Lisa Kiang, *Wake Forest University*
Kathryn Newton, *Shippensburg University*
Donna C. Owens, *Lesley University*
Sadie Pendaz-Foster, *Inver Hills Community College*
Joanne Rondilla, *San Jose State University*
Kendra Simpson, *Rio Salado College*
Madhu Sinha, *Miami University, Hamilton*
Asha Stephen, private practice

I also thank the members of the Asian American Psychological Association. Research on Asian Americans can still be challenging to find, and many members responded to my queries by freely sharing their as-yet-unpublished work and pointing me toward additional resources.

I extend my deepest gratitude to those who courageously trusted me with their stories for this book: Misoo Bang, Kira Omans, KJ Roelke, Cam Lee Small, and others who wish to remain anonymous. I also offer sincere thanks to all of my clients, past and present, who have taught me the importance of naming oppression, bearing witness, and listening for what is unsaid. In particular, I thank those who granted permission to share some of our work together. Nearly four dozen Asian Americans and Canadians also contributed to this project by responding to a request on social media to share their experiences in therapy. Additionally, Moses Farrow provided education about the trauma of international and interracial adoption. Misoo Bang also granted permission to reproduce her captivating artwork both on the cover and within the book, and Drs. Jennifer M. Gómez and Sasha Shen Johfre granted permission to use their figure illustrating the mechanism of cultural betrayal trauma.

Personal support has been extremely important for even imagining that I could write a book, let alone finish one. First, my deepest *pranam*s to my guru, Sri Swamini Svatmavidyanandaji, who embodies the wisdom, compassion, and light that is Vedanta. Janani Chaitanya-ji and Arpan Gauchan-ji provided a steady supply of hot tea, biscuits, and excellent company for our work sessions. I also thank my friend and colleague, Dr. Lori Allen, for always being an enthusiastic supporter in life and in work. I am especially grateful to my husband, Ben, for believing in me and in this project, and for being there during the times when writing about Asian American trauma became emotionally difficult. Finally, I am grateful to my children, Nico and Mason, for their patience during this writing process, and for reminding Mima of the importance of having fun.

User's Guide: Please Read Before Continuing

I am indebted to one of the anonymous peer reviewers for the proposal of this book, who made the following request:

> Can the author consider writing a "User's Guide" that will ask all readers to reflect on their own social positionalities and how those outlooks (often associated with non-Asian / Asian American and non-person of color sensibilities and prejudices) can affect their grasp of Asian Diasporic / Asian American matters? This will be a call for self-reflexivity. It will also explicitly call out the tendencies of many non-Asian American readers to overgeneralize, essentialize, and trap all Asians into static, non-changing, incapable-of-change subjectivities.

In fact, multiple reviewers emphasized the need to address potential bias among the readership toward Asian Americans. The following Perceptions of Asian Americans Quiz is the result. In hopes of making the experience at least somewhat entertaining, I have included links to music videos and other websites in the answers to the quiz. I also encourage readers to take the Asian Implicit Association Test, which is offered online for free by Harvard University. This test can help identify subconscious bias toward Asian Americans: https://tinyurl.com/ImplicitBiasAsian

Finally, I urge readers to consider the trigger warnings and practice self-care while reading this book.

PERCEPTIONS OF ASIAN AMERICANS QUIZ*

1. Name a famous Asian American other than Jackie Chan or Bruce Lee.

_____

For questions 2 through 6, fill in the blanks as quickly as possible with the first things that come to mind.

2. Asian Americans are:

_____   _____   _____

3. Asian women are:

_____   _____   _____

4. Asian men are:

_____   _____   _____

5. When I think of Asian Americans, the image that comes to mind is:

_____

6. When I think of Asian Americans, I feel: _____

7. I get most of my perceptions or knowledge about Asian Americans from (choose top three):

   a. Family
   b. TV, music, or movies
   c. Social media
   d. Friends
   e. News
   f. Colleagues
   g. School

8. _____% of Asian Americans say they are discriminated against.

   a. 20%
   b. 40%
   c. 60
   d. 80%

_____

*Data for quiz answers are based on findings from the LAUNCH (2021) STAATUS Index report.

9. Asian Americans are overrepresented or fairly represented in senior positions within American companies, politics, media, etc.

   a. True
   b. False

10. The most common religion practiced among Asian Americans is:

    a. Buddhism
    b. Christianity
    c. Hinduism
    d. Islam

11. I'm familiar with food from Asian countries.

    a. Yes
    b. No

12. I'm familiar with music/art from Asian countries.

    a. Yes
    b. No

13. I'm familiar with customs from Asian countries.

    a. Yes
    b. No

14. Asian Americans are seen to be just as respected as White Americans.

    a. True
    b. False

15. Attacks against Asian Americans increased during the global pandemic.

    a. True
    b. False

Note to Instructors: You can use the Perceptions of Asian Americans Quiz as a classroom exercise to discuss bias toward Asians and Asian Americans. However, hearing some of these responses can be hurtful (though perhaps not surprising) for Asian American students, especially regarding questions 2 through 6. It may be helpful to create a plan to avoid exposing them to harm.

Answers and More Questions

Question 1: If you struggled with this first question, 62% of Americans could not name a prominent Asian American either. Here is a video from the Late Show with Stephen Colbert called "Here are Some Examples of Asian Americans!" that can help: https://tinyurl.com/SomeAsianAmericans

Questions 2–6: As you probably have guessed, these questions are meant to elicit stereotypes that many people hold of Asian Americans, such as being smart or intelligent, hardworking, kind, thoughtful, and quiet. Note that these are all consistent with the model minority myth that will be discussed extensively in chapter 1. In addition, Asian women have historically been objectified as hot or sexy, while also villainized by the trope of the devious "dragon lady." Asian men, on the other hand, are often viewed as effeminate or wimpy and bad at sports.

Question 7: There is no wrong answer to this question. Just notice what sources are informing your opinions and beliefs. Most people list TV/media in their top three. How representative are those sources? What kinds of stereotypes do they perpetuate? Are there any that are breaking the mold?

One common trope is of the submissive Asian woman paired with a White male savior in multiple forms of media. One example is Bon Jovi's music video for "This Ain't a Love Song": https://tinyurl.com/BonJoviLoveSong

Question 8: The answer is "d." The STAATUS Index report reveals that 80% of Asian Americans, 90% of Black Americans, and 73% of Hispanic/ Latinx Americans say they feel discriminated against in the United States.

Question 9: False. Asian Americans are severely underrepresented in senior positions in companies, media, and politics, holding only about 2.6% of leading positions despite comprising 6.8% of the population.

Question 10: Beliefs about Asian American religious practices are another area of stereotyping. Though 35% of Americans believe Buddhism is the most common religion practiced by Asian Americans, only 8% of Asian Americans identify as Buddhist. The most common religion among Asian Americans is Christianity (38%).

Questions 11–13: Most Americans (75%) say they are familiar with food from Asian countries, but significantly fewer are familiar with customs (44%) and music/arts (37%). Can you name any current Asian American musicians? Here are some recommendations to explore, spanning R&B to indie rock. https://www.teenvogue.com/story/asian-musicians

Question 14: White Americans are by far the most respected ethnic group, with nearly 75% of Americans overall saying White Americans are respected. By contrast, only 33% of Americans say Asian Americans are respected. Hispanic/Latinx Americans (26%) and Black Americans (24%) fare even worse.

Question 15: Despite the news coverage during the pandemic, 37% of White Americans remain unaware of increased racial attacks on Asian Americans. The level of awareness falls along party lines, with 46% of Republicans and 22% of Democrats reporting unawareness of increased anti-Asian racism.

TRIGGER WARNING AND SELF-CARE

I would be remiss if I did not include a trigger warning and advice for self-care in this User's Guide, considering that much of the content of this book addresses various forms of trauma.

If You Identify as Asian or Asian American

Parts of this book may be triggering, as it addresses topics such as racism, childhood abuse, neglect, and other forms of discrimination and violence that our communities have experienced. Therefore, I implore you to please be kind to yourself as you read. Both Asian and American cultures teach us to ignore our emotions and take pride in pushing through pain. However, what I have learned through personal experience is that while resilience is laudable, martyrdom is often dysfunctional. If you also identify as LGBTQIA+, disabled, Hindu, Muslim, or any other marginalized identity, I multiply this plea for self-care tenfold. You've been through enough not to have to push yourself into a state of overwhelm just to read a book. It does not matter if you are a student and a chapter or two from this book has been assigned as required reading. No assignment or grade is worth your mental health. I give you permission not to do the reading or to ask for an alternate assignment. You are worth it.

The same applies to Asian and Asian American faculty members, instructors, therapists, and anyone else who finds some of the information or stories overwhelming at times. Please allow yourself to take a break from it and regulate your nervous system before returning. (I find this music video from the Linda Lindas particularly cathartic: https://tinyurl.com/RacistSexistBoy).

SCAN ME

If You Identify as Other than Asian or Asian American

I urge you to also practice self-care while reading this book, especially if you are a survivor of abuse or other trauma. I also acknowledge that it may be difficult to see how this book relates to you or could benefit you. My hope is that this book can offer insights that directly relate to your life, as well as help you gain an understanding of Asian American cultures. This book differs from most other books on trauma in that it explains how betrayal trauma is particularly harmful. Betrayal trauma is something many people, regardless of ethnicity, have experienced. And if you are part of any marginalized group, you most likely have experienced cultural betrayal trauma in some form, which occurs when someone within your marginalized group causes you harm. Moreover, if you are a health-care professional, researcher, or instructor, the foundational knowledge in this book will increase your ability to work with Asian Americans effectively and will help prevent you from causing inadvertent harm.

Introduction:
A Battle on Two Fronts

THE FIRST FRONT: ANTI-ASIAN RACISM

August 23, 2022, was the kind of summer day that we Oregonians live for—sunny but not too hot, the sky a deep blue streaked with a few clouds. My then seven-year-old son and I were driving home from visiting my mother. I had just stopped at a traffic light when, from the corner of my eye, I saw a dark shape flying toward my car just before it connected with a loud thunk! My son exclaimed with some excitement, "Mommy, I think an apple fell on our car!" At the same time, a pickup truck squealed away around a corner. Puzzled, I looked up. Apple trees are common in Eugene, but there were no apple trees nearby. And an apple wouldn't have fallen sideways, would it? It seemed someone had thrown an apple-sized rock at us, I thought unemotionally.

Despite bracing myself for an event like this throughout the pandemic, it was not until we reached home and my husband angrily stated "That was a racist attack!" that I allowed myself to accept that this was true. I considered the possibility that I could have cut off the pickup on the road, but traffic had been light, and I was in no hurry. None of the other cars stopped around us were hit—just mine. I finally began to feel fear, and it chilled me to realize that someone had likely been driving around armed with a rock within reach, ready to throw. A new dent in the window frame brought home the threat of the situation, as I imagined what could have happened if the rock had gone through the window and hit my son, or if I had not just that day moved his booster seat to the other side of the car, or, God forbid, the perpetrator had fired something more lethal than a rock.

During the pandemic, the expression of anti-Asian racism skyrocketed, driving a steep rise in violent hate crimes, with nearly as many reported in the first quarter of 2021 as in all of 2020 (Levin, 2021). Additionally, between

March 2020 and March 2022, the advocacy group Stop Asian Hate logged 11,500 reports of anti-Asian racism in the United States (*Two years and thousands of voices*, 2022). Those who identify as Asian American and Pacific Islander (AAPI) women, girls, and nonbinary have been the most frequent targets (Pillai et al., 2021). And, despite entering a post-pandemic era, there is no sign of anti-Asian racism abating.

Anti-Asian racism is far from a new phenomenon. One of my first memories of being in first grade involved the ubiquitous chant "Chinese, Japanese, dirty knees . . ." I was excited to entertain my mother with this, one of the first songs I had learned from my friends. Mimicking what they had done, I tugged at the corners of my eyes so they looked like slits. But instead of laughing, my mother responded with a pained expression, her lips drawn taut as she shook her head. "No, that's not a good song," she said. I tried again, repeating the song in case she didn't understand it. She told me to stop but did not explain why, which left me confused and disappointed. In retrospect, I imagine she wanted to spare me the pain of confronting racism at such a young age.

THE SECOND FRONT: INTERGENERATIONAL TRAUMA

The second front of the battle for the majority of Asian Americans is pervasive intergenerational trauma. There is a widespread belief that trauma and mental health issues are low to nonexistent among Asians. The opposite could not be more true: The history of the Asian diaspora is steeped in trauma, including colonialism, oppression, war, and genocide. These collective traumas get passed down through generations within families in the form of domestic violence, addiction, child abuse, mental illness, and neglect.

Outwardly, my own family of origin appeared to be the perfect model minority, an immigrant success story. I did well in school, practiced the violin daily, and attended Chinese language school on Saturdays. But just as routine as school, music lessons, and homework was the perpetual emotional and physical abuse in our home. I also remember an instance of domestic violence occurring when I was about six, though it did not continue. However, as I tell my clients, even one time is enough to be traumatic.

Some of the abuse I experienced intersected with a high degree of pressure to excel academically. This academic pressure is typically born of a desperate quest for survival on the part of immigrant parents, who themselves experienced severe trauma and/or poverty. As sociologist Mimi Khúc (2021) once stated, "The cost of that survival is in the second generation." Khúc posited that even Asian Americans who did not experience childhood abuse as defined in traditionally Western terms still exhibit the effects of achievement pressure in a manner similar to post-traumatic stress. She described her Asian

American students hiding in closets and bathrooms with their laptops while they attended online classes during the pandemic. "I can't let my parents hear me taking this ethnic studies shit!" they would explain (Khúc, 2021).

Until recently, the two battles of racism and intergenerational trauma have been largely unacknowledged by psychology and by Western society in general. This misperception is a fallout of the model minority myth that paints all Asian Americans as successful, with problem-free lives. Neglect is often more painful than abuse, and is a form of discrimination that American culture visits upon Asian Americans as a whole. However, during the pandemic, anti-Asian racism has reached such a crisis point that it, at least, has finally received national attention.

In addition, a growing number of scholars are investigating the relationship between anti-Asian racism and post-traumatic stress among Asian Americans. Unfortunately, childhood abuse and neglect among Asian Americans remain under-investigated domains; the Centers for Disease Control and Prevention (CDC) has yet to publish a single study that includes data on adverse childhood experiences (ACEs) among Asian Americans, despite decades of research on this topic. Instead, Asian Americans are literally labeled "other" when acknowledged at all (e.g., Centers for Disease Control and Prevention, 2019).

ASIAN AMERICANS ARE NOT DOING OKAY

Shreya, an Indian American woman whose story appears in chapter 4, has trouble sleeping at night when her Asian friends travel because she worries they will be attacked. A study of 786 Filipino American and Korean American youth confirmed that discrimination significantly contributed to their increasing distress (Park et al., 2021). Anti-Asian racism is also impacting elders, as they have been among the most frequently targeted (Jeung et al., 2022). Filipina American Elvie Roman, 72, shared that she has anxiety whenever she leaves her home in New York City (Lucente Sterling, 2022). "I'm nervous because I'm old and, you know, I cannot fight because I don't know how to fight. . . . And especially when I go to the subway, I'm really nervous because sometimes you're looking for the police just in case something happened [and] no one [is] there." Researchers have found a linear relationship between racism and Asian American mental health; *each additional racist experience leads to a direct uptick in mental health symptoms* (Wu et al., 2021).

Immigration generation is another factor affecting how racism impacts mental health among Asian Americans. The sharp rise in anti-Asian racism at the outset of the pandemic corresponded with 67% of second-generation Asian Americans reporting symptoms of anxiety and depression (Wu et al., 2021). In contrast, first-generation Asian immigrants reported rates on par with Whites (54% and 53%, respectively). However, after six months, rates of depression and anxiety rose significantly among Asian immigrants, whereas rates among Whites fell significantly. Those of second-generation Asian Americans fell somewhat, but remained the highest of the three groups. As a result, the mental health gap between Whites and both generations of Asian Americans was much wider six months into the pandemic than at the beginning, driven partly by experiences of racism. Physical health is also negatively impacted by experiences of racism among Asian Americans (Lee & Waters, 2021; Litam & Oh, 2021).

Even prior to the pandemic, Asian Americans were reporting high rates of mental health symptoms. A meta-analysis of 58 studies by Kim et al. (2015) found that as many as 35.6% of Asian American adults reported symptoms of depression. As is commonly the case among Asian Americans, there was wide variability by ethnic group and special populations. Estimates of depression were significantly higher for caregivers, mothers, and lesbian, gay, and bisexual people. In addition, reported depression among Korean and Filipino Americans (33.3% and 34.4%, respectively) was twice as high as among Chinese Americans (15.7%). A separate study of Asian Indians aged 55 and older in Canada found similarly high rates of depressive symptoms, with one in five (21.4%) reporting at least a mild level of depression (Lai & Surood, 2008). Southeast Asian refugees, in particular, consistently report high rates of post-traumatic stress symptoms even decades after fleeing war and persecution, with 45 to 86% qualifying for a diagnosis of PTSD (Bang et al., 2023).

Furthermore, suicide disproportionately affects Asian American teens, with 11% having attempted suicide (Yuen, 2000) compared to 7% of teens in general (Cash & Bridge, 2009). Teen Asian American boys are 30 percent more likely to consider attempting suicide as compared to their non-Hispanic White male counterparts (Office of Minority Health, n.d.).

Compounding the toll of racism is a history of childhood abuse and neglect experienced by the vast majority of Asian Americans. Lee and Choi (2018) investigated the link between childhood maltreatment, perceived discrimination, and psychological distress among Asian American women. They found that those who experienced sexual abuse and were exposed to violence during childhood had a significantly greater likelihood of both depressive and anxiety disorders, while childhood physical abuse was significantly associated with a depressive disorder, but not an anxiety disorder. Importantly, perceived discrimination moderated the association between exposure to violence and an anxiety disorder. In other words, experiencing racism heightened the severity of sequelae from childhood trauma. In my own experience, childhood abuse conditioned me to dissociate whenever I experience danger. The confusion and numbness I felt when someone threw a rock at my car is an example. I needed to arrive home safely and have my partner name the racism for me in order to come back to myself and feel my emotions.

BARRIERS TO MENTAL HEALTH SERVICES

Despite high rates of trauma and emotional distress among Asian Americans, they are the least likely to use mental health services among all ethnic groups; Asian Americans are three times less likely to seek mental health services than Whites (Spencer et al., 2010). There are two main forms of barriers to Asian Americans seeking treatment. The first is systemic, a result of the failure of the mental health system to adequately address the needs of Asian Americans. The second is based on Asian cultural norms.

Systemic barriers include:

- Having health issues minimized or ignored by health-care providers
- Lack of language interpreters
- Racial discrimination by mental health providers
- Lack of provider cultural competence

Cultural barriers include:

- Mistrust of authorities due to histories of Western colonization, war, and racism
- Stigma around mental health issues
- Not wanting to bring shame on the family
- Therapy not being part of traditional Asian cultures
- (Lee et al., 2009; Spencer et al., 2010)

Both systemic and cultural barriers reinforce a code of silence adopted by many Asian American families. "Airing the dirty laundry" of the family is considered taboo, and breaking this silence can be seen as an enormous betrayal by family and community members.

The following is my own experience of the pressure to not disclose mental health issues or family violence.

(BREAKING THE) CODE OF SILENCE

At least a few relatives and family friends were aware of the abuse in my family of origin. I remember a loud argument one night between my father and Yeh Yeh, my grandfather, over this issue, but nothing changed. It was unthinkable for a Chinese American family member to call the police or Child Protective Services. The family code of silence became so second nature to me that it never even occurred to me to tell any of my friends. I learned to hold within me the silenced knowings of both racism and family violence.

Silenced knowings, as described by Lorenz and Watkins (2001), are "under-standings that we each carry that take refuge in silence, as it feels dangerous to speak them to ourselves and others" (p. 1).

The burden of carrying silenced knowings is a heavy one. By my junior year in college, I was driving recklessly, tailgating cars in a not-so-subconscious attempt to end my life. After graduation, I found a low-pressure clerical job, but often had to call in sick due to not being able to get out of bed. I had no concept of what depression was, so I had no understanding of what was wrong. Only at the unrelenting insistence of a close friend did I try to seek help.

My first experience with therapy was at a large medical clinic. In the wait-ing room, rows of black vinyl chairs were linked together, airport style. At the time, I worked at a small five-person nonprofit in Oakland's Chinatown called Asian Immigrant Women Advocates. We were in the midst of a social justice campaign on behalf of garment workers that included working nights and weekends, so we spent a great deal of time together. Coincidentally, one of my co-workers and her husband arrived in the same waiting room and sat in the row facing me. However, she did not make eye contact. I kept glanc-ing at her. Did she see me, I wondered? Did she recognize me? Should I say something, or respect her privacy? I ended up leaving when my name was called, neither of us having acknowledged the other's presence. We never spoke of the encounter at work, either. I understood that she had received the same message about maintaining a code of silence as I had. Violating the code meant inviting public shame or imposing that shame on someone else. Best to keep the shame private and save face for each other.

On the other hand, there is now a trend among young Asians and Asian Americans that they are increasingly willing to talk about mental health, as evidenced by the over 60,000 members of the Facebook group, Subtle Asian Mental Health. Dozens of daily posts in the group address intergenerational trauma, racism, and experiences in therapy. I am also seeing this trend among my clients. "So, when can I start talking about my trauma?" an Asian interna-tional student in her twenties recently asked in our first session.

WHY AIR THE DIRTY LAUNDRY?

This book takes a significant risk in its attention to intergenerational trauma and child abuse among Asian American families. First, tiger parents already dominate memes and stereotypes of Asian Americans, and it is far from my intention to reinforce this one-dimensional perception. A second concern is that people may blame Asian Americans for their trauma or pity Asian people as "broken," something I have witnessed in online forums. Finally, some might argue that talking about abuse within families will detract from the focus on current anti-racist efforts. But after much consideration, I have concluded that to be silent is to collude with the oppression of trauma survivors that occurs within Asian American communities. Without airing our dirty laundry, there is no possibility of collective healing. Asian American communities would remain fragmented, stuck in a false narrative of the model minority myth. As the late Jungian psychologist Marion Woodman observed,

> We must be willing to face many cruel truths: those we keep hidden from other people, and those we keep hidden from ourselves. . . . We have to be willing to suffer the loss of those things that have saved us in the past, but which have simultaneously stood in the way of our freedom. (Sieff, 2014, p. 82)

I hope that non-Asian readers of this book can refrain from blanket judgment and appreciate the diversity of various Asian and American cultures, the complex interaction of intergenerational and historical traumas that lead to family violence, and the uniqueness of each person.

My other motivation for writing this book is to further the cause of decolonizing Western psychology. This, too, is a risk, considering the dominance of the medical model and behaviorism in therapy—approaches that center an individual's dysfunction rather than their social and historical context. In doing so, they deny the racialized experiences of Asian Americans and other BIPOC (Black, Indigenous, and other people of color). While there are now many books on the psychology of trauma, I have never seen one that spoke to my specific experiences as an Asian American, let alone an Asian American woman. And yet, Asian American psychology is necessarily trauma psychology. Therapist and co-founder of the Asian Mental Health Collective, Jed Chun (n.d.), explains, "Trauma shouldn't be 'normal,' but for so many of us, it's our reality—and it is intrinsically tied to our identities as immigrants and/ or the children of immigrants."

I think of clients I have met over the course of decades, such as the Cambodian woman who survived being raped by the Khmer Rouge only to have her son killed by gang violence in San Diego. I think of the Indian American woman who was bullied at school and molested by a family friend. I think of the adoptee from China who was the least favorite child in her White family, and the gay Korean student whose parents do not understand why he refuses to get married. I hope this book can serve: 1) as a resource for therapists and researchers about the crisis of racial and intergenerational trauma among Asian Americans; 2) as an impetus and guide to evaluating how they might decolonize their research methodologies and clinical practices; and 3) as a mirror in which Asian Americans and others with oppressed identities can recognize themselves.

There remains an enormous need for culturally sensitive services for Asians and Asian Americans. Culture affects every aspect of how a person experiences trauma, from making sense of what happened and how they feel to how they cope and heal. Although I have been fortunate in my lifetime to receive care from several very gifted and skilled psychotherapists, I have also encountered limitations in their ability to understand the cultural dynamics of my family of origin, such as the need to save face. Nor did any of the therapists I have had ever ask about racism. I wrote this book to help therapists be better able to work with Asian Americans in a trauma-informed, culturally sensitive, and relational manner that honors their strengths.

TOWARD A LIBERATION PSYCHOLOGY OF ASIAN AMERICANS

What does it mean to decolonize psychology and move toward liberation? How do we understand trauma from a decolonized lens? Moreover, how is the decolonization of psychology relevant to the lived experiences of Asians and Asian Americans? These are some of the main questions addressed in this book.

Liberation psychology employs a tension between two forces wherein

> One motion is deconstructive and critical, looking backward at what we have been doing and thinking that is dysfunctional, dissociative, and destructive; the other motion is moving forward, toward new capacities for imagining, voicing, connecting, empathizing, and celebrating self and others in community. (Watkins & Shulman, 2008, pp. 43–44)

Both forces appear throughout the book in the form of suggestions for decolonizing psychology as well as for moving it toward social justice. This approach mirrors a pedagogical method from the Upanishads, spiritual texts that arose in South Asia nearly three thousand years ago, and which form a cornerstone of Hinduism. The Upanishads often begin with what is called *neti neti*, meaning "not this, not that." It is a systematic analysis of what the self is not, but is often mistaken for, such as various aspects of duality. Only after the duality is deconstructed is a vision of nonduality presented. Though the topic at hand is much humbler than spiritual enlightenment, crediting Indigenous wisdom as the original source of modern pedagogical methods is in keeping with the values of liberation psychology.

Liberation psychology was founded in the 1980s by Salvadoran psychologist and activist Ignacio Martín-Baró "as a reaction to dominant Eurocentric psychology's limitations to impart collectivistic, holistic orientations and social justice activism into psychological knowledge, research, and practice" (Torres Rivera and Comas-Diaz, 2020, p. 6). Liberation psychologies address the impact of oppression on oppressed peoples—including oppression by the field of psychology itself—with the aim of decolonizing dominant psychology's knowledge, research, and practice (Torres Rivera and Comas-Diaz, 2020). Therefore, a goal of this book is to critically examine current theory and practice in psychology that is rooted in colonial thought. Focusing on Asian Americans is particularly helpful in highlighting ways colonial thought has caused harm.

Martín-Baró (1996) identified three "urgent tasks" to move toward a Latin American liberation psychology, all of which are also applicable to Asian American psychology. These are recovering historical memory, de-ideologizing common sense and everyday experience, and utilizing the virtues of the people. Each of these tasks supports a process of *conscientization*, which refers to "the awakening of critical consciousness," joining the psychological dimension of personal consciousness with its critical dimension" (Martín-Baró, 1996, p. 18).

Recovering historical memory is necessary to recover collective traumas that were dismissed, suppressed, and/or rewritten in a manner that benefited the ruling power. De-ideologizing common sense and everyday experience refer to the need to "study and analyze the dominant messages in light of the experiences of those living on the margins" (Torres Rivera, 2020, p. 45). Psychology and psychiatry hold many assumptions that therapists take for granted, such as the medicalization of mental illness and the tenuousness of empirical support for therapies that are promoted as such (discussed in chapter 5).

Both recovering historical memory and de-ideologizing what is assumed to be common sense rely upon the virtues of the people. The collectivism of Asian American cultures promotes a sense of solidarity and altruistic willingness to help each other through what is currently an exceptionally difficult time. I wanted to center these virtues and simultaneously offer a rich diversity of voices, as I represent but one perspective as a straight, cis-gendered, second-generation, and (mostly) able-bodied Chinese woman who practices Hinduism. Liberation psychologies regard *testimonios* as vital sources of truth from those with marginalized and oppressed identities. My hope is that these testimonios will move and inform readers more than theory or data ever could. Therefore, this book contains three forms of sharing Asian American voices.

The first is in the form of individual stories based on interviews I conducted with Asian Americans who entrusted me with their personal stories. Some gave permission to share their full names, while others preferred anonymity for a variety of reasons. Those stories with altered names have a first name only. Regardless, they all took a risk in sharing their story with me, someone they had not met before, and even more, allowing me to tell it publicly. Each of them shared that their motivation for doing so was to help others.

Second, I have included case studies and examples that are composites of clients I have worked with for the past two decades. These cases do not represent any single person, and I have altered potentially identifying details.

Finally, I created an online survey asking Asian Americans to share anonymously about their experiences of therapy. These responses are included in chapter 6.

The first three chapters of this book argue for recognition of the various forms of historical and intergenerational trauma that many Asian Americans and their families have experienced. The anti-Asian racism of the pandemic is far from new. Centuries of European colonization in Asia set the stage for a similar treatment of Asian Americans when the United States was founded.

Chapter 1 critically examines the model minority myth and how it masks the diversity of Asian American lived experiences. The myth also belies a history of anti-Asian racism and America's own role as a colonizing power. This history necessitates an ecological conceptualization of trauma, which is introduced in chapter 2. Betrayal trauma theory is a means of understanding how relational trauma—including racial and intergenerational trauma—causes harm. It also explains that it is adaptive for a victim not to recognize being betrayed when they are dependent upon the perpetrator for their well-being. As with many racist experiences I have had, along with being abused as a child, the need to preserve vital relationships took precedence over feeling hurt or wronged. Cultural betrayal trauma theory in particular addresses the consequences when one member of a minority group is harmed by another group member. It also speaks to intersectional identities of marginalized members within Asian diaspora communities who identify as LGBTQIA+, female, and/or disabled.

Building upon cultural betrayal trauma theory, chapter 3 dispels the myth that child maltreatment is rare among Asian Americans. It provides a detailed review of extant research on adverse childhood experiences (ACEs). There is substantial overlap between ACEs and betrayal trauma, since many of the items refer to childhood abuse and neglect, which typically implicates caretakers. Unfortunately, rates of emotional, physical, and sexual abuse among Asian Americans are at least as high, if not higher, than the general US population. Multiple studies indicate that one in four Asian diaspora women and one in eight Asian diaspora men are sexually abused as children. A recent study found that in California, home to the largest proportion of Asian Americans, 12.5% of Asian and Pacific Islander children were the subjects of CPS reports by age 7 (Parrish et al., 2020). Therefore, the repeated narrative of Asian Americans as having low rates of childhood maltreatment is a form of epistemological violence.

As much as this book is about how betrayal trauma permeates Asian American lived experiences, it is also about healing from betrayal. The second half of this book critically examines the practice of psychotherapy, especially regarding trauma, and suggests ways to decolonize it using a liberatory framework. Only then can a therapist help a client increase their capacity to trust others. The process of decolonizing psychotherapy begins with the therapist developing increased self-awareness of their biases and internalized racism. It also requires making a conscious effort to understand the client's worldview. Chapter 4 presents a new instrument for self- and client assessment of trauma, the Rings of Betrayal Inventory, that helps with these efforts.

Next, chapter 5 addresses the need to dismantle the power-over model of therapy that idealizes the therapist as the expert. It provides case examples of the harm this model can cause when working with Asian Americans. This chapter also recommends using relational-cultural therapy (RCT), one of the only therapeutic approaches that directly tackles oppression in the therapeutic relationship and contextualizes the client's experience of trauma. This orientation is ideal for working with Asian Americans and other oppressed groups.

Few books that address therapy center the expertise of clients. I wanted to provide therapists with the rare opportunity to hear from Asian American clients directly and benefit from their wisdom. Therefore, chapter 6 is devoted to the input of dozens of Asian Americans who volunteered to share their positive and negative experiences of therapy and offer recommendations for working with Asian Americans.

Finally, no volume related to liberation psychology is complete without encouraging advocacy for social justice. Each chapter concludes with recommendations for moving psychology toward liberation. Additionally, chapter 7 is a call to psychology training programs to embrace institutional courage by decolonizing their curricula and to dismantle systemic racism against and sexual harassment of psychology graduate students.

The end of every chapter features actionable steps to decolonize psychology and advance it toward liberation and social justice. Additionally, quite a few instructors have requested video resources to accompany the book. In response, a variety of links to YouTube videos, films, websites, and documentaries supplement the material of each chapter. Almost all are accessible for free.

Trauma affects all aspects of one's life—much more than could be covered in one book. Nonetheless, I hope this volume can help start more conversations about working with Asian Americans in therapy. Although writing this book has required me to confront some painful truths about the deeply rooted anti-Asian racism in America, it has also given me a sense of purpose and hope. Amid a crisis, we can each make a small contribution toward making the world a better place to live. I honor the work of therapists and counselors everywhere who have been lifelines to their clients during the pandemic and beyond.

Chapter One

The Model Minority Myth and Anti-Asian Racism, Past and Present

Vishvam is a first-generation Indian American and disability activist. His 10-year-old daughter has muscular dystrophy and requires intensive medical care. Through his local gurudwara, he is working to change stereotypes of disability. He supplements his income as a music teacher by working nights as a taxi driver, where he is often the target of racism. Riders will sometimes refuse to get into Vishvam's taxi when they see him. Recently, a group of passengers demanded that he remove his turban and began kicking the back of his seat while he was driving. He is starting to have nightmares about driving the cab and has been more irritable with his family.

Laura is a high school senior in the Midwest. She was adopted from Korea when she was four years old by a White, heterosexual couple who divorced when she was eight. She is one of only two Asian students in her school. Laura does not identify as Korean American but also does not identify as White. She feels as though she doesn't belong anywhere. During the pandemic, she experienced racist bullying at school. Her parents tried to reassure her by telling her they do not see her as Asian, which made her feel angry and more confused.

Jordan identifies as nonbinary and multiracial. Their father is Black, and their mother is Indonesian. They have a few friends in the queer community, but all are White and have difficulty understanding why Jordan is still closeted from their family. Jordan's therapist is also encouraging them to come out and has made that one of the goals of therapy. Additionally, she wants Jordan to disclose being sexually abused by a relative. As a result, Jordan feels their therapist doesn't "get" them culturally, but is also afraid to discontinue therapy because they need help coping with the trauma of the abuse.

1

Charles is a fourth-generation Filipino American. He and his wife own a hotel, where business was heavily impacted by the COVID-19 pandemic. They also experienced increased racism from hotel guests. Although the business is now recovering, the racism continues. Charles feels depressed and burned out, and has been avoiding going to work. He and his wife are active members of the Catholic Church and have been praying for Charles to feel better, but they feel ashamed of sharing about his depression with their friends.

Minh is the daughter of Vietnamese immigrants. Her parents moved into her home a year ago, as they could no longer safely live alone. She and her husband, who have three young children, have been arguing more often since then. He would prefer that her parents move into a care facility. Minh feels he does not understand her cultural values of caring for her parents in their home, because he is White. In addition, living with her parents is reactivating traumatic memories of childhood abuse and making her feel more distant from her own children. She is also experiencing racial microaggressions at work, where she feels she is judged more harshly than her colleagues.

Jeong Hoon just moved to Madison, Wisconsin, from Seoul, Korea, to attend college. He feels isolated and self-conscious about speaking English, especially after someone made fun of his accent when he was ordering food over the phone. He also broke up with his boyfriend just before moving to the United States, which compounds his loneliness. Jeong Hoon does not feel he fits in with the local gay community, where he has experienced being fetishized and sometimes avoided altogether in clubs.

Xiao Mei, an undocumented immigrant, lives with her sister's family. She cares for her sister's two young children during the day in exchange for room and board and works at a Chinese restaurant at night, where she is owed two months in back wages by her employer. In therapy, she disclosed that her sister is physically abusive toward her, and that she is only allowed to leave their home to go to work. Otherwise, she is cooking, cleaning, and providing child care. Xiao Mei does not speak English and has nowhere else to go. She feels trapped and hopeless and has been having thoughts of suicide.

These vignettes are an amalgam of true stories from the news and Asian and Asian American clients I have worked with for the past two decades. Seven vignettes can seem like a lot to digest at once. I initially began with four, but the vast diversity under the umbrella term "Asian American" required more. Even seven vignettes seemed too few to me, which is why you will find many more stories in the form of testimonios and case examples throughout this book. In addition to demonstrating the diversity of Asian Americans, I also wanted to share a common theme—how the collective trauma of racism intersects with intergenerational trauma and multiple oppressed identities to create complex lived experiences.

It may be helpful to pause and notice any thoughts or emotions reading the vignettes has evoked. Perhaps there is surprise at the diversity of experiences and identities or the various forms of trauma that Asian Americans can experience. You may even register disbelief, which is understandable, considering how Asian American experiences have historically been erased from the headlines. Reactions I have also encountered commonly include dismissal or disinterest, one of the most painful responses one can receive, since we are hard-wired to be social beings. As journalist Charles Blow (2012) has written, *"One doesn't have to operate with great malice to do great harm. The absence of empathy and understanding are sufficient."* On the other hand, there may be a sense of recognition if you identify with elements of these stories, whether you are Asian American or not, leading to a range of emotions such as sadness, anger, or hopelessness.

According to liberation psychology, it is necessary to "name the losses—psychological, interpersonal, symbolic, economic, and environmental—that whole communities have suffered due to colonialism and its present incarnation as neoliberal policy" (Watkins & Shulman, 2008, p. 29). In doing so, communities can reshape the dominant narrative. Thus, this first chapter addresses the erasure of the lived experiences of Asian Americans, including historical trauma, in the wake of the model minority myth, which characterizes all Asian Americans as high-achieving, hardworking, and having strong family values. Its effect, as with any racial stereotype, is one of erasure. It is the erasure of diverse identities and experiences, of a history of colonization and colonial trauma, of other collective historical traumas, and of systemic racism in the government, in workplaces, educational arenas, religious institutions, and throughout American culture. As actor Steven Yeun once quipped, "Sometimes I wonder if the Asian American experience is what it's like when you're thinking about everyone else, but nobody else is thinking about you" (Kang, 2021).

Numerous scholars have argued that the model minority myth is in actuality a pernicious lie that seemingly praises Asian Americans while serving as a tool of oppression (e.g., Chang, 2011; Uyematsu, 1971; Yi & Museus, 2015; Yi et al., 2020). Other familiar racist tropes of Asian Americans include being viewed as a perpetual foreigner, and as sneaky or conniving. Asian women are hypersexualized, while men are stereotyped as undesirable nerds or buffoons. The model minority lie acts like a magical cloak of invisibility, dismissing the harm of all other racist stereotypes.

The myth/lie has become such a dominant narrative that it has pervaded psychology and psychotherapy. There is a pervasive belief that trauma and mental health issues among Asian Americans are extremely low to nonexistent. Even when trauma is acknowledged, it is often dismissed as irrelevant. Therefore, decolonizing psychology's relationship to Asian Americans begins with researchers and clinicians exploring how the pervasive model minority myth has influenced their perceptions of Asian Americans. This includes recognizing the vast diversity of ethnic groups encompassed by the umbrella term "Asian American," as well as the long history of racism and racialized violence toward Asian Americans in the United States.

THE COLLECTIVE LIE

Referring to his home country of El Salvador, Martín-Baró (1996) wrote, "The established power structure has concealed reality and systematically distorted events, producing a Collective Lie" (p. 188). In the United States, the model minority myth arose in the 1960s as a collective lie that characterized Asian Americans as exemplary citizens among people of color in the United States. Since then, it has been used to drive a wedge between Asian and Black communities, spreading the false belief that racial discrimination can be overcome with a high work ethic and family values. However, the model minority myth continues to pervade American culture. The following comment posted on social media exemplifies common arguments made in its favor:

> Statistically, Asians in the USA outperform Whites at every resolvable metrics [*sic*]. They study better in schools and colleges, have higher incomes, lower crime, and homelessness, lower divorce rates, lower number of children out of wedlock . . . Sure, some Asian groups do better and others do worse. Still, their overall performance makes it very difficult to claim that [the United States] is [*sic*] powered by White supremacy. (Itin, n.d.)

Ironically enough, this post was written in response to a news article highlighting the harm of the model minority myth (Róisín, 2019). However, it can be helpful to unpack the beliefs shared in this post, as it succinctly captures the essence of the myth and pervading views of Asian Americans. The post includes four of the main ways in which the myth is highly problematic.

First, *the myth negates the diversity of Asian Americans*, instead treating them as a monolithic group. This biased belief is exemplified in the above comment with the words "they" and "overall," and by the assumption that average statistics can represent Asian Americans. The author also minimizes the concept that "some Asian groups do better and others do worse." There is enormous diversity in terms of ethnicity, generation status, income, disability, sexual orientation, religion, education, and other markers of socioeconomic status among Asian American communities who trace their roots to countries representing 60% of the world's population.

Second, *the model minority myth has been used to argue that American society is in a post-racial state where racism is no longer an issue.* This is found in the commenter's claim that the success of some Asian Americans is proof that "the United States is not powered by White supremacy," essentially a denial of institutional racism. In this manner, the myth has been used to 1) disavow any racism against Asian Americans; 2) discredit the struggles of other Black, Indigenous, and people of color (BIPOC); and 3) foment dissension among Asian Americans and other BIPOC. In other words, some argue that if Asian Americans can succeed as an ethnic minority group, then the struggles of Black Americans and other people of color must be due to something cultural and not due to racism. This argument ignores the vast differences between Asian American and Black American histories, particularly slavery. The legacy of slavery continues to thrive on anti-Black racism in American institutions and culture. Marital trends are just one example. Of all new interracial marriages in 2008 with a White male, White–Hispanic marriages were the most common (46%), followed by White–Asian (26.9%), and then White–Black (6.9%; Pew Research Center, 2012). Disproportionate rates of incarceration, poverty, and health disparities are among many of the additional ongoing, pervasive elements of racism against Black Americans.

The model minority myth is not the only form of racial bias regarding Asian Americans. Other stereotypes that coexist with the myth include viewing Asian Americans as perpetual foreigners, evidenced by the question "Where are you from?" often addressed to Asian Americans. Still, another is that of being sneaky and untrustworthy, which is incorporated into the hypersexualization of Asian women in being portrayed as evil "dragon ladies." Another form of hypersexualization is the "lotus blossom"—the exotic yet docile and submissive Asian American woman. These biases often play out in everyday life on dating apps. Lillian Sun, an Asian American woman, received so many racist comments on Tinder that she started an Instagram meme account (@ thefleshlightchronicles) to raise awareness and validate the experiences of other Asian American women (Jackman, 2018). Comments like, "I want to try my first Asian woman," and "I need my yellow fever cured" are among the least graphic, while many others describe sexual violence in explicit detail. On the other hand, Asian American men get emasculated and shunned on dating apps as the "least desirable" of all ethnic groups. Jason, a 29-year-old Los Angeles resident, shared common responses he received on a dating app (Brown, 2018):

I don't date Asians—sorry, not sorry.
You're cute . . . for an Asian.
I usually like "bears," but no "panda bears."

"It was really disheartening," Jason says, adding, "It really hurt my self-esteem." Comments such as these directly contradict a corollary of the model minority myth—affluence as protection—or the belief that Asian Americans are shielded from racism due to socioeconomic status.

Like the dismissal of racism, the third way the model minority myth is harmful is that *it leads to overlooking health disparities among Asian Americans*. The underestimation of the death toll of COVID-19 among Asian Americans is a recent example (Yan et al., 2021). Most media stories covering the disproportionate impact of COVID on Black, Latinx, and Native American groups fail to mention Asian Americans. However, there is substantial evidence that recorded COVID-19 deaths among Asian Americans are severely undercounted, including 37% more deaths than usual among Asian Americans from January to October 2020. In comparison, there were only 9% more deaths among Whites in the same period. Yan et al. (2021) argue that it is also important to disaggregate data by ethnicity rather than treat Asians as a monolith to understand mortality patterns. For example, in New York City, Chinese Americans had the highest mortality rate of any ethnic group (Marcello et al., 2020), while in California, Filipino and Vietnamese Americans have borne a disproportionate burden of COVID-19 deaths (Lin, 2020).

Yan et al. (2021) link racial biases stemming from the model minority myth to the high mortality burden on Asian Americans, as well as its erasure. "The myth perpetuates the perception that Asian Americans do not have disparities and therefore are unworthy of resources, which leads to a lack of data or inaccurate data for this population that reinforces the misperception that Asian Americans do not have disparities . . . *For Asian Americans, the absence of evidence is often not the evidence of absence, but the evidence of neglect due to racism*" (italics added). The ongoing oversight of Asian Americans results in blocking the allocation of vital research funding. Between 1992 and 2018, clinical research projects funded by the NIH that included subgroups of Asian Americans or NHPIs (Native Hawaiian and Pacific Islanders) comprised a paltry 0.17% of the total NIH budget (Đoàn et al., 2019).

In addition to physical health, the model minority myth also directly influences impressions of Asian mental health. In one research study, some participants read a newspaper article describing Asian American success while others did not. Then, they all were presented with a vignette of an Asian American with symptoms of depression and anxiety. The participants primed with the model minority myth rated the subject's mental health as better than those who did not read the newspaper article (Cheng et al., 2017).

Finally, the model minority myth *minimizes the lived experiences of Asian Americans, experiences that are often pervaded with trauma, past and present*. In her memoir, *Minor Feelings: An Asian American Reckoning*, second-generation Korean American author Cathy Park Hong (2020) incisively describes the paradox of the model minority myth.

> When I hear the phrase, "Asians are next in line to be White," I replace the word "White" with "disappear." Asians are next in line to disappear. We are reputed to be so accomplished, and so law-abiding, we will disappear into this country's amnesiac fog. We will not be the power but become absorbed by power, not share the power of Whites but be stooges to a White ideology that exploited our ancestors. This country insists that our racial identity is beside the point, that it has nothing to do with being bullied, or passed over for promotion, or cut off every time we talk. Our race has nothing to do with this country, even, which is why we're often listed as "Other" in polls and why we're hard to find in racial breakdowns on reported rape or workplace discrimination or domestic abuse.

Racialized trauma in the United States perpetrated against Asian Americans has largely been omitted from American history books just as it has been with Black, Indigenous, and Latinx Americans. However, the journey toward healing for Asian Americans, as well as the country, necessitates a reckoning with historical traumas, such as multiple massacres of Asian Americans in the late 1800s and the incarceration of 120,000 Japanese American families in concentration camps during World War II, that have given rise to the current wave of violence against Asian Americans.

The remainder of this chapter explores these four mechanisms of harm by the model minority myth in more detail as they relate to trauma among Asian Americans. First, however, it may help to examine whether there is any truth to the model minority myth. In other words, is there something special about Asian cultures that breeds success and that is lacking in other ethnic groups, as the myth contends?

ARE CULTURAL VALUES RESPONSIBLE FOR ASIAN AMERICAN SUCCESS?

In their book, the *Asian American Achievement Paradox*, sociologists Jennifer Lee and Ming Zhou (2015) tackle the model minority myth from a new lens, questioning the assumption that there is something cultural about Asian American achievement. In other words, are the values of hard work, education, and family ties responsible for the portion of Asian Americans who are high-achieving?

Lee and Zhou point to two main contributors to the success of some Asian Americans. First, most immigrants are already selected within their countries of origin to have a higher level of education than average. In addition, the 1965 Immigration and Nationality Act created a significant shift in Asian immigration, eliminating quotas based on country of origin and prioritizing foreign-born applicants with high levels of education and skills. Thus, the Act led to what Lee and Zhou term "hyper-selectivity," the phenomenon of Asian immigrants being both more highly educated in their countries of origin and more highly educated than the average American. Hyper-selectivity, in turn, results in a specific mind-set based on class that they term the "Asian success frame." To support the success frame, immigrant parents band together to share knowledge about navigating the US educational system.

Furthermore, Asian American students benefit from higher expectations of teachers and guidance counselors, which provides external support for the success frame. The educational system becomes a self-fulfilling prophecy, evoking the well-known stereotype threat research of Claude Steele (e.g., Steele, 2018, pp. 752–56; Steele & Aronson, 1995), who found that when negative stereotypes are present (e.g., girls are bad at math, Black students score lower on standardized tests), members of the targeted group perform worse than usual. Asian Americans, on the other hand, benefit from a stereotype boost. In a cycle of reinforcement, higher achievement increases stereotypes about Asian Americans, which further boosts the expectations of teachers and guidance counselors.

Lee and Zhou (2015) further argue that the success frame benefits from the belief of Asian immigrant parents that effort is more important than ability. In contrast, the opposite is true among native-born American parents. I extend their argument to include the massive historical traumas that occurred in many Asian countries—such as Partition in India, the Vietnam War, and the Cultural Revolution in China—which led to importing the success frame. Families turned to education as a means to escape from poverty and political turmoil. My grandfather, a lawyer, politician, and supporter of the Kuomintang party that opposed the Chinese Communist government during the Cultural Revolution, experienced persecution of himself and his siblings. Consequently, he urged my father to avoid politics and study engineering instead.

UNSEEN DIVERSITY: CHOPSTICKS VERSUS SPOONS

When I first began eating at Thai restaurants, I always asked for a pair of chopsticks, believing that using chopsticks was the proper way to eat all Asian food. My parents had raised me to reject the spoons and forks offered in most Chinese restaurants. But then, one time, I noticed the server in a Thai restaurant frown as they brought me a pair of chopsticks, which puzzled me. With some Internet research, I learned afterward that Thai people usually prefer to use a fork and spoon to eat. Not using chopsticks is seen as a symbol of pride in rejecting attempts by Chinese missionaries to colonize Thailand. Though the fork and spoon came to Thailand via France, their adoption was seen as a choice rather than an imposition.

The issue of chopsticks versus spoons may seem trivial, but it is symbolic of the many more considerable differences among various South, Southeast, and Eastern Asian cultures. These include religion, family structure, economic status, the arts, histories of being colonized and colonizers, government, and geopolitical relationships.

Ethnic Diversity among Asian Americans

The United States is home to the largest number of Asian diaspora in the world, where 22 million Asians and Asian Americans represent over 50 ethnic groups and 100 languages. An additional 6.1 million Asian diaspora live in Canada. For the past two decades, Asian Americans have consistently been the fastest-growing ethnic group in the United States and are projected to surpass 46 million by 2060, surpassing the Latinx population (Budiman & Ruiz, 2021).

Coined by activists Emma Gee and her partner Yuji Ichioka in 1968, the term "Asian American" originated as a political term created to unite diverse ethnic groups with origins from Asian countries during student protests against the Vietnam War (Lee, 2015). "Asian American" was never meant to define a particular ethnic group. Instead, it was modeled upon the successful organizing of the Black Power Movement and the American Indian Movement. According to Ichioka, "There were so many Asians out there in the political demonstrations, but we had no effectiveness. Everyone was lost in the larger rally. We figured that if we rallied behind our own banner, behind an Asian American banner, we would have an effect on the larger public. We could extend the influence beyond ourselves, to other Asian Americans" (Kambhampaty, 2020).

In this book, I use both of the terms "Asian" and "Asian American." The term "Asian" refers specifically to people who are typically first-generation immigrants from an Asian country and who do not identify as American. Many international students fall under this category. I use "Asian American" as it was originally developed by Gee and Ichioka, although at times, for brevity, I may also use it to include all Asians living in America. Regardless, even the term "Asian" is imperfect.

There is a saying that "there are no Asians in Asia." People from Asian countries, which comprise 60% of the global population, do not call themselves Asian. Instead, they refer to themselves based on their country of origin, e.g., Thai, Japanese, Korean, Indian, Filipino, Chinese, etc. The same is true for many Asian Americans, who often identify themselves as Filipino American, Indian American, Burmese American, and so on, rather than, or in addition to, Asian American. Other people of Asian descent living in the United States, usually first-generation immigrants or temporary residents, such as international students, prefer to use the term "Asian" rather than "Asian American." Further, some with Asian heritage do not define themselves as Asian or Asian American at all.

A large majority of Asian Americans (83%) identify as single-race. However, the proportion of multiracial Asian Americans is growing at an extremely rapid rate. Between 2000 and 2010, the population of adults with a White and Asian background, the largest biracial group among Asian Americans, increased by 87% (Parker et al., 2015). Though imperfect, in this book, the term "Asian American" is also used for those of Asian heritage living in the United States who are multiracial. I feel it is important to do so, as multiracial Asian Americans are sometimes excluded from Asian American arenas, as are international adoptees.

There is also variation in who is identified by American culture as Asian. Today, "Asian American" is commonly assumed to represent only East Asians. As a result, Chinese, Korean, and Japanese Americans receive the most attention, while other ethnic groups are often overlooked, such as South Asians (Bangladeshi, Bhutanese, Indian, Pakistani, and Punjabi), Southeast Asians (Burmese, Cambodian, Hmong, Lao, Thai, and Vietnamese), and Filipinos/Pinoy. More complex ethnic identities, such as being multiracial or being raised in a multiracial household, even if one is not multiracial themselves, are also typically unacknowledged.

Furthermore, it would be too reductionist to consider ethnicity as a person's primary identity. For example, KJ Roelke, whose story follows, describes how being disabled was a primary identity that superseded being Korean American for much of his life (personal communication, November 4, 2021). However, his journey around ethnic identity and other identities continues to evolve. Language around identity is also important. In referring to his being disabled, I wanted to respect KJ's use of identity-first language (e.g., disabled people) as opposed to person-first language (e.g., person with a disability). Disability advocates and scholars also support the use of identity-first language (Dunn and Andrews, 2015).

KJ's Story

Twenty-eight-year-old KJ Roelke was adopted from Korea by a White couple in Dallas, Texas, when he was six months old. He now co-hosts *The Janchi*

Show, a podcast that explores the experiences of Korean American adoptees. KJ describes wrestling with five main spheres of identity over his lifetime: adoptee, disabled person, Korean / Korean American, Asian American, and Christian. According to KJ, "They're really like a Venn diagram—there's a huge amount of crossover, and yet they do exist in really specific distinct parts in my brain."

For example, he explains how exploring his Korean roots has led him on a spiritual quest. His adoptive parents identify as Christian, and religion played a central role in his upbringing. He attended a private Christian college in the Midwest before returning to Dallas, where he lives now with his wife. "I guess I'm actually trying to, like, find my way into Buddhism sort of as I reconnect with my own Korean American heritage . . . like thinking about how I can expand my worldview as I move towards non-dual thinking as a part of kind of reclaiming my own culture, like whether it's Confucianism or Buddhism or whatever." KJ asks, "How do I break out of where I currently am to better understand where I came from, and how does that then shape who I want to be today?"

George Floyd, Racism, and Asian American Identity

The murder of George Floyd and the coinciding rise of anti-Asian racism galvanized KJ and two of his friends to start *The Janchi Show* podcast, which was "born out of this urgent need to express some type of allyship with social justice." Early episodes explored how embracing Asian American identity can be used as a means for uniting around social justice with the Black Lives Matter movement. For KJ, therefore, his exploration of ethnic identity was interwoven with the political, which he described as a period of "forced self-racialization and identity work" imposed by rising anti-Asian racism. He shares, "I found myself in the rock and the hard place of fearing for my life in a way that I had never done before, and also being married to a White woman, and knowing the town that we lived in . . . It's not great for either of us to go get groceries right now . . . Still, one of us has to do it, and so that was just such a hard, hard thing. But anytime I heard a loud car roll by, my heart rate would elevate, and I would, like, tense up, and I would just be ready for someone to yell something at me or, God forbid, stick a gun out the window."

Some adoptees from Asian countries do not necessarily identify as Asian American; for much of his life, KJ did not either. He shares that his wife "pointed out that whenever I would talk about Asian Americans, I would use 'they' or 'them' and not 'we' . . . like I had no ownership in that community. So that really represents a clear line of demarcation for me—that even while I knew that I was Korean and celebrated being Korean, I had no idea what it meant to be an Asian American."

Evolving Ethnic Identity and Relationships

The process of ethnic identity development requires courage, as it can risk changing relationships with loved ones. KJ shared how his exploration of identity has affected his relationships with his family members, such as with his mother. It has led to difficult conversations with her, whom he describes as "a conservative Christian who means well." They strive for acceptance of each other, and at the same time, KJ describes how his mother's disagreement with the views he expressed in his podcast made him feel more alone, saying, "When your mother says, 'You know I still love you—I just don't agree with you' it sounds like, 'Well, I'm not in this fight with you. I'll watch, but I'm not going to wrestle with it the way you are.' And that's a privilege."

Increasingly identifying as Asian American has also required KJ and his wife, Sarah, to grapple with the implications of being in an interracial relationship—a label they had not used prior to the pandemic. KJ shares, "From 2020 on, Sarah and I have properly realized that we're in an interracial marriage . . . We've been married now for 5 years, and we've been together—it'll be 13 years in February. It wasn't until year 12 of our relationship that we realized, 'Hey, we're in an interracial relationship, and that has certain implications, and that means certain things.' So, in a big way, on top of all the change forced on us by the pandemic, and also self-imposed by moving back to Dallas, there has been a real sense of 'How do we relate to each other?' and 'What does it mean to be in an interracial marriage?' and also, 'What does it mean for me as an Asian man and person of color to relate to my White wife?' And on the one hand, I'm gaining all this new language and gaining all of these, especially adoptee, but generally, just non-White friends, and this sense of community online is really growing. And yeah, so it's changed our dynamic in some really interesting ways, and we've had to have some really intentional conversations. At the same time, it's done some really good things in continuing to grow my empathy for what it means to be a woman in America. And then we're thinking about how we raise children when we have kids . . . and those ideas [have] shifted greatly in the past year and a half."

Native Hawaiians and Pacific Islanders

Asian Americans and Pacific Islanders are often grouped as a single category, commonly labeled AAPI for short. Such an allyship can be advantageous in amplifying the voices and needs of both groups. However, after much consideration of Native Hawaiian and Pacific Islander (NHPI) perspectives, which includes the privilege of working with NHPI mental health therapists and clients in Hawaii, I have come to agree with many NHPIs that they have more in common with Indigenous cultures than Asian or Asian American cultures. In addition, NHPI voices are often lost in conversations around AAPI.

According to first-generation Samoan American and executive director of the nonprofit Empowering Pacific Islander Communities (EPIC), Tavae Samuelu, "The intent of API [*sic*] is inclusion, but the impact, the long-term impact has been erasure" (Yu, 2021).

NHPIs have also inherited a unique and complex relationship with colonialism that includes being colonized by both Western and Asian countries, resulting in multiple forms of intergenerational trauma and racism. Finally, Indigenous NHPI modes of healing differ from those of Asian countries. Therefore, they deserve to be given careful consideration. I also acknowledge that this is an imperfect solution. As a professor of Hawai'ian studies, Lilikalā Kame'eleihiwa has observed, NHPIs "benefit from the work that Asians are doing on different issues around racism and bias," and ongoing alliances are needed to highlight the condition of NHPIs (Yu, 2021).

Economic Disparity among Asian Americans

Films such as *Crazy Rich Asians* and the Netflix series *Bling Empire* perpetuate the model minority myth that all Asian Americans are incredibly wealthy and well-educated. The reality is much more complex. Asian Americans are the most economically divided racial or ethnic group in the United States, with those in the top tenth of the income distribution earning 10.7 times more than those in the bottom tenth. Furthermore, this income inequality is rising faster among Asians than all other ethnic groups (Kochnar & Cilluffo, 2018).

While Asian Americans do have the highest median income level and educational attainment of all ethnic groups in the country, they also experience a higher rate of poverty (12.3%) than non-Hispanic Whites (9.8%; DeNavas-Walt et al., 2012). In 2014, the highest poverty rate by any ethnic group in New York City was among Asian Americans (29%). Hmong, Laotian, Bhutanese, and Cambodian Americans are especially at risk for poverty. The difference in poverty rates becomes even more significant when cost of living is accounted for, since Asian Americans are concentrated in areas of the country with the highest cost of living, primarily California (30%) and the Northeast (19%; Austin, 2013; Budiman & Ruiz, 2021). According to an analysis by the National Academy of Sciences, *the adjusted poverty rate among Asian Americans (16.1%) is about 155% more than that of White Americans (10.4%;* Austin, 2013; Dalaker, 2005).

Asian American immigrants with limited English proficiency, who are undocumented, or who do not have a college degree, often have no choice but to enter low-wage manual labor jobs, where wage theft and exploitation are common. Restaurants, nail salons, and garment industry sweatshops are among the most common settings for the exploitation of undocumented Asian Americans, where wage theft and other labor violations are commonplace (Milkman, González, & Narro, 2010; Nguyen-Ngo, 2020). Underlying the sizable economic disparity among Asian Americans are the vastly different socioeconomic backgrounds from which they come. While about half of Asian immigrants have completed bachelor's degrees or more, some of the most deprived and vulnerable also originate from Asian countries (Platonova & Urso, 2013). About one-fifth of Asian immigrants (22%) to the United States and one-third to Canada (31%) are considered low-skilled labor. It may be surprising to learn that 1 in 7 Asian immigrants are undocumented, comprising 1.5 million (14%) of the almost 11 million estimated undocumented immigrants in the United States (Capps et al., 2020).

The pandemic disproportionately affected those working in the service industries, including many Asian Americans. Among those with high school degrees or less in California, over twice as many Asian Americans (83%) filed unemployment claims than non-Asians (37%; Mar & Ong, 2020). Asian Americans with some college education were also disproportionately impacted, with 35% claiming unemployment versus 22% for the rest of the California labor force (Mar & Ong, 2020). Moreover, during the lockdown in New York City, Asian unemployment jumped from 3.4% to 25%—the largest increase among all ethnic groups (Yee, 2021). In addition, all of these employment statistics are likely underestimates, since 28% of Asians and Asian Americans do not speak English (Budiman & Ruiz, 2021), which is a barrier to filing for unemployment. These data also do not capture the 1 in 7 Asian immigrants who are undocumented (Yee, 2021).

Diversity in Generations

Asians have been migrating to the United States for centuries. On October 18, 1587, several decades before the Pilgrims landed at Plymouth Rock, Filipino sailors arrived at what is now called Southern California. Nearly two hundred years later, in 1763, Filipino immigrants established their first settlement in Louisiana. In the nineteenth century, Asian laborers, mainly from China, began arriving in increasing numbers. This movement coincided with the Chinese coolie trade to South America, an extension of the African slave trade, that lasted several decades, from 1847 to 1874 (Lee, 2015). "Coolie" literally translates to "bitter work" in Mandarin. Chinese coolies were typically recruited through kidnapping, deception, and coercion. The coolie trade shaped the American view of Asian laborers as cheap, servile workers who take away jobs from Whites.

The long history of Asian Americans in the United States has resulted in a large diversity of immigrant generation status, a touchstone of identity for Asian Americans. Some Asian Americans can trace their family history in the United States for many generations. On the other hand, the majority of Asian Americans (57%) are first-generation immigrants (Budiman & Ruiz, 2021).

"First generation" is a label for those who immigrated in their lifetimes, whether they are naturalized citizens, temporary or permanent residents, asylum seekers, or unauthorized migrants. It is also sometimes used to refer to offspring (i.e., the first generation to be born in a country). However, for this book, I will refer to the offspring of immigrants who are not immigrants themselves as second generation, which is a more common practice. The term "1.5 generation" refers to those who immigrated with their parents as young children. The second generation of Asian Americans is young, with a median age of 19 years old, which is half the median age (38 years old) of the rest of the US population. Understandably, a new immigrant will have a very different lived experience than a second-generation Asian American due to acculturation and language differences, as well as citizenship status, and these experiences will continue to evolve with future generations.

It is also important to recognize that not all Asian Americans are voluntary immigrants. The United States is home to approximately 125,000 Asian American adoptees, with the majority adopted from China and South Korea (US Department of State—Bureau of Consular Affairs, n.d.). Most international adoptees are transracially adopted—that is, they are adopted into White families, often living in White suburbs. However, international adoption has declined significantly since its peak in 2004, mainly because of increased restrictions in China, Korea, Russia, and Guatemala (Westerman, 2018).

The political climate in the United States during the Trump administration had a profound effect on patterns of migration. For example, Chinese students have become increasingly wary of studying in the United States due to fears of deportation, restrictive immigration policies implemented during Trump's presidency, and safety concerns (Wan, 2020). As a result, Canada has seen a 33% increase and the UK a 28% increase in admissions to Chinese students from 2017–2018 (Wan, 2020). It is still unclear how the COVID-19 pandemic has affected migration patterns, but ongoing political tension between the United States and China continues to inhibit immigration.

HISTORICAL AND INTERGENERATIONAL TRAUMA: KNOWING AND REMEMBERING, WOUNDED AND WOUNDING

Many are unaware of the pervasive history of trauma among Asian diaspora, including centuries of Asian immigrant history, trauma in countries of origin, colonial oppression, and institutionalized racism. However, knowing about and remembering the histories of Asian Americans is necessary for any attempt at helping Asian Americans heal. As Yusin (2017) has observed, trauma is not just a wound that lives in the past, but one that has the capacity for continual wounding. In this manner, trauma due to colonization is not only historical but ongoing. For Asian Americans, the past lives in the present through historical and intergenerational trauma.

Historical Trauma

The terms "historical trauma" and "intergenerational trauma" both highlight the lasting effects of trauma over time. As a result, they are often used interchangeably; however, they are theoretically distinct (Gone, 2013).

Historical trauma is defined as:

> A collective complex trauma inflicted on a group of people who share a specific group identity or affiliation . . . It is the legacy of numerous traumatic events a community experiences over generations and encompasses the psychological and social responses to such events. (Evans-Campbell, 2008, p. 320)

The concept of historical trauma has most often been applied to the Holocaust and the genocide of Native Americans. However, there is a small but growing body of literature on historical trauma and Asian Americans, particularly related to the mass incarceration of Japanese Americans and Canadians during World War II. In addition, many Asian immigrants also have experienced historical trauma in their countries of origin due to war, famine, and/or genocide.

Intergenerational Trauma

The impact of historical trauma upon subsequent generations is defined as intergenerational trauma, as depicted in figure 1.1. That is, intergenerational trauma is a secondary effect of historical trauma; it also does not depend on whether the trauma occurred in the collective (Gone, 2013, Cromer et al., 2018). Unlike large-scale historical trauma, intergenerational trauma typi-

Figure 1.1.

Note. Historical trauma and intergenerational trauma are distinct but related. Historical trauma leads to intergenerational trauma. Image description: An arrow points from a box labeled "Historical Trauma" into a box labeled "Intergenerational Trauma."

cally manifests within individuals and family systems. Therefore, conflating historical and intergenerational trauma can mask differences in the ways they impact mental health (Cromer et al., 2018).

Among Asian Americans, intergenerational trauma often intersects with differing acculturation levels across generations. The memoir and graphic novel, *The Best We Could Do*, by Thi Bui (2017), illustrates this phenomenon. Much of the book recounts her parents' life in Vietnam, the trauma of the Vietnam War, and the family's dangerous escape from the country. However, it also explores their new life as immigrants in the United States. In one scene, an explosion occurs in the family's apartment building. Bui's family members reflexively hide as they did during the war, to avoid being found by Communist soldiers, but Bui realizes they need to leave the building, and leads them to safety. Such responsibility for the family's survival often falls to the children of immigrants and refugees who acculturate more rapidly than their parents. It's common for 1.5- and second-generation children to serve as interpreters for their parents and to assume adult roles in helping their parents navigate institutional systems such as welfare, schools, and work.

The Los Angeles Chinatown Massacre

Founded in 1938, the Phoenix Bakery in Chinatown, Los Angeles, is known throughout Southern California for its Chinese desserts. A two-hour drive from my family's home in San Diego, the Phoenix Bakery was a place of pilgrimage for us. Their *lao-po bing*, four-inch discs of flaky layers of pastry encasing a sweet winter melon filling, were the ultimate prize. Some days when we arrived, the bakery would already be sold out of them, but when we were lucky, my father would buy up all that was left, triumphantly carrying a large pink box back to the family station wagon, where we would devour the first ones right away. We would ration the rest, allowing the pink box to occupy half the space in our freezer for the next month. Unknown to my family then, and to most residents of Chinatown today, the Phoenix Bakery also happens to be located just a mile north of the original Chinatown of Los Angeles, the site of one of the largest lynchings in recorded US history.

On October 24, 1871, a White rancher was shot and killed when he initiated a gun battle with members of a Chinese gang (Zesch, 2012). He died an hour later, at 6:00 p.m., and by evening, a mob of 500 people had circled the block that constituted Chinatown. The local sheriff ordered his deputies to shoot anyone who tried to flee. As a rumor spread that "the Chinese were killing Whites wholesale," the mob overran the block and began a killing spree, climbing to rooftops and punching holes in them to shoot at the people inside. There was no escape through the streets where Chinese people were beaten, tortured, and shot. Every business was looted, resulting in the loss of thousands of dollars. In little more than three hours, the following people were lynched while crowds of witnesses laughed and jeered (Zesch, 2012):

- Ah Wing
- Dr. Chee Long "Gene" Tong, physician
- Chang Wan
- Leong Quai, laundryman
- Ah Long, cigar maker
- Wan Foo, cook
- Tong Won, cook and musician
- Ah Loo, 15 years old
- Day Kee, cook
- Ah Waa, cook
- Ho Hing, cook
- Lo Hey, cook
- Ah Won, cook
- Wing Chee, cook
- Wong Chin, storekeeper

Three more were shot and killed:

- Johnny Burrow
- Ah Cut, liquor maker
- Wa Sin Quai

Someone had cut off the finger of one of the lynched to steal his ring and torn off his pants as part of the robbery, so that he was hung mutilated and half-naked. The rioters also botched several attempts at hanging their first victim, Ah Wing, essentially torturing him before he died. Only 10 of the 500 rioters were prosecuted, of whom 8 were convicted. However, all convictions were overturned on appeal due to the technicality that the indictment did not name one of the victims, Dr. Gene Tong, as having been murdered. Afterward, "society agreed to drop all mention of the incident," one local recollected (Zesch, p. 216). Several of the killers eventually became prominent politicians and law enforcement officials.

Today, a highway runs across the land of the original Chinatown. One of the sites of the lynchings is now an entrance to a mall parking lot. According to the *Los Angeles Times*, "The massacre was buried so deeply that even those with deep roots in Chinatown did not know it happened until generations later. Gay Yuen, who was born and raised in Los Angeles's Chinatown, and even taught Chinese American history, did not learn about it until she retired and joined the board of the Chinese American Museum" (Shyong, 2021).

Not long after the Chinatown massacre, anti-Chinese hate was codified in national legislation, with strong support from Angelenos. The Page Act of 1875 banned immigration by Chinese women, followed by the Chinese Exclusion Act in 1882, which also banned Chinese men. Similar legislation would follow over the next several decades to curtail immigration from Japan, South Asia, Southeast Asia, and the Philippines. Such race-based immigration policy was not officially abolished until 1965.

For decades after the Los Angeles Chinatown massacre, mass violence ensued against Chinese immigrants and other Asians. In 1885, at least 28 Chinese miners in Rock Springs, Wyoming, were slaughtered, and dozens more were wounded by a group of White miners who blamed them for economic struggles (Lew-Williams, 2018). No charges were filed against the perpetrators. A similar massacre occurred in Oregon in 1887, where at least 34 miners were ambushed and killed for their gold (Nokes, 2009). Three of the six perpetrators were brought to trial, but none were convicted. Historian Lew-Williams (2018) estimates that between 1885 and 1887, there were at least 86 killings of Chinese people and more than 168 forced or attempted evictions of Chinese communities.

Forgotten American Colonialism: The Philippine-American War

Anti-Chinese hatred at the turn of the twentieth century broadened to other Asian ethnic groups, fueling the little-known but brutal Philippine-American War from 1899 to 1902. The war led to the United States becoming a colonial power and ruling over the Philippines for nearly 50 years. Before United States rule, the Philippines had been a Spanish colony for almost 300 years, during which time Spain exploited natural resources such as wood, sugar, and hemp to make rope for ships. Spain also sought to extinguish Indigenous culture through the domination of the Catholic Church, which appropriated most of the land and levied taxes. Resistance by Filipinos to colonization continued throughout these centuries, and eventually coalesced in the Filipino nationalist movement in the mid-1800s (Jones, 2012).

From 1896 to 1897, the Filipino Revolution—led by Andres Bonifacio, and later, Emilio Aguinaldo—fought to overthrow the Spanish government, until a peace treaty was negotiated. Aguinaldo accepted exile in Hong Kong in return for promises of reforms by the Spanish government, which never manifested. While in Hong Kong, he was approached on behalf of the US Navy by Captain Edward P. Wood, commander of the US gunboat *Petrel*. Wood offered arms and proposed an alliance if Aguinaldo returned to the

Philippines to lead the revolution on land while the United States attacked the Spanish fleet in Manila. When Aguinaldo asked about US intentions, Wood assured him, saying, "The United States, my General, is a great and rich nation and neither needs nor desires colonies" (Aguinaldo & Pacis, 1957, p. 31). Another diplomat, US Consul General Spencer Pratt, also pledged the same, though he demurred when Aguinaldo pressed for an agreement in writing. "The government of the United States is a very just and powerful government," Pratt promised (Aguinaldo & Pacis, 1957, p. 33).

The following year, in 1898, American forces quickly defeated the Spanish navy and then, with the support of the Philippine Revolutionary Army, defeated the Spanish on land. Aguinaldo subsequently declared independence for the Philippines, which went unrecognized by the United States or Spain. In the subsequent Treaty of Paris, Spain sold ownership of the Philippines to the United States. To Filipinos, Spanish imperialism had been replaced by US imperialism. The ensuing Philippine-American War resulted in an estimated 200,000 Filipino civilian casualties, mainly due to famine and disease. American forces placed civilians in concentration camps, and executed prisoners, including children. The political cartoon in figure 1.2 references an order by General Jacob Smith for American troops to kill any Filipinos over the age of 10 on the island of Samar after the US Army suffered a major defeat there.

Furthermore, the army systematically practiced what they called the "water cure," a form of torture developed during the Spanish Inquisition. The water cure entailed forcing a victim's mouth open and pouring water down their throat until their stomach was so engorged that it became taut. Soldiers would then beat the victim's stomach with their fists until water, and gastric juices, would erupt from the victim's mouth and nose. Victims experienced a sensation of drowning and excruciating pain as their internal organs stretched and convulsed (Jones, 2012). The water cure is like the waterboarding practiced by US soldiers in Vietnam and, more recently, by the CIA. These practices were not outlawed until 2009, by President Obama.

The following clinical vignette illustrates the importance of conceptualizing mental health in a historical context when working with Asian American clients:

Edgar, a first-generation Filipino American in his 60s and an army veteran, had been plagued by panic attacks for years. They occurred so frequently that he had stopped driving for fear of causing an accident. I asked Edgar about his parents and grandparents. He shared that he was close to his mother, but that his father, a veteran of World War II in the Philippines, was "very strict," a description many of my Asian American clients use when referring to physical and emotional abuse. His father's father, Edgar's grandfather, was an orphan, having lost both parents during the Philippine-American War. He, too, was "very strict" toward Edgar's father. "So, you not only have your own trauma

Figure 1.2.

Note. "Kill everyone over ten." —Gen. Jacob H. Smith (Davenport, 1902) Image description: A firing squad of American soldiers prepares to shoot at blindfolded Filipino children with their backs turned to the soldiers. A vulture perches amidst American flags. The caption at the bottom reads, "Criminals because they were born ten years before we took the Philippines."

that you experienced as a child and then trauma from the Vietnam War, but you are carrying in your body the history of wars and trauma of the whole Philippines." Nodding vigorously, Edgar said, "Yes! That's right!" His shoulders, which had been hunched together tightly, relaxed, lowering several inches. "It seems to me," I continued gently, "that it's pretty understandable to be having panic attacks then, isn't it?" His eyes moist with tears, Edgar nodded again.

A RESURGENCE OF ANTI-ASIAN HATE

According to the model minority myth, anti-Asian racism is a long-ago and inconsequential relic of the past two centuries. A White client of one of my supervisees expressed shock at the rise in anti-Asian racism during the pandemic. "Doesn't everyone love Asians?" she asked. It is important to note that "competence, moral worth, and respectability are no safeguards against racism and xenophobia" (Lee, 2021, p. 181). On June 23, 1982, a Chinese American man, Vincent Chin, was beaten to death in a racially motivated attack when disgruntled Detroit autoworkers mistook him for Japanese, as they blamed Japanese automakers for losing their jobs. Chin's two killers were fined $3,000 and sentenced to probation, with no jail time, leading to a national outcry by Asian American communities. The current wave of violence targeting Asian Americans is a chilling reenactment of Chin's death and centuries of anti-Asian violence.

There are signs that American culture is waking from a collective oblivion to Asian American struggles. The steep global rise in anti-Asian racism during the COVID-19 pandemic has, for the first time, centered Asian diaspora in mainstream media for a sustained period. This attention appears to be influencing public opinion. A poll of Americans conducted a year after the start of the pandemic in the United States found that a majority (60%) believe that discrimination against Asian Americans has risen during this time (Tang & Fingerhut, 2021). Still, many Americans express surprise, such as this poll participant, who commented, "I really wouldn't think [Asian Americans] are facing any kind of discrimination because I happen to think they're very well educated—most of them—and they don't face that much scrutiny . . . However, ever since the pandemic began and it was labeled a 'China thing,' that's where it all began" (Tang & Fingerhut, 2021).

The following is a very abbreviated list of violent acts toward Asian Americans during the pandemic.

March 16, 2021: In a deadly rampage now known as the "spa shootings," a man in Atlanta, Georgia, gunned down eight people in three locations, six of whom were Asian American women:

XiaoJie "Emily" Tan, 49—mother, wife, spa owner
Daoyou Feng, 44—recent immigrant
Suncha Kim, 69—mother, grandmother, wife
Soon Chung Park, 74—mother of five, wife
Yong Ae Yue, 63—mother of two, grandmother
Hyun Jung Grant, 51—mother of two, former teacher
Delaina Ashley Yaun, 33—mother of two, wife
Paul Andre Michels, 44—brother, military veteran

Additionally, Elcias Hernandez-Ortiz, age 30, and a recent immigrant and father, was gravely wounded.

Immediately after the shootings, Captain Jay Baker, a spokesperson for the sheriff's office in Cherokee County, where five of the victims were killed, offered sympathy for the perpetrator, saying, "He was pretty much fed up and had been at the end of his rope, and yesterday was a really bad day for him, and this is what he did." The same sheriff also dismissed any possibility of racial motivation for the shootings, attributing the attacks to sexual addiction. Advocates such as Sung Yeon Choimorrow, the executive director of the advocacy group, National Asian Pacific American Women's Forum (https://www.napawf.org/), have pointed out that for Asian American women, sexism and racism have always been intertwined (Dewan, 2021). "I'm telling you, most of us didn't sleep well last night," she said in the wake of the shootings. "Because this was what we had feared all along—we were afraid that the objectification and the hypersexualization of our bodies was going to lead to death."

March 17, 2021: Pakistani American college student Nafiah Ikram was exiting her car outside her home in New York when a stranger ran up and threw acid in her face, causing permanent disfigurement and partial blindness (Annesse, 2021).

April 17, 2021: Four members of the Indianapolis Sikh community were among the eight slain at a FedEx facility. Two of the victims, Amarjit Sekhon and Jasvinder Kaur, were related and had applied for their jobs together a year earlier (Acevedo, 2021). They worked the night shift together and were sitting in a car outside the facility, waiting for their shift to begin. Perhaps they were chatting about their families. Jasvinder was planning on attending her two-year-old granddaughter's birthday party in a few days. Or perhaps they were sharing a snack Amarjit had prepared for them. She was the primary breadwinner of the home for her two sons and her disabled husband, and her family described how she expressed her love for them through home-cooked Indian meals.

April 25, 2021: John Huynh, 29, had only been married five months before being stabbed to death in an unprovoked attack outside his apartment in Bothell, Washington. The son of a factory worker and a seamstress raised in Pennsylvania, Huynh's family described him as a father figure to his younger sisters and an avid mountain biker (Meyer, 2021).

May 5, 2021: Two elderly Asian American women, aged 63 and 84, were waiting at a bus stop in San Francisco when they were stabbed without warning (Associated Press, 2021). Both were hospitalized and managed to survive the attack.

July 17, 2021: Than Htwe, a recent immigrant from Myanmar, was on a rare outing with her son Kyaw Zaw Hein in New York (Knoll, 2021). As they walked up a flight of stairs to exit the subway, someone yanked Kyaw's backpack so hard that he fell backward. He reached for his mother, and they both tumbled down the stairs and lost consciousness. When he awoke, he saw his mother lying next to him in a pool of blood. She died from her injuries in the hospital eleven days later.

August 7, 2021: While out for a run in San Francisco, an Asian American woman was assaulted when someone jumped out of a car with three other passengers and grabbed her. The car window shut on her arm, and she was dragged for half a block down the street. Though she survived the attack, she was left with a ring of teeth marks on her hand where one of the perpetrators bit her (Lim, 2021).

October 23, 2021: A 30-year-old Asian American man was beaten with sticks by three men and two women in Manhattan. "What are you doing here, Asian?" the victim reported one of the perpetrators saying (Parascandola, 2021).

November 2021: Olympic gold medalist Sunisa Lee was waiting for an Uber with her friends, all of Asian descent, when they were startled by a group speeding by in a car, yelling racist slurs like "ching chong" and insisting they "go back to where they came from." One passenger, Lee says, sprayed her arm with pepper spray as the car sped away. "I was so mad, but there was nothing I could do or control because they skirted off," she recalls. "I didn't do anything to them, and having the reputation, it's so hard because I didn't want to do anything that could get me into trouble. I just let it happen" (Kim, 2021).

Fall 2022: As sociology professor Jennifer Lee was jogging on the grounds of the Institute for Advanced Study in Princeton, New Jersey, an older, White woman she passed began screaming at her. "You're threatening my life by breathing hard while jogging past me! You're F*CKING threatening my life by breathing on me!" (Lee, 2022)

January 11, 2023: An 18-year-old student at Indiana University was stabbed multiple times while riding a local bus. According to National Public Radio (Kim, 2023), "the suspect told police she stabbed the victim because the victim was 'Chinese,' adding that it 'would be one less person to blow up our country.'"

These instances of violence represent only a fraction of the thousands of attacks that have continued to be committed against Asian Americans since the start of the pandemic. Between March 2020 and March 2022, the advocacy group Stop Asian Hate logged 11,500 reports of anti-Asian racism in the United States These reported incidents reflect a 369% surge from prior to the pandemic, in 2019 (Levin, 2021). AAPI women and girls were targeted twice as often as men (Pillai et al., 2021), and nonbinary Asian Americans also reported heightened discrimination (Pillai et al., 2021). The rate of incidents continued to escalate during the pandemic; nearly as many hate crimes were reported in the first quarter of 2021 as in all of 2020 (Levin, 2021).

Despite a global perception that anti-Asian racism is solely a "US problem," there is evidence that it has risen throughout the West (Human Rights Watch, 2020). Canada has an even higher number of anti-Asian racism reports per Asian capita than the United States, with Asian Canadian women similarly reporting hate crimes twice as often as Asian men (project 1907, 2021).

In the UK, complaints of anti-Asian racism filed with UK police in the first quarter of 2020 surpassed the total reports in all of 2019. Reports of increasing violence toward Asian diaspora have also spanned Europe, Australia, and New Zealand (Human Rights Watch, 2020; Haynes, 2021). In addition to the violent street racism that is the focus of media attention, anti-Asian hate and discrimination manifest as bullying and harassment in schools, workplaces, and any social venue, including social media.

Racial Microaggressions

Racial microaggressions are a form of racism whose appearance is much less dramatic than many of the overt and violent acts described in this chapter, but are ubiquitous in the lives of BIPOC. Like other forms of racism, they have a direct, negative impact on mental health (Nadal et al., 2014) and physical health (Nadal et al., 2017). A single microaggression is enough to impact mental health (Nadal, 2011), while the accumulation of microaggressions creates more mental health problems (Nadal, Griffin, et al., 2014) and erodes self-esteem (Nadal, Wong, et al., 2014).

Sue et al. (2007) describe microaggressions as "brief, everyday exchanges that send denigrating messages to people of color because they belong to a racial minority group" (p. 72). They often arise from unacknowledged biases that "other" BIPOC. For example, a well-intentioned White friend once said to me with good intentions that she does not see me as Asian, but just "like everyone else." It felt painful to have my ethnicity erased in that simple statement. However, my friend immediately recognized that what she said was problematic, and apologized. Unfortunately, this awareness is far from the norm. More often, microaggressions are overlooked and dismissed by the perpetrators, who have the power to define reality (Sue et al., 2007; Sue et al., 2008). This results in a gaslighting dynamic that has the pernicious effect of causing the victims to doubt their interpretation of reality and, thereby, themselves.

SUMMARY: MOVING TOWARD LIBERATION

Asian Americans represent many cultures, socioeconomic statuses, generational statuses, and other intersecting identities. The model minority myth attempts to mask this rich diversity. Listening to individual testimonios, such as the story of KJ Roelke, and the many others that follow in this book, can help to humanize Asian Americans beyond the stereotypes. Additionally, researchers should disaggregate data on Asian Americans rather than treating them as a monolith.

The model minority myth also obfuscates centuries of anti-Asian racism in the United States. The current crisis of anti-Asian violence is yet another of many waves of anti-immigrant and anti-Asian persecution. This historical trauma persists over time as intergenerational trauma, affecting parenting, and leading to high rates of family violence and neglect, detailed in chapter 3.

But first, chapter 2 extends the argument that trauma must be understood in context. It presents an ecological model that integrates various forms of betrayal trauma. Betrayal traumas are relational forms of trauma in which the perpetrator is a person or an institution upon whom an individual relies for their well-being (Freyd, 1996). Examples include a parent abusing a child or an employer refusing to stop discrimination in the workplace. Chapter 2 also explains how betrayal is a key mechanism by which historical and intergenerational trauma cause harm. Therapy for all people, regardless of ethnicity, may be enhanced by a better understanding of the processes that contribute to oppression. Finally, chapter 2 presents an ecological model of trauma among Asian Americans that integrates historical, intergenerational, and betrayal traumas across social spheres.

Moving toward a liberation model of psychology requires acknowledging one's subjectivity—that all people have emotional responses to race, and we are all participants, knowingly or not, in creating narratives of race. Therefore, I end this chapter as it began, with a self-check-in. How did it feel to read about the historical atrocities against Asian Americans? What specific emotions did it evoke? Personally, learning more about past and current anti-Asian violence in the United States left me feeling irritable, depressed, and fatigued, and I found myself being less present with my family. Fortunately, I found a process group specifically for Asian American therapists that has been an invaluable space to explore how race and racism have affected us and our relationships. It is an example of the many ways Asian Americans have united to support each other during the pandemic. I hope that each person, regardless of ethnicity, can likewise find the support they need to engage in their own process of conscientization.

ADDITIONAL RESOURCES

- Bieber, J., Gong, S., Young, D., Fifer, S. J., Tsien, J. (2020). *Asian Americans* [TV Series]. WETA Washington, DC; Center for Asian American Media; PBS; Independent Television Service; Flash Cuts; Tajima-Peña Productions. https://www.pbs.org/show/asian-americans/

This five-part film series produced by PBS chronicles the history of Asian Americans and describes their contributions and challenges.

- Jubilee. (2021, June 30). *Dine with Hasan Minaj, Eugene Lee Yang, and Michelle Kwan | Recipe for change* [Video]. YouTube. https://tinyurl.com/recipe4change

  Asian American activists and celebrities discuss Asian American culture and experiences of racism in this one-hour video, produced by Jubilee.

- *I experience being Asian American differently than my peers* [Video]. (2021, March 3). Decibel; PBS. https://tinyurl.com/AsAmDifferently

  Asian American members of the Austin LGBTQIA+ community share their experiences of having multiple marginalized identities in this brief (five-minute) video, produced by PBS.

Chapter Two

Rings of Betrayal: Contextualizing Asian American Trauma

My oldest son seemed to want to walk from the time he was born; as a baby, he loved to be held upright and push his feet into my lap. At just nine months old, he was ready to take his first steps. Balancing on wobbly legs, he firmly grasped one of my fingers in each hand, and together we toddled around the house. His delight in this newfound power was infectious, while at the same time, his tight grip on my fingers made clear his need for not just physical but emotional support. My son's experience in learning to walk is an example of the importance of social attachment for healthy child development. As observed decades ago by the developers of attachment theory, a child's caretakers are the "secure base" from which children explore the world and to which they can return for reassurance (Salter, 1940).

ATTACHMENT, HEALTH, AND HAPPINESS

We learn who we are through our relationships with each other, beginning with our primary caretakers, then extending to other family members, friends, teachers, and the larger world. Through others, we learn the measure of our worth as human beings, how to make meaning of events that happen to us, and what they mean about us. Through others, we find our place in time and culture. Judith Herman states, "A secure sense of connection with caring people is the foundation of personality development" (p. 52, 2015). As we grow older, we continue to develop relationships with the world around us and reassess our self-image based on the messages we receive in these relationships. Research has repeatedly found that the quantity and quality of our social connections are directly linked to our mental and physical health. In one of the most extended studies on health that has spanned 80 years, the

Harvard Study of Adult Development found close relationships to be the central factor in what keeps people happy, more than money, fame, social class, IQ, or even genes (Vaillant, 2012). Though this study focused on men, the link between social support and health has been established for people in general (e.g., Thoits, 2011; Umberson & Montez, 2010), including those with trans and nonbinary gender identities (Weinhardt et al., 2019). Additional benefits of supportive relationships include lowering the risk of depression, anxiety, and PTSD in the general population (Mehnert et al., 2010), and among some refugees (Schweitzer et al., 2006).

Leong et al. (2013) found that increased social networking among Asian Americans can serve as a protective factor against depression, anxiety, and substance abuse. Still, it is important to note that social support cannot be ethically recommended as a blanket rule without considering culture. Research has revealed that Asians and Asian Americans may benefit more from an implicit form of social support defined by not disclosing problems rather than explicit social support that involves talking about stressors (Taylor et al., 2007). For example, sharing a meal with someone or spending time together can be implicit forms of support.

Conversely, having fewer and lower-quality social connections increases the risk for numerous health issues, such as hypertension, cancer, myocardial infarction, slower wound recovery, impaired immune function, and chronic inflammation (Berkman & Syme, 1979; Ertel et al., 2009; Everson-Rose et al., 2005; Kiecolt-Glaser et al., 2002; Reynolds & Kaplan, 1990; Robles & Kiecolt-Glaser, 2003; Umberson & Montez, 2010). Having little social connection may have a more significant effect on BIPOC than Whites. Research among Black Americans with a chronic illness, diabetes mellitus, has found a higher mortality risk for those with few to no social connections compared to White peers in similar circumstances (Liu, 2011). More research is needed on the potential interaction of social connection and trauma on the health of Asian Americans.

Despite the clear connection between relationship quality and health, the current dominant medical model of mental health continues to focus solely upon diagnoses based on symptoms presented by individuals and discounts sociocultural or historical context. For example, trauma is characterized as an individual's inner experience that includes symptoms such as anger, fear, panic, and dissociation. Similarly, much of contemporary psychotherapy focuses almost exclusively on treating symptoms without first understanding their origins. I once attended a workshop led by a preeminent expert on acceptance and commitment therapy (ACT), a form of behavioral therapy. When I asked her about the importance of someone's story about why their trauma happened, she replied curtly, "That and a dime will get you a cup of coffee."

An exclusively behavioral perspective negates the fact that racism and colonialism harm BIPOC and other marginalized people. As the introduction to this book emphasizes, the majority of Asian Americans face two main forms of relational trauma—racism and intergenerational trauma. Therefore, one cannot responsibly discuss Asian American psychology— or provide psychotherapy—without placing trauma in context. That is, theories of psychology that do not consider cultural and historical contexts (which is most of them) perpetuate a colonial, Western-dominant mentality. According to Chakira Haddock-Lazala (2020), "Central to understanding the zeitgeist of contemporary psychology is its denial and avoidance of the social realm—more specifically, it struggles to attend to and conceptualize the importance of social context, social (in)justice, oppression, and their link to social identity and mental health" (p. 149). Therefore, new models are needed to center marginalized people's voices and highlight their oppression, *because their stories matter.*

This chapter continues by examining the importance of social connection and how it applies to Asian Americans. I then introduce betrayal trauma theory, which contextualizes the harm of trauma by identifying the importance of the relationships in which it occurs (Freyd, 1996). Another critical means of understanding Asian American experiences is cultural betrayal trauma theory, which extends betrayal trauma theory by identifying racism and discrimination as factors in causing harm for members of marginalized groups (Gómez, 2017, 2019). Finally, I present an Asian American model of betrayal trauma that incorporates historic trauma due to colonization by Western powers in Asian countries and systemic oppression within the United States.

Betrayal is a key mechanism of oppression, and history is rife with examples. In the United States, these include repeated broken treaties between the federal government and Native American tribes, the broken promise to honor the sovereignty of the Philippines, as detailed in chapter 1, and the failure for centuries of a racist judicial system to convict perpetrators of hate crimes. Whether the betrayal trauma occurs within a family, a culture, or an institution, it can negatively impact mental health. Betrayal trauma theory offers a profoundly different way to understand trauma. When people think of trauma, a car accident or war often comes to mind. However, the most harmful aspect of trauma is not so much what happens *to* an individual as *between* individuals. In other words, *while the individual may bear the burden of post-traumatic stress, dysfunctional, oppressive relationships are most often the origin of harm.* Because betrayal trauma points to the fundamental need for functional relationships in healthy human development, it is necessary to consider mental health in a social and historical context. This premise is central to the growing movement to decolonize psychology.

SOCIAL CONTEXT, TRAUMA, AND ASIAN AMERICANS

The importance of social context in understanding trauma is especially true for Asian Americans, for at least several reasons. The first is that Asian cultures of origin tend to have more fluid social boundaries and family structures than Western cultures. The distinction between immediate and extended family can be blurred, so that "family" often includes multiple generations of family members, extended relatives, and sometimes even family friends. Furthermore, in many Asian cultures, children are taught to call others uncle, aunt, grandma, or grandpa out of respect, even if they are not directly related.

A primary example of having more fluid boundaries and family structures is that Asian diaspora families are more likely than White families to live in multigenerational households. It is traditional in many Asian cultures to take care of the elderly within the home, extend help to relatives in need, and have grandparents assume a significant role in child care. In Canada, about one in five South Asian and Chinese Canadian households live with at least one parent, compared with one in ten of the general Canadian population (Statistics Canada, 2019). A similar trend exists in the United States, where 29% of Asian Americans live in multigenerational family households (Cohn & Passel, 2018).

At the same time, it is essential to recognize that there can be wide variation among Asian ethnic groups. While 27% of South Asian grandparents in Canada live with their grandchildren, the same is true for only 6% of Korean Canadian grandmothers and 3% of Japanese Canadian grandmothers (Todd, 2016). There can also be generational differences; Asian immigrants report greater family cohesion and ethnic identity than their US-born counterparts (Leong et al., 2013), so the prevalence of multigenerational households may decrease with each subsequent generation.

A second reason why sociocultural context is essential in understanding the Asian American experience is language. About 71% of Asian American adults were born in another country, and most speak a language other than English at home. In addition, nearly half of first-generation immigrants report not speaking English proficiently (Budiman & Ruiz, 2021). Not speaking English or the language increases interdependence upon group members for help with translation and finding resources, adding to the importance of forging connections within one's ethnic group for first-generation immigrants.

The desire to preserve one's cultural heritage is another motivation for forming bonds with ethnic group members. Burmese refugee Mu, whose story is featured in the documentary *Mu and the Vanishing World* (Beltrán & Leung, 2020), describes her dream to build a home where various people from various ethnic tribes can come and wear their traditional clothes freely, as well as practice their religious rituals (*DisOrient screening World Refugee Day: Q&A: Mu and the vanishing world* [Video], 2021). The many Asian ethnic communities in the United States, from Little Manilas, Mumbais, and Saigons to Koreatowns, Japantowns, and Chinatowns, are evidence of the importance of cultural bonds among Asian American groups.

A third reason is that being part of a minority group increases the need to band together in a shared identity for security in the face of racism (Gómez, 2012). In addition to social networking being helpful for Asian Americans in general, research has also found it particularly helpful in coping with increased anti-Asian racism during the pandemic (Lee & Waters, 2021; Yang, Tsai, & Pan, 2020).

Finally, historical and intergenerational trauma, which for many Asian Americans are inseparable from a history of Western colonization, are an intrinsic part of the Asian diaspora experience. Many immigrants and refugees left their home countries due to war, extreme poverty, and persecution. Even if they did not, their parents and grandparents often experienced these forms of trauma. As a result, they may transmit the effects of post-traumatic stress through sudden rages or extreme anxiety directly to their children, who can, in turn, pass down their inherited trauma to subsequent generations.

For all of these reasons—familial, societal, racial, colonial, and historical—the experiences of Asian Americans cannot be decontextualized. A new framework is needed to understand trauma among Asian Americans accurately. Betrayal trauma theory, which places trauma in context, provides the beginnings of a pathway toward that understanding.

BETRAYAL TRAUMA: THE RUPTURE OF ATTACHMENT

When a relationship that hinges on trust is ruptured, or, in extreme cases, never developed at all, "the traumatized person loses her basic sense of self" (Herman, 2015, p. 55). This includes not only relationships with individual people, but also with institutions, culture, and society. Thus, trauma can only be accurately understood in its social context (e.g., Freyd, 1996; Harvey, 1996; Herman, 2015; Tang & Freyd, 2012). As Judith Herman, author of the classic text *Trauma and Recovery*, writes,

Traumatic events . . . shatter the sense of connection between individual and community, creating a crisis of faith . . . the damage to the survivor's faith and sense of community is particularly severe when the traumatic events themselves involve the betrayal of important relationships. The imagery of these events often crystallizes around a moment of betrayal, and it is this breach of trust which gives the intrusive images their intense emotional power. (Herman, 1992/2015, p. 55)

Betrayal trauma theory, developed by Jennifer Freyd (1996), offers a contextual framework for understanding trauma. It identifies the betrayal of trust in a close, dependent relationship as a key mechanism that causes lasting harm in cases of abuse. As a result, interpersonal trauma at the hands of someone close or more powerful results in more mental health risks than that of someone less close and less powerful. A substantial body of research has demonstrated that trauma high in betrayal can result in more severe symptoms consistent with post-traumatic stress disorder (PTSD), as well as depression, anxiety, suicidality, and dissociation than when the relationship is less close, or there is no relationship at all (e.g., DePrince & Freyd, 2002; Freyd et al., 2005; Goldsmith et al., 2012; Edwards et al., 2012; Gómez, 2021; Tang & Freyd, 2012). These findings support Herman's assertion that "*Psychological trauma is an affliction of the powerless*" (Herman, 2015, p. 33). This is not to say that traumas low or moderate in betrayal do not have any impact; these, too, can be quite harmful and have severe, lasting effects.

Examples of trauma high in betrayal include sexual, physical, or emotional abuse within a family or at the hands of someone in a position of power. Traumas considered moderate in betrayal include being assaulted by a stranger, being harassed at work, and bullying, although, again, these can also be highly impactful events. Traumas lowest in betrayal include events that do not involve harm deliberately inflicted by other people, such as car accidents and natural disasters.

For many Asian Americans, betrayal may be an even more salient factor in trauma, partly due to broad and interdependent connections with their families and communities. Betrayal trauma committed by a relative, such as an uncle or teacher, may feel as impactful as that perpetrated by a direct caretaker, due to fluid family boundaries. Though high betrayal often refers to perpetrators who are immediate family members, for Asian Americans, relationships outside the parent-child dyad can be considered close or even dependent, since many live in multigenerational households or maintain close contact with relatives in the community.

The following is the story of Korean American artist Misoo Bang (personal communication, May 20, 2021), whose work appears on the cover of this book. Her story illustrates the painful effects of betrayal trauma in the form of being sexually abused by a family member from the age of 10 into her teens.

Misoo's Story

Though she was born in the Bronx, Misoo Bang was raised in Korea by her father from the age of one. When she was 18 years old and still in high school, her father died, and she had to move to the United States to live with a mother she did not know (Cotton, 2021). At the time, the only way to communicate with friends in Korea was to write a letter that took two weeks to arrive and would take two additional weeks to receive a reply. Not being able to speak any English and feeling lost in her new school, Misoo describes finding solace in art to cope with intense loneliness and a newly diagnosed chronic illness (Bang, 2021).

Recovering Traumatic Memories through Art

Later, when Bang became pregnant, she again turned to art, this time to express the inexplicably intense anxiety she felt for her future child's safety. She began to draw images of an ominous presence she calls "the Bunnyman," a tall humanoid figure with rabbit's ears. In some scenes, the Bunnyman appears to be stealing the fetus from her womb (see figure 2.1); in others, the Bunnyman is giving children candy and leading them away on a parade. Bang also became obsessed with collecting broken porcelain dolls that she would sketch in contorted positions of being raped. Eventually, after years of drawing these dolls, she would recognize she had been repeatedly raped herself. In Misoo's words, "Understanding that what happened to me as a child affected how I was thinking and the work I was making was a big shock, because I never really had the courage [until then] to connect [my] history with what I was making. I didn't have the courage to understand why am I suicidal, why was I hurting myself,

Figure 2.1.

Note. Misoo Bang. (2009). *Twinkle Twinkle.* [Oil pastel and color pencil on paper]. Image description: A dark blue sky lit with stars forms the backdrop. A humanoid rabbit with a pink face and black arms reaches out from behind a pregnant woman to grab her fetus. The woman has a bloody nose and a frozen smile.

why did I feel entrapped. To understand that was a big turning point in my artist career. It was like a lost piece of a puzzle that was missing the whole time, and when I figured out that memory was affecting my life the whole way, finally, I could see the big picture of what I was doing, why I was so scared, and why I was making these very disturbing images of dolls."

For many years after realizing she was sexually abused, Misoo used art to recover memories of the traumas and to process the related pain and terror. This process required her to trust her intuition, and she describes the importance of engaging her entire body in the creation of larger-than-life paintings spanning 15 feet across and 5 feet tall, which, to her, represented an enormous bed. Many of the paintings include hair that she painstakingly drew strand by strand. In one such painting, titled *I Am the Barrier* (2014; figure 2.2), Misoo drew thick, dark locks of a mother's hair over finer child's hair. She estimates she spent over 300 hours drawing hair. "Everything hurt—knees, backs, wrists," she described. Yet she recognized that the more physical labor she put into the work, the more she could physically impart the strength of the mother. Then, to represent "losing something precious," Misoo poured black ink all over the canvas. Immediately, she panicked at the sight of what she felt was ruined work, and once more got down on hands and knees to scrub away the ink, using everything she could think of, including her nails. She realized as she was scrubbing that she was fighting her perpetrator. As she uncovered areas of the original hair, she saw that the mother was still there, protecting the child.

Figure 2.2.

Note. Misoo Bang. (2015). *I am the Barrier.* [India ink and pencil on paper]. Image description: Thick swirls of long, dark hair catch the light and are partially covered by splashes of black ink.

Using art, Misoo was able to transform her relationship with her perpetrator from one of helplessness to empowerment. However, she denied believing in recovery. "How can I recover something that was never there?" she asked, referring to the loss of a childhood free of abuse. Still, she asserted she has attained a sense of peace with her memories.

Publicly Disclosing Sexual Abuse

While being sexually abused carries an enormous amount of stigma for any victim, it has become somewhat more acceptable to discuss in the West, where it has been addressed by celebrities, news media, and in self-help books. However, for Asians and Asian Americans, talking about sex, especially sexual abuse, is often still considered taboo (Futa et al., 2001; Moghal et al., 1995; Okamura et al., 1995, Rao et al., 1992). Therefore, Misoo's openness in disclosing her sexual abuse is both courageous and unusual. Regarding her extended family, Misoo states, "They know I am giving a lot of talks about [being sexually abused], but they never acknowledge it." She adds, "My family thinks I am bringing shame on them in talking about it."

Experiencing Racism and Sexism

Racism and sexism are additional forms of trauma Misoo has experienced as an Asian immigrant in the United States. A frightening incident occurred when she was walking home alone and a car full of young, White people drove by and started yelling, "Go back to your own country!" (Murray, 2021). She was so shaken by what happened that she moved from the small Vermont town where she lived at the time to a larger city that she felt would be safer. She also began carrying pepper spray with her whenever she left her home. She described how her Asian American friends wear hoodies and sunglasses when out in public to disguise their race.

How Common Is Betrayal Trauma among Asian Americans?

One of the most extensive surveys of betrayal trauma includes over 800 teens and young adults (Gamache Martin et al., 2016). Among this community sample, 58% had experienced at least one low betrayal trauma, 65% had experienced moderate betrayal trauma, and 47% had experienced high betrayal trauma. Women, on average, experienced more betrayal traumas than men. Information on those who identify as nonbinary was not available.

In research I conducted focusing on Asians, Asian Americans, and Pacific Islanders (API) living in the United States, 277 adults answered questions about various forms of betrayal trauma (Tang, 2009). Of this group, 95% identified as Asian or Asian American, and 5% as Pacific Islander. The group ranged from young college students to older community members. All identified as either male or female, and none identified as nonbinary, though it was an option on the survey.

Reported abuse rates varied depending upon the type of trauma (close or not close) and age, and are shown in table 2.1. Younger women (under 25 years old) were more likely to report being attacked by someone close as a child and as an adult than women 25 years or older. Rates of reported sexual abuse were similar for the two age groups, ranging between 10 to 11%, respectively, by someone close, and 5 to 11%, respectively, by someone not close.

Young API men reported adult sexual assault with surprising frequency, at 20% for close perpetrators and 19% for not close perpetrators. On the other hand, none of the API men over 25 reported being sexually abused by someone close, and only 5% reported being sexually abused by someone not close. The large difference in reporting rates may reflect changing attitudes toward disclosing sexual abuse between the generations and greater recognition of what constitutes sexual abuse among the younger generation.

Physical abuse was measured by asking respondents whether they were attacked by someone close as a child and as an adult. In retrospect, the use of the word "attacked" may have led to lower reports of physical abuse compared to other studies that use the word "hit" instead, since respondents may have been hit by someone but did not consider it an attack. Estimates of physical abuse among Asian diaspora range between 25 to 82% among men (Meston et al., 1999; Schoen et al., 1998; Sieben et al., 2019a) and 22 to 69% among women (Meston et al., 1999; Sieben et al., 2019a).

Table 2.1.   Rates of Betrayal Trauma among APIs

	% Women		% Men	
Age	< 25	>= 25	< 25	>= 25
Attacked by someone *close* as a child	9.9	6.1	15.0	9.4
Attacked by someone *not close* as a child	2.0	2.8	9.4	10.0
Child sexual abuse by someone *close*	10.3	11.3	12.5	0.0
Child sexual abuse by someone *not close*	5.2	11.3	7.8	5.0
Attacked by someone *close* as an adult	9.9	1.0	5.0	7.8
Attacked by someone *not close* as an adult	2.0	2.8	9.4	2.5
Adult sexual abuse by someone *close*	9.0	12.7	18.8	7.5
Adult sexual abuse by someone *not close*	4.9	12.7	17.2	2.5

Note. (Tang, 2009)

Overlooking and Forgetting Betrayal

Betrayal trauma theory provides an explanation as to why betrayal is often overlooked or even forgotten, as in Misoo Bang's story. The ability to detect betrayal is often adaptive, alerting one to potential threats. However, recognizing betrayal can at other times be too painful and/or even dangerous, and the risk of losing a relationship can feel like a threat to survival (Freyd, 1996; Gómez & Freyd, 2019). According to betrayal trauma theory, individuals therefore suppress natural reactions to betrayal, such as anger, outrage, or fear, blocking normally integrated processes of processing and memory (De-Prince & Freyd, 1999; Freyd, DePrince, & Zurbriggen, 2001). In other words, the goal of maintaining a sense of being loved and protected can cause adults and children alike to forget about abuse and overlook evidence of betrayal.

Those who have experienced betrayal trauma as children can have a more difficult time seeing when someone is behaving in a harmful way in adult relationships. In their book *Blind to Betrayal: Why We Fool Ourselves We Aren't Being Fooled* (2013), Freyd and her co-author, psychologist Pamela Birrell, begin by telling the story of Julie, a well-respected lawyer in her 40s. Julie decides to surprise her husband at a bar, but when she shows up, she witnesses him walk up to another woman and kiss her. Nonetheless, she believes her husband when he tells her he does not know the woman.

People in similar situations often berate themselves, saying, "Why was I so stupid?" and "Why didn't I see this sooner?" However, unawareness of betrayal happens automatically and is out of one's conscious control. It is not that Julie chose to believe her husband. In a sense, her past conditioning to overlook betrayal short-circuited her ability to think objectively (Freyd & Birrell, 2013).

As Freyd (1996) explains, we can both know and not know something simultaneously. That is, the memory gets stored out of our conscious awareness, making it more difficult to access. Cognitive psychologists call this "implicit memory" or "implicit knowledge." Our brains use implicit memory to help us take shortcuts in thinking. For example, once we learn how to ride a bike, we can do it repeatedly without having to think about each step involved. Sometimes, we can even drive a familiar route to work using implicit memory.

Attachment theory and current neuroscience both support the premise that betrayal trauma involves implicit memory outside of conscious awareness. "Attachment theory is essentially a regulatory theory, and attachment can be defined as the interactive regulation of biological synchronicity between organisms" (Schore, 2000, p. 23). In particular, the brain's right hemisphere is specifically impacted by early social experiences, up to age three (Geschwind & Galaburda, 1987; Schore, 1994, 1998), and is largely responsible for storing early emotional experiences (Semrud-Clikeman & Hynd, 1990). The right hemisphere is also dominant in infants and adults for processing the facial expressions of others (Indersmitten & Gur, 2003; Semrud-Clikeman & Hynd, 1990). Schore (2000) argues that since the right hemisphere is dominant for implicit learning, early learning about close relationships is encoded in implicit-procedural models. Being implicit, these models work at a subconscious level.

Racism and Betrayal Trauma Theory

Racial trauma has only recently begun to receive more attention in psychological research. Some scholars have applied betrayal trauma theory to explain the harm of racism. Susana Ming Lowe et al. (2012) describe the case of Jan, a Korean American staff member of a college counseling center. At closing time, one of her co-workers, a White male, mistook her for an international student. He gesticulated at her as if she could not speak English and yelled at her to leave. Enraged and in tears, Jan sought help from her clinical supervisor, who facilitated an "empty chair exercise" in which Jan could imagine confronting the perpetrator. At first, she confronted the co-worker. Then, she noticed that his appearance changed in her imagination into a little boy, also White, who had taunted her on the school bus when she was a little girl. She had forgotten about him until that moment, but experienced a surge of emotion as she yelled what she described as "A lot of really sort of immature responses. It was more like shut up, shut up! . . . You don't know anything!"

Using betrayal trauma theory to explain Jan's forgetting, Lowe et al. (2012) theorize that Jan blocked out the memory of being taunted on the school bus because confronting her childhood bully as a young girl may have been too painful and threatening for her. Children are ill-equipped to defend themselves, either physically or emotionally. One of the few coping strategies available to them is to internalize the rupture in the relationship as their fault. They learn to overlook and forget about abusive behavior in order to preserve a relationship. Young Jan likely recognized that confronting her bully meant risking having his behavior condoned by the entire class, assuming they were mostly non-Asian. Forgetting about the bullying helped preserve her membership in her peer group (conditional as it was), which is central to a child's healthy development. It is important to note that while Jan was not dependent upon the boy as a caregiver, racism has the power to completely ostracize someone from their social peers, not just from the perpetrator.

Betrayal and Shame

Shame is a direct result of the need to preserve an important relationship in the face of betrayal trauma (Platt & Freyd, 2015; Freyd & Birrell, 2013).

Platt and Freyd (2015) investigated levels of shame and dissociation among a cohort of 124 female-identifying college students (79% White, 16% Asian or Asian American, 7.3% Hispanic, 1.6% Black, and 4% "other"). They randomly assigned participants to one of two conditions. In the "interpersonal threat condition," participants were shown images that implied relational violence, such as a man grabbing a woman and a boy with a black eye. In the other condition, participants were shown images that involved non-interpersonal threats, such as a tornado and an auto accident. Those with a history of high but not low betrayal trauma had increased levels of shame and dissociation after viewing the images.

The shame response preserves a relationship in two ways: 1) It prevents the victim from reacting to abuse by confronting the perpetrator or running away from them, both of which risk a rupture in the relationship; and 2) The victim's response is instead one of submitting and appeasing, which is more likely to elicit a caregiving response from the perpetrator and increase the likelihood of safety (Keltner & Harker, 1998). For trauma survivors, the perspective provided by betrayal trauma theory that it is adaptive not to have conscious feelings when a trauma high in betrayal occurs can help mitigate shame.

While shame can be adaptive when one's safety is threatened, repeated betrayal trauma produces chronic shame (Freyd & Birrell, 2013). Chronic shame can have a wide range of consequences, including depression (Scheff, 2001), PTSD (Leskela et al., 2002; Robinaugh & McNally, 2010), and dissociation (Izard et al., 1993). The relationship is also bidirectional. Feeling dissociated or disconnected from others can trigger acute shame (Dorahy et al., 2021). Further, survivors can develop secondary shame, or what Lewis (1990) calls "feeling traps," in which they feel ashamed of feeling ashamed. For example, suppose Jan's supervisor had not helped her process her emotions with the empty chair exercise. In that case, she may never have understood that the intensity of her response to workplace racism was informed in part by the humiliation of past racial trauma. As a result, she may likely have blamed herself for having such an intense response to being belittled by her coworker.

Sudha's story, which follows, is a case example based on Asian American clients I have worked with.

Sudha's Story

Sudha, a second-generation Indian American and college student, sought therapy to help with debilitating depression preventing her from eating or doing any of her schoolwork. She was in danger of losing her scholarship if she failed her classes. Her parents were also helping to finance her education, covering the costs of rent and food. Sudha insisted that nothing remarkable had happened to her as a child. I asked whether her parents had ever hit her, careful not to use the word "abuse." For many Asian and Asian American clients, the term "abuse" feels culturally insensitive. It is associated with a Western perspective that does not recognize Asian cultural norms.

"All of my friends got hit by their parents," Sudha replied. "It's no big deal for Indian families." However, as we explored her past over the next few months, she recounted her mother's frightening rages during which she would call Sudha worthless and ungrateful. Sudha also remembered repeatedly being beaten with a stick when she did not receive perfect marks on an exam. Like many survivors of abuse, Sudha would sometimes express surprise at the intensity of the emotions accompanying a memory that arose during therapy. She would also doubt the validity of the emotions, saying, "I feel like I'm being a baby." Sudha recalled being told by aunts and uncles to have patience with her mother, who worked long hours to support the family while her father was unemployed.

According to betrayal trauma theory, it is adaptive for young adults like Sudha, who are still financially dependent upon their parents, to avoid acknowledging betrayal trauma. To maintain a close relationship with their parents, they may internalize any conflict by assuming all of the blame. Shaming oneself is a common result, as Sudha did in calling herself a "baby." However, betrayal trauma theory does not fully capture Sudha's experience as it relates to her cultural context. What happens when one member of an oppressed ethnic group is harmed by another member of that same group? How are other group members likely to respond, and why?

CULTURAL BETRAYAL TRAUMA THEORY

Cultural betrayal trauma theory (CBTT) advances betrayal trauma theory by underscoring the harm of pervasive racism in the dominant culture (Gómez, 2017, 2019). By considering broader societal influences, it provides a postcolonial perspective of trauma. As Gómez explains, Black communities practice "(intra)cultural trust," both a legacy of collectivist West African cultures and a mechanism to guard against the harm of racism. Thus, the breach of (intra) cultural trust when one Black person abuses another results in a greater degree of betrayal than when the perpetrator is outside the ethnic community.

A growing number of research studies support the influence of cultural betrayal trauma on mental health for other oppressed groups as well. One study of US college students compared experiences of sexual violence among marginalized groups (BIPOC, foreign nationals, Muslims, and non-heterosexuals) to dominant group members (defined as all others; Gómez & Freyd, 2018). Over one-third (35%) of the BIPOC group comprised Asian and Pacific Islanders. The study found a stronger association between sexual

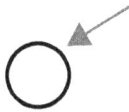

a) **Traditional Model of Trauma:** Traditional models of trauma expect that individuals have defenses (represented by circle) to trauma.
Arrow = all forms of trauma

b) **Betrayal Trauma Theory:** Betrayal trauma theory[1] contextualizes trauma in interpersonal relationships with trust and/or dependancy, which creates unique vulnerability (perforated defenses) to traumatic betrayal.
Arrow = betrayal trauma

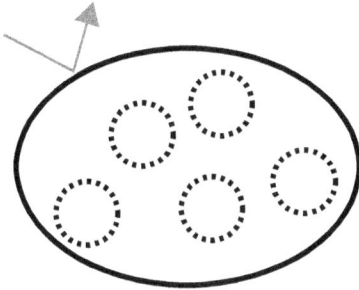

c) **(Intra)Cultural Betrayal Trauma:** Cultural betrayal trauma theory[2] contextualizes betrayal trauma within larger sociocultural dynamics. Cultural minorities pool defense resources (represented by ellipse) to buffer against societal trauma.
Arrow = societal trauma

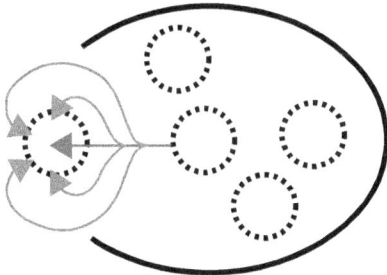

d) **Cultural Betrayal Trauma:** A member of a cultural minority has uniquely vulnerable defenses to betrayal of (intra)cultural trust. When a victim is violated by a perceived in-group perpetrator, the victim's (intra)cultural trust is also betrayed.
Arrow = cultural betrayal trauma

Figure 2.3. Traditional Models of Trauma versus Betrayal Trauma and Cultural Betrayal Trauma

Note. From "Jennifer M. Gómez, PhD: Cultural betrayal trauma theory" by J. Gómez, n.d. (https://jmgomez. org/cultural-betrayal-trauma-theory/). Reprinted with permission from S. Shen Joffre & J. Gómez. Image description: A series of four images (a through d) depict models of trauma. Image (a) depicts a circle with an arrow pointing toward it, representing a traditional model of trauma in which individuals are expected to have defenses. Image (b) represents Betrayal Trauma Theory. There are two circles, each with a section drawn with a dotted line to represent vulnerability. An arrow originates from one circle and ends in the other, representing the relational nature of trauma. Image (c) demonstrates intra-cultural trust in which perforated circles are enclosed together within a solid boundary. Image (d) depicts the process of cultural betrayal trauma in which one of the intra-cultural members is attacked by another. This is shown by arrows drawn from one perforated circle to another.

violence and symptoms of post-traumatic stress for marginalized group members assaulted by members within their identity groups than for dominant group members. This result suggests that cultural betrayal trauma plays a primary role in the mental health consequences of interpersonal violence. Beyond cultural betrayal, membership itself in a minority group also increased the frequency of symptoms. In other words, there are unique factors about being part of a minority group that exacerbate post-traumatic stress other than the perpetrator's ethnicity. Figure 2.3 illustrates the difference between traditional models of trauma that are focused on the individual versus betrayal trauma and cultural betrayal trauma theories that situate relational trauma in its sociocultural context.

Cultural betrayal trauma theory has also been explicitly examined in relation to Asians and Asian Americans. A study that compared experiences of cultural betrayal trauma in the form of physical, sexual, or emotional abuse by other Asians or Asian Americans to those perpetrated by someone of a different ethnic group found that cultural betrayal trauma was associated with increased symptoms of post-traumatic stress, including dissociation, hallucinations, and hypervigilance (Gómez, 2017). These results indicate that CBTT is relevant to Asian Americans with trauma perpetrated by other Asians or Asian Americans, adding a unique layer of harm beyond trauma perpetrated by someone outside the ethnic community.

As in both Sudha and Misoo's cases, cultural betrayal trauma can also take the form of failure by ethnic group members to protect or advocate for the victim, such as asking the victim to have compassion for their parents, or not reporting the abuse to authorities. The need to join in solidarity against racism and discrimination, coupled with Asian collectivist values, results in blaming the victim, which exacerbates their shame.

INSTITUTIONAL BETRAYAL TRAUMA

I had been working with my client Shizuko for several months when one day, she arrived to a session very tearful and angry. An employee of a student dining hall had refused to serve her, although they took orders from others in line immediately before and after her. Shizuko, an international student from Japan for whom English was a second language, described having a freeze response and being unable to speak, partly for fear the server would laugh at the way she spoke.

Shizuko filed a complaint through the college's designated channel for reporting discrimination, but received no response. She contacted them again a week later and was referred to an international student coordinator, who questioned whether Shizuko had actually experienced racism. Finally, she contacted the dining hall director, who, after another week, told her they would discuss the matter with the employee in question. Shizuko never received an official apology from the college and was never informed of any disciplinary action taken against the employee. For weeks after the incident, Shizuko felt humiliated, helpless, and ashamed, an outcome that might have been mitigated had the college been more responsive to her complaint. This failure of the college to protect Shizuko and its impact on her mental health exemplifies institutional betrayal trauma.

Institutional betrayal trauma highlights the power disparity that exists between institutions and those that depend upon them, such as employees, customers, and students. It refers to "wrongdoings perpetrated by an institution upon those dependent upon that institution" (Platt et al., 2009). Institutional betrayal directly applies to Asian American experiences to describe systematic racial trauma perpetrated by the government and other institutions. The targeting of Southeast Asian immigrants for deportation by US Immigration and Customs Enforcement (ICE) (*Inside the numbers: How immigration shapes Asian American and Pacific Islanders communities*, 2019) is a contemporary example of institutional betrayal trauma. Institutional betrayal is also a frequent mechanism of harm in historical trauma, extending back through centuries of Western colonialism across the globe.

Institutional Betrayal, Historical Trauma, and Ethnic Identity

The legacy of colonialism continues to affect current generations. A study focusing on a diverse group of Native Americans by Cromer et al. (2018) found associations between historical and institutional betrayal trauma and intergenerational trauma. The more years parents and grandparents had spent in boarding school, the more likely the participant experienced childhood betrayal trauma (emotional and physical abuse, sexual abuse, and witnessing domestic violence).

The researchers also asked participants how often they thought about the effects of historical trauma, such as the loss of language, traditional family systems, and traditional healing practices. An association emerged between acculturation to White culture and having less awareness of the effects of historical trauma. Conversely, those who identified more with Native American culture thought more often about historical trauma. These findings are consistent with institutional betrayal trauma theory, since identifying with the perpetrators of historical trauma appears to create a need to look past collective suffering. In other words, institutional "betrayal trauma theory explains the enduring negative impact of colonization. Trauma that occurred to colonized people who were forced into a dependent relationship with their oppressors exacerbates the traumatic impact because of a need to maintain closeness for survival" (Cromer et al., 2018, p. 101).

Japanese American Internment: "Betrayal by a Trusted Source"

The incarceration of 120,000 Japanese Americans during World War II is one of the starkest examples of institutional betrayal toward Asian Americans in US history. The majority were US citizens, half of whom were children. An additional 22,000 were relocated and incarcerated in Canada. Most lost their belongings, homes, and businesses. When trauma occurs on a collective level such as this, it persists through generations of the individual and collective unconscious in the form of internalized racism and shame.

The novel *Obasan* (Kogawa, 1994) illustrates how this is the case for Naomi Nakane, a 36-year-old Japanese Canadian schoolteacher. Naomi is *Sansei*, or third generation, her grandparents being immigrants from Japan. The novel begins in the year 1972, and Naomi is introduced as a solitary figure with few friends in the small town of Cecil, in the province of Alberta, where she teaches. In the classroom, the students taunt her for being a "spinster," and deliberately mispronounce her Japanese last name. As the story progresses, we learn that the classroom racism is not only the cause of new wounds, but is also a vehicle through which racial trauma from the past perpetrates ongoing wounding.

Naomi is also coping with the disappearance of her mother, who never returned to Canada after leaving for Japan during World War II, when Naomi was six years old. Around the same time, her family was forcibly separated, with some sent to one internment camp while Naomi, her brother, and her grandmother were sent to another. Even after the war, Japanese Canadians were not allowed to return home, and were forced to work on farms for meager wages until 1949. Naomi eventually learns that her mother was severely wounded when the United States dropped an atomic bomb on Nagasaki, and did not want her children to know about her condition. Placed in this context of repeated racial trauma, the teasing by Naomi's students multiplies in significance.

In Naomi's story, we see the impact of historical trauma—the bombing of Nagasaki and the imprisonment of Japanese American and Japanese Canadian citizens—upon Naomi. It also illustrates how the connection to her family acts as a counterpoint to the chronic loss and isolation she experiences. The collectivism of her culture is a source of strength and solace through her grandmother and uncle.

Historical trauma is not only defined by the events but also by their broad psychological and cultural impact (Gone, 2013). These impacts extend beyond narrowly defined symptoms of PTSD. Intense shame, a sense of betrayal, depression, anxiety, impaired relationships, and a fractured sense of self correlate with symptoms associated with what is called complex trauma (Cole, 2006). According to Nagata et al. (2015), the incarceration of Japanese

Americans was a collective trauma that changed their very identity and shattered their pride in being American citizens.

Lew (2016) interviewed Japanese Americans who had been incarcerated during World War II. She found that one of the major impacts was a sense of betrayal, leading to decreased trust in the US government and feeling less safe. According to one survivor of the prison camps, who was incarcerated at age four,

> When you are treated like less than a fucking snake, I mean goddamn, what does that do for you as human being with feelings, you are red blooded human being like anybody else, you have your feelings, your pride, your intellect, etc., you know? (p. 44).

Incarcerated Japanese Americans also expressed increased empathy for other oppressed groups, such as Blacks and Latinos. In addition, they displayed increased activism and a sense of community empowerment.

ECOLOGICAL MODELS OF TRAUMA

An ecological model accounts for the many levels of social relationships that affect an individual's well-being. It is especially useful for conceptualizing historical and intergenerational trauma experienced by many Asian Americans. Bronfenbrenner (1977) was one of the first to propose an ecological model of child development that acknowledged the need to consider the child's environment. This model describes the child at the center of nested social structures, beginning with those with the most influence, such as family, peers, and teachers (the microsystem). Surrounding the microsystem is the exosystem, which consists of settings that do not directly involve the child, such as the parents' workplace, parents' friends, and the neighborhood. Bronfenbrenner emphasized the importance of the interaction between the microsystem and exosystem in what he called the mesosystem. Parent interactions with a child's teachers are one example of the mesosystem network. At a broader level is the macrosystem, which comprises cultural values and beliefs. Finally, there is the chronosystem, representing changes in the environment over time, such as historical events, the pandemic, or, at an individual level, stages of life.

Trauma researchers have used Bronfenbrenner's ecological model to conceptualize the multiple layers of relationships that can be sources of trauma and affect how an individual interprets trauma. Bronfenbrenner's model, however, assumes a homogenous culture and does not account for racial differences within a dominant culture.

Recognizing the usefulness of Bronfenbrenner's model for conceptualizing the social contexts of trauma and its shortfall in not addressing issues of race and ethnicity, Neville and Heppner (1999) developed what they termed CIEM-SAR: a culturally inclusive ecological model of sexual assault recovery. They observed that ethnic identity and culture influenced the responses of trauma survivors to assault. For example, Neville et al. (2004) found cultural differences among Black and White sexual assault victims in their cultural attributions of why they were sexually assaulted. African Americans were more likely to internalize the "Jezebel" and had a greater tendency to blame themselves, leading to lower self-esteem than their White peers. Chinese rape survivors have been found to express a distinctly Chinese cultural construction of rape, focused on self-blame (Luo, 2000). A priority on preserving family honor and valuing female virginity made recovery more difficult, and sometimes, nearly impossible, in cases when rape survivors are forced to marry their perpetrators. In addition, Campbell et al. (2009) observed that victim-blaming and self-blame occur at all levels of social structure of the ecological model, not just from larger society, as Neville and Heppner proposed.

Gómez (2019) adapted Bronfenbrenner's model to illustrate sociocultural levels of betrayal trauma for Black Americans. It explicitly names discrimination in dominant American culture as a component of the macrosystem, describing its manifestation in the exosystem, such as police brutality, Black criminalization in the media, and a racist judicial system. These broad social contexts exert pressure upon the microsystem of Black individuals and communities that exist within them.

AN ASIAN AMERICAN MODEL OF BETRAYAL TRAUMA

The Rings of Betrayal Model (figure 2.4), is an ecological approach to contextualizing the traumatic experiences of Asian Americans. Expanding upon Gómez's model of cultural betrayal trauma for Black Americans (2019), the Rings of Betrayal Model also includes Bronfenbrenner's chronosystem that accounts for the influence of time. As depicted by the model, institutional and cultural betrayal traumas can cross spheres of influence, as indicated by the labels. Institutional betrayal trauma spans all the social systems that involve institutions, from the mesosystem to the chronosystem. Similarly, cultural betrayal is more likely to occur in both the microsystem and the mesosystem that comprise Asian American communities and families.

Chronosystem: History and Time

The chronosystem is vital to include from a decolonizing perspective because colonization, oppression, war, and other widespread traumas pervade the history of Asians and Asian Americans. The chronosystem thus provides the

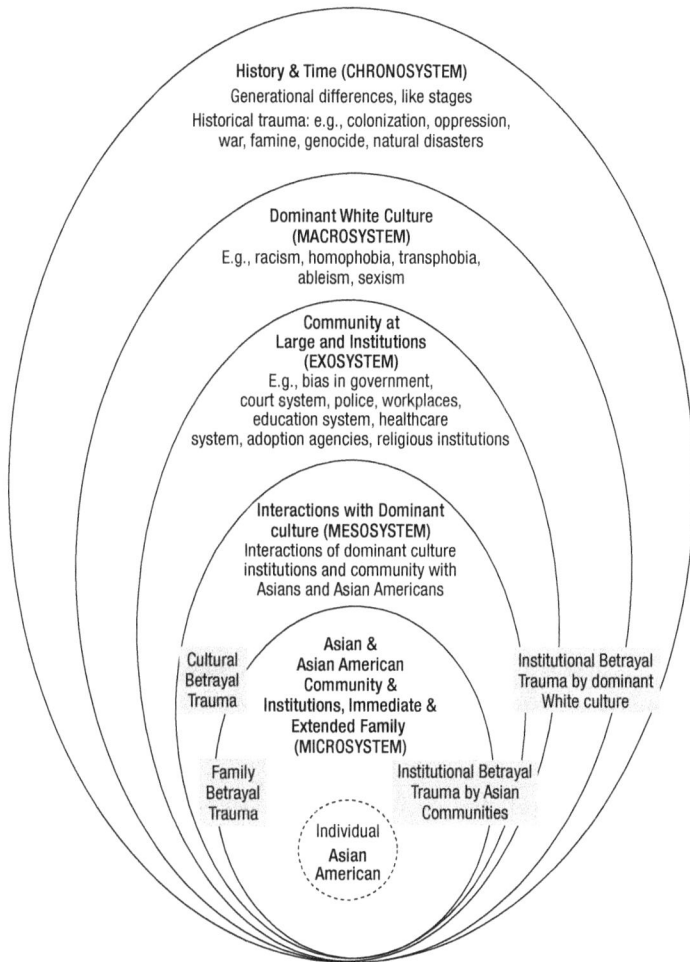

Figure 2.4. The Rings of Betrayal Model for Asian Americans

Note. Adapted from "Jennifer M. Gómez, PhD: Cultural betrayal trauma theory" by J. Gómez, S. Shen Joffre, & R. L. Gobin, 2018 (https://jmgomez.org/cultural-betrayal-trauma-theory/). Reprinted with permission. Image description: six concentric circles, each representing a social sphere. The outermost ring is the Chronosystem and is labeled "History & Time," which includes generational differences and life stages as well as historical trauma. It is followed by the sphere labeled "Dominant White Culture (Macrosystem)," which includes racism, homophobia, transphobia, ableism, and sexism. The third ring, "Community at Large and Institutions (Exosystem)," represents bias in government, the court system, police, workplaces, the education system, the healthcare system, adoption agencies, and religious institutions. The fourth ring, called "Interactions with Dominant Culture (Mesosystem)," represents interactions between the community at large and dominant institutions with Asian and Asian American communities, institutions, and families who occupy the next ring, Microsystem. Finally, nested within Asian and Asian American communities is the individual. The boundary around the individual is perforated, representing the more collectivist values and shared identity of many Asian Americans with their families and communities. Institutional Betrayal Trauma by the dominant culture can occur within the four outer rings. Cultural betrayal trauma, institutional betrayal trauma by Asian American communities, and family betrayal trauma occur predominantly within the mesosystem and microsystem.

context for systematically perpetrated oppression, which often manifests as institutional betrayal trauma.

The chronosystem can also include recent changes, such as the global pandemic associated with the weaponization of racism against Asian Americans. Within an individual, the chronosystem can represent different stages of life, from birth to old age, or changes in ethnic identity. Further, the chronosystem helps conceptualize how historical trauma can lead to intergenerational trauma.

Macrosystem: Dominant White Culture

The macrosystem includes cultural biases such as racism, sexism, ableism, homophobia, and transphobia that pervade the dominant culture. These forms of bias manifest in all social structures within the macrosystem, resulting in institutional betrayal and interpersonal traumas on an individual level. In the United States, the macrosystem is based on Western belief systems. However, first-generation immigrants will often have grown up with another macrosystem from their country of origin as well.

Exosystem: Dominant Culture Institutions

This sphere comprises dominant culture, i.e., White, Western communities and institutions. These institutions comprise workplaces, US government agencies, the judicial system, schools, corporations, and many others. Any of these institutions upon which people such as employees, students, and citizens depend can be a source of institutional betrayal trauma. Therefore, the types of institutional betrayal are many and varied.

The targeting of immigrants by the federal government is one example. In a model of psychological well-being for Mexican immigrants, Jensen (2007) identified fear of deportation as a stressor in the exosystem. During the first year of the Trump administration, ICE arrests of undocumented immigrants without a criminal record more than tripled over the prior year (*Inside the numbers: How immigration shapes Asian American and Pacific Islanders communities*, 2019). ICE also began targeting Southeast Asian refugees, many of whom arrived in the United States as young children whose parents had fled war. Approximately 15% of Asian Americans are undocumented. These discriminatory practices affect not only them, but also their families, and whole communities.

The judicial system is often another source of institutional betrayal. A well-known example regarding Asian Americans is the case of Chanel Miller, who was sexually assaulted on the campus of Stanford University. The perpetrator, a White male student at Stanford, was convicted of three charges of felony sexual assault. However, the judge at the trial for this crime expressed sympathy for him, giving him a light sentence of six months in jail, of which he only served three.

In chapter 7, I address the pandemic of racism (Brunsma et al., 2017; Clark et al., 2012; Maton et al., 2011; Yamazaki-Jones, 2023) and sexual harassment (Cantor et al., 2015; Rosenthal et al., 2016; Schneider et al., 2002) experienced by psychology graduate students within their own departments. Much of the discrimination is driven by faculty and staff. Therefore, the failure of universities and departments to protect the students is emblematic of institutional betrayal.

Microsystem: Asian Community, Immediate and Extended Family, the Individual

The microsystem includes Asian American institutions and community organizations, immediate and extended family, and the individual. In most ecological models, the extended family is placed within the exosystem, two layers removed from the individual. In this Asian American model, extended family is located within the microsystem, reflecting the more fluid boundaries between immediate family and extended family that often exist among Asian diaspora. Even when interactions with extended family are infrequent, these relationships can assume a degree of closeness and authority that extends beyond Western norms. For example, aunts, uncles, and even family friends may have input over an individual's choice of major in college, career path, or potential candidates for marriage.

Examples of Asian community organizations include Asian language schools for children, Asian American social justice organizations, and ethnicity-based associations. Additionally, places of worship for many Asian Americans center around culture and language, such as a Sikh or Hindu temple, or Filipino Catholic or Chinese Baptist church. Asian American organizations provide legal, social, and spiritual support. However, they can at times commit institutional betrayal trauma that is simultaneously cultural betrayal. For example, army combat veteran Tegh Singh described how his gurudwara is not accessible to people like him who suffer from post-traumatic stress. "[They] have no intentionally quiet spaces, and create crowding, even on low attendance days. We have parking lots with blocked fire lanes, wide open spaces intentionally turned into narrow walkways, funneling us into massive rooms with three out of five exits permanently blocked. My choice is then difficult—risk a panic attack or stay home" (Kaur, 2021).

The exploitation of immigrant labor in the restaurant industry is another example of institutional betrayal within Asian communities. Asian American immigrants with limited English proficiency, who are undocumented, or who do not have a college degree often have no choice but to enter low-wage manual labor jobs where wage theft and exploitation are common. Restaurants are one of the most common settings for exploiting undocumented Asian Americans (Nguyen-Ngo, 2020). The Korean Immigrant Workers' Alliance, a nonprofit advocacy group, estimates that $1.4 billion in wages are stolen yearly by restaurant owners (Koreatown Immigrant Workers Alliance, n.d.). According to a 2012 report by Desis Rising Up & Moving (DRUM), South Asian restaurant workers make less than half of what the average New Yorker makes per hour, and a staggering 74% are paid less than minimum wage.

In addition to institutional and cultural betrayal trauma that can occur in this sphere, family betrayal trauma can also be present. A more recently identified form of betrayal trauma, family betrayal trauma refers to instances when family members fail to prevent or respond supportively to child abuse perpetrated by a trusted other (Delker et al., 2018). For BIPOC, family betrayal trauma often overlaps with cultural betrayal trauma. For others, family betrayal can be perpetrated by non-Asian family members.

It is also essential to recognize that although a focus on cultural betrayal trauma will apply to many Asian Americans, there is also wide variation among individual experiences. For example, most Asian American adoptees are adopted into White families and, as a result, may not live with Asian family members or be raised within an Asian American community. Also, some Asian Americans live in areas where there is little to no Asian American community, which is very different from those who live in areas with high concentrations of Asian Americans, such as California and New York.

Mesosystem: Community Interactions

Traumas that occur in the mesosystem are defined by the interaction between the Asian community and the exosystem. It is a unique sphere in that it includes both cultural and institutional betrayal traumas. Examples of institutional betrayal trauma at this level are one's parents getting deported, or one's teacher getting fired for discussing critical race theory. Cultural betrayal traumas here may be responses to these institutional betrayals, such as defending the government's or school's actions—in other words, blaming the victims.

Part of the complexity of Asian American narratives is that a particular event can be categorized under multiple social spheres. For example, an Asian American employee of a predominantly White institution, such as the education system, can commit cultural betrayal trauma against an Asian American student. In this case, the betrayal is both institutional and cultural.

DECOLONIZING ASIAN AMERICAN PSYCHOLOGY

I return to the questions asked in the introduction to this book: What does it mean to decolonize psychology and move toward liberation? How do we understand trauma through a decolonized lens? Moreover, how is the decolonization of psychology relevant to the lived experiences of Asians and Asian Americans?

Decolonizing psychology begins with recognizing that human suffering occurs in the context of historical trauma and oppression (Bhatia, 2017; Gone, 2021). Ignoring social and cultural contexts invalidates the oppression experienced by women, BIPOC, disabled people, and LGBTQIA+ communities. Many of what are labeled mental disorders are closely linked to traumatic experiences, including historical trauma, oppression, and racism. Ignoring this fact dismisses trauma victims' lived experiences and blames them for having disorders rather than understanding the leading cause as an interpersonal one. Understanding that betrayal is a fundamental mechanism of how trauma causes harm runs counter to the traditional Western view of trauma.

This chapter presents a new model of understanding Asian American lived experiences that recognizes the intersection of many types of betrayal trauma in time and allows for variation in individual experiences.

We can decolonize the field of psychology by:

- Recognizing the fundamental importance of human relationships to well-being. This is especially relevant to Asian Americans, who often have more fluid social and familial ties due to their culture and the need to band together for safety.
- Understanding that disconnection and betrayal are how trauma causes lasting harm (Freyd, 1996; Harvey, 1996; Herman, 2015; Tang & Freyd, 2012).

We can understand trauma through a decolonized lens by:

- De-pathologizing symptoms of post-traumatic stress by locating illness and dysfunction in oppressive relationships rather than individuals, whether between parent and child or dominant and minority culture. To do so means, in many cases, viewing mental illness less as an illness and more as intense suffering caused by prolonged experiences of trauma and betrayal.

Finally, the decolonization of psychology is relevant to the lived experiences of Asian Americans because psychology needs to be decolonized in order to be culturally relevant. In actionable terms, this means:

- Developing new, culturally relevant theories and models that situate trauma in its sociocultural context. Cultural betrayal trauma theory is one such model.
- Developing an awareness that institutional betrayal, cultural betrayal, and family betrayal are forms of trauma experienced by the majority of Asian Americans.
- Considering Asian American trauma through an ecological perspective that intersects with layers of various forms of betrayal trauma, from institutions to individual families.

The opening chapter of this book argues for the need to dispel the model minority myth and acknowledge the historical and social context of Asian American trauma. In doing so, it focuses on forms of institutional betrayal in the outermost levels of the Rings of Betrayal Model.

The next chapter shifts the focus to intergenerational trauma within Asian American communities. Again, the model minority myth is implicated in the false narrative that child abuse, particularly sexual abuse, among Asian Americans is rare. I describe how this bias in psychological research is a form of epistemic violence (Teo, 2010).

ADDITIONAL RESOURCES

- Montgomery College. (2021, May 18). *Athenaeum Symposia artist Misoo Bang: The journey of the giantess* [Video]. YouTube. https://tinyurl.com/MisooBang

  Misoo Bang presents her story of trauma and healing through her artwork, spanning two decades.

SCAN ME

- *DisOrient screening world refugee day: Q&A: Mu and the vanishing world* [Video]. (2021). Eventive. https://tinyurl.com/Mu-and-the-Vanishing-World

  In this interview with Burmese immigrant Mu and the two directors of the documentary, *Mu and the Vanishing World* (https://www.muandthevanishing.world), she describes her perspectives on the making of the documentary and shares about her current life in the United States.

SCAN ME

ACEs High or Low? Biases in Research on Child Maltreatment among Asian Americans and Asian Canadians

The two million members of *subtle asian traits*, a Facebook group started by a few second-generation Asian Australian high school students, bond over inside jokes that reference experiences uniquely shared by young Asian diaspora. SAT, as it is called for short, features memes about boba tea cravings, parents who hoard plastic bags and hotel soap, and Asian-themed pop art. At the same time, it is peppered with dark humor about child abuse, such as polls asking about whether spiky durian fruit or bamboo sticks were used more often for corporal punishment. Rather than expressing shock, fellow members post laughing emojis because it is their shared experience. Occasionally, a member will also ask a direct question about whether emotional or physical abuse is "normal." The poster does not have to explain to this group that what they mean to ask is, "Because this is a regular part of Asian culture, is it okay, or is it wrong?" The experience of childhood abuse is so common among Asians and Asian Americans that, at times, comments in response to posts about abuse even veer toward normalizing it.

Beyond the home, the practice of hitting children is institutionalized in the very education systems of Asian countries (Chen et al., 2021; Ghosh & Pasupathi, 2016; Omi, 2019). Despite being officially banned in most Asian countries, teacher beatings of children in school with implements such as sticks and canes are still commonplace, as is verbal abuse. These practices continue to receive broad support from parents in countries such as India, China, and Japan, where teachers are revered and their practices not questioned. In addition, many Asian parents fear that children will not learn discipline if they are not physically punished (Chen et al., 2021; Ghosh & Pasupathi, 2016).

The normalization of physical and verbal abuse as a form of discipline appears to transcend generations and immigration. Amy Chua's best-selling book *Battle Hymn of the Tiger Mother* shocked Westerners by portraying a "strict"

Asian parenting style. She candidly describes yelling at her daughters, calling them "garbage," and threatening to destroy their toys to motivate them to practice music. Additionally, several large-scale studies on the prevalence rates of child maltreatment among Asian diaspora in Canada and the United States point to high rates of physical, emotional, and sexual abuse, as well as neglect (Maker et al., 2005; Meston et al., 1999; Schoen et al., 1998; Sieben et al., 2019a; Sieben et al., 2019b). Since there are so few epidemiological studies measuring rates of childhood abuse in either Canada or the United States, I have included data from both countries in this chapter.

In stark contrast are perspectives that child abuse among Asian Americans is low. An example is sociologist Jennifer Lee's (2014) essay, "Why Asian American Parents Don't Spank Their Kids," in which she argues that physical abuse is less common among Asian immigrant families than the general population due to their having high levels of education. The narrative of child abuse being rare among Asian Americans is lent cachet by the US Centers for Disease Control and Prevention (CDC). Their "Facts at a Glance" is a one-page online resource on child maltreatment (CDC, 2014). One of these glancing facts is "The 2012 rates of victimization per 1,000 children were 14.2 for African Americans, 12.4 for American Indian / Alaska Natives, 10.3 for Multiracial, 8.7 for Pacific Islanders, 8.4 for Hispanics, 8.0 for non-Hispanic Whites, and *1.7 for Asians*" (italics added). Additionally, some of the literature indicates low rates of childhood maltreatment among Asian Americans (Ima & Hohm, 1991; Rao et al., 1992; Sacks and Murphey, 2018; US Department of Health & Human Services, Administration for Children and Families, Administration on Children, Youth and Families, Children's Bureau, 2021).

So, which is the true story—is abuse common or uncommon among Asian Americans? And what accounts for the conflicting results in research on childhood abuse among Asian Americans? To answer these questions, this chapter provides a critical examination of the research methods used by the relevant studies. It also explores factors contributing to the undercounting of abuse among Asian Americans, including cultural barriers and racial bias in behavioral science research. First, though, it can be helpful to become acquainted with one of the most common methods of assessing childhood trauma and other stressful events—adverse childhood experiences surveys.

ADVERSE CHILDHOOD EXPERIENCES

Adverse childhood experiences, aka ACEs, are potentially traumatic or highly stressful events that occur to children, such as being abused or neglected, having a parent with a mental illness, or a parent in jail. It is important to know that an ACE is not necessarily a traumatic experience. However, there is substantial overlap between ACEs, family betrayal trauma, and cultural betrayal trauma, since the abuse items typically implicate caretakers.

The first ACE survey conducted by the CDC was one of the largest of its kind (Felitti et al., 1998). It asked 214,157 adults living in 23 states across the United States about childhood traumas and stressors. The results surprised researchers for two reasons. The first was that they learned ACEs are extremely common. Nearly two-thirds (64%) of respondents reported experiencing at least one ACE, and 1 in 6 reported four or more ACEs.

The second surprising finding was that ACEs appeared to have long-term consequences for physical health. The more ACEs the respondent experienced, the greater the likelihood they had of developing chronic illnesses in adulthood, such as osteoporosis, cancer, and heart disease. The study also found that ACEs were linked to an earlier death. These results have since been replicated in other studies of ACEs. The CDC estimates that up to 1.9 million cases of heart disease and 21 million cases of depression could have been potentially avoided by preventing ACEs (Centers for Disease Control and Prevention, 2019).

Changes in the mind and body can also manifest before adulthood. Among children with ACEs, critical areas of the brain responsible for long-term memory, problem-solving, and emotional regulation are shrunken and have less neural connectivity than children without ACEs. As a result, children with ACEs can have difficulty concentrating in school and with remembering new information, and may exhibit acting-out behaviors.

ACEs and Racism

For several decades, research has repeatedly shown that racism impacts physical and mental health just as other adverse experiences do (Bernard et al., 2020; Chae et al., 2015; Krieger et al., 1993; Paradies, 2017; Williams & Williams-Morris, 2000). Additionally, chapters 1 and 2 of this book demonstrate how historical and present-day racism are not only forms of trauma but often involve a high degree of relational betrayal, exacerbating their harm. However, the original ACE studies conducted by the CDC surveyed primarily White and middle- to upper-middle-class adults, and did not include racism as an adverse event. Some states now include racism in their survey of ACEs. So that you can calculate your own ACE score, this chapter includes a questionnaire (see textbox 3.1, below) that includes the original items from the CDC survey with a few additional questions about racism, bullying, and poverty, developed by the Philadelphia ACE Project.*

*The Philadelphia ACE Survey was used with permission from the Health Federation of Philadelphia and Philadelphia ACE Research and Data Committee. Funding for the Philadelphia ACE Survey was provided by the Robert Wood Johnson Foundation, with additional support from the Thomas Scattergood Behavioral Health Foundation, and the Stoneleigh Foundation. Data were provided by the Public Health Management Corporation's Center for Data Innovation, Southeastern Pennsylvania Household Health Survey, 2012.

TEXTBOX 3.1.   ACE QUESTIONNAIRE

PRIOR TO YOUR 18TH BIRTHDAY:

Were you bullied by a peer or classmate?

No___   Yes___

Did you see or hear someone being beaten up, stabbed, or shot in real life?

No___   Yes___

Sometimes people are treated badly, not given respect, or are considered infe-rior because of the color of their skin, because they speak a different language or have an accent, or because they come from a different country or culture. Did you feel that you were treated badly or unfairly because of your race or ethnicity?

No___   Yes___

Did a parent or other adult in the household often, or very often: swear at you, insult you, put you down, or humiliate you? Or act in a way that made you afraid you might be physically hurt?

No___   Yes___

Did a parent or other adult in the household often, or very often: push, grab, slap, or throw something at you? Or ever hit you so hard that you had marks or were injured?

No___   Yes___

Did an adult or person at least five years older than you ever: touch or fondle you or have you touch their body in a sexual way? Or attempt or actually have oral, anal, or vaginal intercourse with you?

No___   Yes___

Did you often, or very often, feel that: No one in your family loved you or thought you were important or special? Or that your family didn't look out for each other, feel close to each other, or support each other?

No___   Yes___

Did you often, or very often, feel that: You didn't have enough to eat, had to wear dirty clothes, and had no one to protect you? Or that your parents were too drunk or high to take care of you, or take you to the doctor if you needed it?

No___   Yes___

Were your parents ever separated or divorced?

No___ Yes___

Was your mother or stepmother often, or very often: pushed, grabbed, slapped, or had something thrown at her? Or sometimes, often, or very often: kicked, bitten, hit with a fist, or hit with something hard? Or ever repeatedly hit for at least a few minutes, or threatened with a gun or knife?

No___ Yes___

Did you live with anyone who was a problem drinker or alcoholic, or who used street drugs?

No___ Yes___

Was a household member depressed or mentally ill, or did a household member attempt suicide?

No___ Yes___

Did a household member go to jail or prison?

No___ Yes___

Now add up your "Yes" answers: ___ This is your ACE Score.

CONFLICTING RESEARCH ON ACES

Not all children experience ACEs equally; income disparity and ethnicity are two of the most significant factors when it comes to being at risk for ACEs (Slack et al., 2017). Children from low-income families report greater numbers of ACEs than those from wealthy families. It is also commonly acknowledged that Black and Latinx children in the United States experience more ACEs than White children. However, research studies concerning ACEs among Asian Americans have yielded conflicting results.

One large-scale study asked nearly 8,500 US college students about 11 ACEs, including forms of childhood abuse and neglect (Sieben et al., 2019a). On average, Asian and White students experienced equal rates of total ACEs. However, there was a significant difference between the two groups in the types of ACEs they experienced. White people were more likely to report living with a parent with mental illness or addiction, while Asians and Asian Americans were more likely to indicate witnessing domestic violence and being physically, sexually, or emotionally abused.

In contrast, ChildTrends, a US-based research organization, asked 50,000 parents about their children's ACEs in a national survey (Sacks & Murphey, 2018). While 40% of White children's parents reported that their child experienced at least one ACE, only 25% of Asian children's parents did so. However, there are several crucial differences between this ACE survey and other typical ACE surveys, such as the one by Sieben et al. (2019a). The first is the omission of all questions about child maltreatment. In other words, *their list of ACEs did not ask about physical, sexual, or emotional abuse, the very items that Asian Americans reported experiencing more frequently than Whites in the Sieben (2019a) study.* Therefore, it is highly likely this omission led to undercounting the ACEs of Asian American children.

Secondly, the ChildTrends survey substituted the questions about maltreatment with asking parents whether their child had "been the victim of violence or witnessed any violence in his or her neighborhood." However, physical abuse is often normalized as discipline and not considered violence by Asian parents. Therefore, asking about violence will also result in an undercount. Finally, the ChildTrends survey relied upon parent disclosures given to an authority figure (in this case, the researcher). The next section further examines why this is a culturally insensitive practice.

THE PROBLEMS WITH RELYING ON ABUSE REPORTS AMONG ASIAN AMERICANS

Empirical research on child abuse falls into two main categories. The first type comprises self-report questionnaires, which are typically administered by paper or online. Therefore, they do not require direct interaction with another person, which grants a sense of anonymity. The second type relies upon the abuse being reported to authorities by an adult who is often a parent, healthcare provider, or police officer. Both forms of research have issues with bias and inclusiveness, such as Western-based recruitment strategies that neglect to involve trusted community leaders, and the lack of Asian-language versions. However, the reliance upon reports of abuse to authorities is additionally problematic, and disproportionately affects Asian Americans and Asian Canadians.

Cultural Betrayal Trauma and the Motivation to Disbelieve Survivors

Research indicates that Asian Americans are more likely to disbelieve claims of child abuse than other ethnic groups. In the study of sexual abuses cases by Rao et al. (1992) described above, Asian American caretakers (23.4%)

were over three times more likely to disbelieve the report of abuse than White caretakers (6.7%), and over twice as likely to do so as Black (10.2%) and Hispanic American (11.3%) caretakers. These findings echo those of Wong (1987), who conducted focus groups with Southeast Asian refugees to learn about their perceptions of child sexual abuse. She found that many did not believe child sexual abuse was a problem in their community, and that if it happened, it would only be perpetrated by a stranger and not a family member.

People are more likely to dissociate from the knowledge that abuse occurred when this knowledge threatens a relationship (Freyd, 1996; Goldsmith et al., 2004). In doing so, they dissociate themselves from the stigma and shame that accompanies those who are abused. Additionally, according to cultural betrayal trauma theory, the pressure to not know is even higher within Asian American and Asian Canadian communities, due to the need to protect themselves from White supremacy (Gómez, 2017). These and other cultural factors, such as loss of face, can result in greater suppression of reporting among Asian diaspora relative to other ethnic groups.

Loss of Face

Even when abuse is acknowledged, Asian Americans are significantly less likely to disclose abuse than Whites (Foynes et al., 2007). Rao et al. (1992) found that Asian American primary caretakers, such as mothers, were half as likely to report abuse to authorities as other non-Asian caretakers. A study of child sexual abuse hospital referrals in the UK found that South Asian children disclosed less frequently than White children, and family members were less likely to initiate concerns to medical staff (Moghal et al., 1995). Other researchers have also found that Asian children may likely recant allegations of child sexual abuse to preserve the integrity of the family (Okamura et al., 1995).

Loss of face is a dominant cultural construct in most, if not all, Asian cultures. "Face" is the social esteem accorded an individual or group, usually in the fulfillment of social norms and expectations. "Loss of face" is often described as synonymous with shame (Yeh & Hwang, 1999). Indeed, there are many similarities, and shame is one of the direct results of losing face. However, loss of face is a unique cultural construct that can be differentiated from a Western concept of shame (Zane & Yeh, 2002). The main distinguishing feature of loss of face is based upon the collectivist nature of Asian cultures. Face is a collective commodity that belongs not only to the individual but to a group, such as extended family, business, school, sports team, or country. Thus, loss of face results in shame for an individual as well as the collective group of which the individual is a member. As Cathy Park Hong, author of *Minor Feelings: An Asian American Reckoning*, wrote, "I grew up in a culture where to speak of pain would not only retraumatize me but traumatize everyone I love, as if words are not a cure but a poison that will infect others. Denial is always the salve, though it is merely topical" (2020, p. 157).

In addition to collective shame, another consequence of losing face is the withdrawal of social support from family and friends (Shon & Ja, 1982). Although the loss of social support can have a detrimental impact on any individual, in a collectivist culture in which identity and self-worth are based mainly upon group membership, this loss can have even more profound implications than in an individualist society (Tang, 2009).

Lower rates of disclosure among Asian Americans are likely due to fear of losing face and the subsequent withdrawal of social support by others (Foynes et al., 2007; Futa et al., 2001; Ima & Hohm, 1991; Tang, 2009). Adhering to Asian values, including loss of face, is associated with the non-disclosure of abuse by someone close, such as a parent or caregiver (Foynes et al., 2014). Further, when members of a focus group of Southeast Asian refugees were asked how they would respond to sexual assault, most reported that they would keep the assault a secret within the family for fear of community rejection and blame (Wong, 1987).

Additional barriers to parent disclosure include not knowing whom to report to, other than the police, and language barriers. Futa et al. (2001) observed, "Given the presence of misperceptions and the lack of awareness of resources for child sexual abuse victims, it is not surprising that the Asian American community is reporting lower rates of sexual abuse and is perhaps more likely to keep sexual abuse a secret" (p. 192).

SELF-REPORT QUESTIONNAIRES

Self-report questionnaires essentially ask people about their own experiences. While underreporting in retrospective surveys happens as well, they result in much higher rates of disclosure than those relying on parent reports or cases reported to authorities. A meta-analysis by Stoltenborgh et al. (2011) comprising 217 international studies showed the rates of child sexual abuse to be more than 30 times greater in studies relying on self-reports than in reports to officials, such as CPS. Without exception, studies on Asian Americans follow this same pattern—those that rely on reporting ongoing child maltreatment find relatively low abuse rates in absolute terms, and compared to other ethnic groups. On the other hand, self-report surveys find abuse rates among Asian Americans at about equal or higher levels compared to other ethnic groups. Most of the surveys regarding child maltreatment among Asian Americans focus on adults (e.g., Meston et al., 1999; Robertson et al., 2016; Sieben et al.,

2019a), although one addresses adolescents (Schoen et al., 1998). The following sections examine the literature on various forms of child maltreatment.

CHILD SEXUAL ABUSE

The narrative of child sexual abuse being lower than the national average among Asian Americans is shared repeatedly in research articles and government websites (e.g., Ima & Hohm, 1991; Kenny & McEachern, 2000; Rao et al., 1992; US Department of Health & Human Services, Administration for Children and Families, Administration on Children, Youth and Families, Children's Bureau, 2021; Zhai & Gao, 2009). Two studies are typically cited to support this belief, both relying upon the abuse being reported to an authority. Like the ChildTrends study, the National Center on Child Abuse and Neglect (1999) asked parents whether they had abused their children. This study found lower rates of sexual abuse among Asian families than among other ethnic groups. The other is a study by Ima and Hohm (1991), who reviewed 158 medical charts of cases identified as child maltreatment at an Asian American mental health clinic in San Diego, California. The cases reviewed in this study were all referred by Child Protective Services (CPS), a nationwide agency in the United States that investigates reports of child abuse. CPS receives reports from professionals that are mandated to report suspicions of abuse, and from the public. Ima and Hohm found that only 4.9% of the cases were related to child sexual abuse, which is significantly lower than the national average at the time, of 12.3% of CPS cases.

Similarly, Rao et al. (1992) reviewed 2007 patient charts at the Child and Adolescent Sexual Abuse Resource Center in San Francisco, California. They found that Asians were disproportionately underrepresented, at 6.6% of all the cases, despite comprising 29% of the general population in San Francisco at the time. Asian Americans also represent a disproportionately low percentage of all abuse cases investigated by CPS agencies nationwide. In 2018, fewer than 1% of all reported cases to CPS were Asian (US Department of Health & Human Services, Administration for Children and Families, Administration on Children, Youth and Families, Children's Bureau, 2021), whereas Asians and Asian Americans comprise 5.4% of the total US population.

In contrast, studies that use self-report questionnaires to ask people about their own histories of abuse have found high rates of child sexual abuse in the Asian community. Multiple studies suggest that about 1 in 4 Asian American and Asian Canadian women have been sexually abused. These include a survey of 470 Asian college students in Canada, in which 25% of women and 11% of men reported being sexually abused (Meston et al., 1999). Similarly, a survey of 368 South Asian adults living in the United States found that a quarter (25.2%) reported being sexually abused as children (Robertson et al., 2016). The authors did not differentiate rates of abuse by gender, but the majority of their sample identified as female (77.7%). Of the respondents, 13.8% of them reported abuse involving exposure to media with sexual content; 21.5% reported abuse involving touching; 4.5% reported attempted sexual intercourse; and 3.5% reported forced sexual intercourse. Two other studies have also found double-digit rates of sexual abuse among Asian Americans and Asians living in the United States, ranging from 17% to 25%, respectively (Foynes et al., 2014; Gomez, 2017). These data also reflect an aggregate of gender identities.

According to the literature, Asian American boys are at much higher risk of sexual abuse than White boys. A survey of thousands of adolescent boys in the United States, from grades 5 through 12, found that Asian American boys reported sexual abuse at three times the rate of White boys (9% vs. 3%; Schoen et al., 1998). A recent study by Sieben et al. (2019a) of college students found a similar pattern, with Asian / Pacific Islander men more likely to have been raped as children than White men, at a statistically significant level.

Having multiple oppressed identities compounds the risk of sexual abuse. Lesbian, gay, and bisexual Asian American and Pacific Islander students were more likely than others to report being sexually assaulted as children (Sieben et al., 2019b).

How do these rates compare to global rates of sexual abuse? A meta-analysis of data from 65 studies spanning 22 countries found that 7.9% of men and 19.7% of women had suffered some form of sexual abuse before age 18 (Pereda et al., 2009). In the United States, the CDC reports that 11.3% of youth identifying as female and 3.5% identifying as male have been raped. These percentages were even higher among gay, lesbian, and bisexual students (21.9%) than among heterosexual students (5.4%). These statistics do not include other forms of sexual abuse, such as being exposed to media with sexual content, being touched sexually, or being forced to touch someone else sexually. When those experiences are included, teen girls are at the highest risk, with 16.4% reporting experiencing a sexual offense in the past year (Finkelhor, 2015).

In summary, the scientific evidence clearly refutes the narrative that child sexual abuse is rare among Asian American and Asian Canadian communities. To date, seven epidemiological studies have found that about *1 in 4 Asian American and Asian Canadian women and 1 in 10 Asian American and Asian Canadian men have been sexually abused.* Furthermore, both groups are significantly more at risk for sexual abuse than their White counterparts. As difficult as it can be to believe such astronomic numbers, these rates are of the same magnitude as those found globally by other studies, signifying an epidemic of child sexual abuse worldwide.

CHILD PHYSICAL ABUSE, EMOTIONAL ABUSE, AND NEGLECT

As in the case of sexual abuse, findings of high rates of other forms of child victimization from survey research contrast with the underrepresentation of Asians in reports to CPS. Most survey research indicates that child physical abuse among Asian Americans and Asian Canadians is higher than the national average for Americans. Estimates of physical abuse among Asians range between 25 to 82% among men (Meston et al., 1999; Schoen et al., 1998; Sieben et al., 2019a) and 22 to 69% among women (Meston et al., 1999; Sieben et al., 2019a).

The wide range of findings may be partly explained by the number of questions asked. Meston et al. (1999), the authors of the study with abuse findings in the upper range, asked more detailed questions about each form of abuse. Wyatt and Peters (1986) have suggested that asking multiple questions about abusive experiences can lead to finding higher prevalence rates. Asking additional questions also led to findings that approximately one in five of the women (19%) and one-third of the men (34%) reported being beaten severely enough to have bruises, broken bones, and/or require medical care.

Among Asian Americans and Asian Canadians, reports of emotional abuse range between 50 to 88% of women and 41 to 93% of men (Meston et al., 1999; Sieben et al., 2019a). In terms of reports of neglect, 46% of Asian Canadian women and 64% of Asian Canadian men reported neglect, such as having food or water withheld for more than a day, or being locked out of the home without appropriate clothes or shoes in the winter (Meston et al., 1999). Compared to Whites, these rates of physical and emotional abuse and neglect among Asian-identified participants were consistently higher (Meston et al., 1999; Schoen et al., 1998; Sieben et al., 2019a).

Research also suggests that lesbian, gay, and bisexual Asians are at higher risk of abuse than Asians who identify as heterosexual (Sieben et al., 2019b). Among the same Minnesotan college students, researchers found that ACEs were more frequent among lesbian, gay, and bisexual API college students, who reported an average of 2.8 of 11 ACEs compared to heterosexual API students, who averaged 1.8 ACEs. This study did not include those who identify as trans, queer, intersex, or asexual. Lesbian, gay, and bisexual API students were more likely to report being sexually assaulted and verbally and physically abused as children (Sieben et al., 2019b). These results are consistent with other studies on LGBTQIA+ groups, who consistently show higher prevalence rates of childhood victimization (e.g., physical or sexual abuse, parental neglect, witnessing domestic abuse) than their heterosexual peers (Andersen & Blosnich, 2013; Friedman et al., 2011). These studies underscore the need to consider intersecting identities when addressing ACEs to identify youth most at risk for maltreatment.

In summary, survey research has consistently found high rates of child abuse and neglect among Asian Americans and Asian Canadians. Given that the majority of Asian American and Asian Canadian men and women report being physically and/or emotionally abused, and at least 17 to 25% of women and 9 to 11% of men have been sexually abused, it is safe to conclude child maltreatment among these communities is quite high. Contrasting opinions reference data based on flawed methodologies that exclude any rigorous epidemiological or retrospective survey data. For example, I return to Lee's (2014) essay cited at the beginning of this chapter, which presumed low rates of physical abuse among Asian Americans. The answer to how she arrived at this conclusion is that she relied on research from ChildTrends.

EPISTEMOLOGICAL VIOLENCE IN PSYCHOLOGY

In the now-classic book on understanding abuse survivors, *Trauma and Recovery*, Dr. Judith Herman begins by observing that the study of trauma is one of episodic amnesia. "Periods of active investigation have alternated with periods of oblivion. Repeatedly in the past century, similar lines of inquiry have been taken up and abruptly abandoned, only to be rediscovered much later" (2015, p. 7). While this description is profoundly apt regarding the study of trauma among White people, trauma among Asian diaspora has never been "taken up" in any meaningful sense. In fact, the narrative that it is minimal continues to dominate research. The lack of questioning of this narrative heretofore implicates the model minority myth and perpetuates the history of erasure of the Asian American experience by psychology.

That the CDC, ChildTrends, and others have overlooked published epidemiological research that has been repeatedly replicated speaks to a systematic and entrenched racial bias in research institutions. In other words, how Western research is conducted and interpreted is historically rooted in a paradigm that centers White culture as the norm and all else as "Other" (Bhatia, 2018; Bhatia, 2020; Teo, 2008). The result is epistemological violence.

Epistemological violence in empirical psychology refers to the interpretation of data in a manner that does harm by othering a group of people. As Teo (2008, p. 52) explains, "The term *epistemological* suggests that . . . speculations are framed as knowledge when in reality they are interpretative speculations regarding data. The term *violence* denotes that this 'knowl-

edge' has a negative impact on the 'Other' and that the interpretative speculations are produced to the detriment of the 'Other.' The negative impact
can range from misrepresentations and distortions to a neglect of the voices
of the 'Other,' to statements of inferiority, and to the recommendations of
adverse practices or infringements concerning the 'Other.'" The interpretation of data to mean Asian diaspora experience low rates of abuse is one
example of epistemological violence.

The use of the "Other" category, a catchall for those identifying as Asian,
Pacific Islander, Native American, and multiracial, in ACE research is another manifestation of othering Asian Americans (e.g., Centers for Disease
Control and Prevention, 2010; Giano et al., 2020; Goldstein et al., 2020).
Often, Asian Americans are eliminated altogether by not being mentioned at
all, even in studies examining the role of racial differences in the prevalence
of ACEs (e.g., Maguire-Jack et al., 2020; Slopen et al., 2016).

Researchers typically justify the use of "Other" as a category by citing too
few numbers of participants among specific groups for meaningful analysis
(Goldstein et al., 2020). In one large-scale national survey of ACEs by the
CDC of 144,017 individuals, only 1% were Asian, although Asian Americans
comprise 5.9% of the US population (Merrick et al., 2019). However, chronic
inattention to this issue also points to a colonial research paradigm in its failure to address barriers to participation for Asian diaspora. As a result, federal
health-care data in general on Asian Americans is extremely limited (Devers
et al., 2013). As Thalmayer et al. (2021, p. 116) write, "Psychology still has
a long way to go to become a science truly representative of human beings."

DECOLONIZING PSYCHOLOGICAL RESEARCH

Research in psychology has great potential to cause harm by neglecting to
consider cultural factors in the methodology, and by being influenced by stereotypes, such as the model minority myth. Far from being rare, ACEs and childhood abuse are staggeringly common among Asian diaspora. That psychology
and medicine have largely ignored this reality is a manifestation of the erasure
of the Asian diaspora experience through colonial oppression that is expressed
in all our institutions, including those of science. Researchers must investigate
this epidemic further so that survivors know they are not alone, so that counselors understand its magnitude and import, and so that more resources can be
allocated to Asian communities to combat child maltreatment.

Barriers to participation by Asian diaspora in health-care research include a
low rate of language proficiency (about 30% of US Asian adults do not speak
English proficiently); a greater reluctance to participate in health research
than other ethnic groups; and sensitivity to certain types of questions, as

well as different cultural interpretations of the questions (Devers et al., 2013; Gao, 2016; Liu et al., 2019). One method of addressing the underrepresentation of a group is to employ a technique called oversampling. As its name implies, oversampling means intentionally sampling more members of a particular group in a survey to obtain an adequate representation of that group (Vaughan, 2017). A variety of techniques have been developed to oversample subgroups (see Kalton [2009] for examples). In addition, Devers et al. (2013) observe that Asian Americans are more likely to participate in written or online surveys than those conducted by phone.

The following are suggestions for adopting anti-racist processes in conducting research:

- Develop awareness of our own internalized biases, which includes the model minority myth.
- Increase diversity among researchers who will bring unique expertise and perspectives.
- Practice cultural humility: Conduct thorough literature reviews and consult with experts familiar with the communities being examined.
- Discontinue the practice of "othering" Asians and recognize the use of "Other" as a racist practice. Instead, name Asian, Native American, Pacific Islander, and multicultural as distinct ethnic groups in analyses (Roberts et al., 2020).
- Justify the racial demographics of samples just as researchers must justify sample sizes (Roberts et al., 2020), or at least explain limitations in the research methods as to why these groups were omitted, including identifying plans to address barriers to sampling these groups in future research.
- Address barriers to participation by oversampling, translating survey questions into Asian languages, avoiding phone interviews, and conducting community outreach to increase the likelihood of participation in research.

Child maltreatment is a cultural and systemic problem, not one that lies within any individual or even an individual family. The model minority myth paints an idealized image of family harmony among Asian Americans. As a result, abuse victims feel isolated and abnormal, a condition ripe for breeding shame. As Herman (2015, p. 1) writes in the opening of *Trauma and Recovery*, "Remembering and telling the truth about terrible events are prerequisites both for the restoration of the social order and for the healing of individual victims." The next chapter of this book addresses how to begin this process of contextualizing trauma in the realm of psychotherapy.

ADDITIONAL RESOURCES

• Sangra, B. (Director). (2019). *Because we are girls* [Film]. National Film Board of Canada.

    Because We Are Girls is a documentary directed by Baljit Sangra (2019) that shares the story of three Indian Canadian sisters who publicly accuse a relative of sexually abusing them when they were children.

• NBC News. (2017, October 10). *Christine's story: Raising awareness about domestic violence | NBC Asian America* [Video]. YouTube. https://tinyurl.com/Christinedv

    Witnessing domestic violence is a common item in ACE surveys. In *Christine's Story*, Christine Lee shares her story of leaving an abusive relationship, and her hopes that Asian Americans will become more willing to talk about intimate partner violence.

Chapter Four

Beginning Therapy with Asian Americans: Therapist Self-Awareness and Client Worldview

Asian, Asian American, and other BIPOC clients often present with intersecting marginalized identities and complex histories of trauma, as explored in this book's first three chapters. However, many therapists are unprepared to address the interplay of oppression and internalized racism with historical and intergenerational trauma. As Dr. Kenneth Hardy once stated, "My training had prepared me in a way that I was a pretty good, decent White therapist" (Wyatt, n.d.). As a result, *Where do I begin?* is a common question among trainees and even seasoned therapists. The Multicultural and Social Justice Counseling Competencies (MSJCC; Ratts et al., 2015, 2016), endorsed by the American Counseling Association, recommends beginning with oneself. The MSJCC identifies four domains:

1. Counselor self-awareness
2. Client worldview
3. Counseling relationship
4. Counseling and advocacy interventions

Although these domains are listed in a developmental order, each represents an area of growth that should continue throughout therapy. Counselor self-awareness is a necessary first step, but "becoming culturally skilled is an *active process*, . . . is ongoing, and . . . is a process that *never reaches an end point*" (Sue & Sue, 1990, p. 146). This chapter addresses the first two of the four developmental domains of the MSJCC (chapters 5 through 7 address the latter two). It also presents the Rings of Betrayal Inventory, a tool that can be used for assessing one's own trauma history and that of BIPOC clients. Case examples and interviews with Asian Americans are also included, to help deepen understanding of Asian American experiences. These testimonios can also be used as an opportunity to practice using the Rings of Betrayal Inventory.

BEGINNING WITH YOU

The MSJCC describes the first domain of competency, counselor self-awareness, as follows: "Privileged and marginalized counselors develop self-awareness, so that they may explore their attitudes and beliefs, develop knowledge, skills, and action relative to their self-awareness and worldview" (Ratts et al., 2015, p. 5). The practice of beginning with self-examination is consistent with a liberation approach. Martín-Baró strongly advocated for a process called *conscientization*, a term earlier advanced by Fanon and Freire. Conscientization is a response to injustice that promotes "a critical consciousness of the objective and subjective roots of social alienation" (Martín-Baró, 1996, p. 42). This consciousness is not only individual, but is an understanding of one's social identity. This social identity, in turn, is rooted in historical memory that is often hidden or overlooked by those in power.

Implicit Bias and Internalized Racism

Implicit or unconscious bias refers to generalizations and preconceptions outside conscious awareness (*Unconscious bias*, n.d.). Nonetheless, they constantly influence our emotions and behavior. These biases can be based on race, body size, age, or any number of attributes. Whereas all people hold unconscious biases, internalized racism refers specifically to individuals who have been oppressed and have internalized that oppression. Pyke (2010) defines it as "the individual inculcation of the racist stereotypes, values, images, and ideologies perpetuated by the White dominant society about one's racial group, leading to feelings of self-doubt, disgust, and disrespect for one's race and/or oneself" (p. 553). In other words, racism may lead Asian Americans to feel their ethnic culture is inferior to White culture. As a result, they may harbor a conscious or unconscious desire to be White.

From the ages of four through seven, I lived with my parents in a small, rural town in Pennsylvania. I remember experiencing a couple of instances of overt racism (one was the Chinese/Japanese, dirty knees song that I describe in the introduction). But overall, I remember my experience there as a positive one, and I had quite a few friends. However, when I reread my first-grade journal a few years ago, I was shocked to see that I had wished for long blond hair and blue eyes. Even by such a young age, I had somehow learned that being White was better. It is, however, important to recognize that this form of internalized racism does not necessarily apply to all Asians or Asian Americans.

There are many steps one can take toward developing self-awareness of internalized bias. A few include taking the Implicit Association Test (see user's guide, at the beginning of this book), exploring these issues in psychotherapy, and educating oneself about the histories and cultures of other ethnic groups. Another essential step is to understand one's own traumas in a historical and social context. I developed the Rings of Betrayal Inventory as a tool that can be used for this purpose.

The Harm of Self-Ignorance

A former therapist once told me in our initial meeting, "Since I am White, there are some things I may not understand about being Asian American. I hope you can help me with that and teach me what it means to be Asian American." While she intended to be helpful, her words left me feeling hurt, angry, and confused. Here was yet another instance where the burden of educating someone about my culture was put on me. Wasn't it her job to educate herself? I would have felt more supported had she said, "Since I am White, there are some things I may not understand about being Asian American. I am working on learning more about Asian American cultures and recognizing my own racial biases. I also welcome feedback if I say something hurtful or make a mistake." Often, we do the best we can with the therapist we have, which is the course I chose in this situation. However, I did not raise any issues related to race or racism with her, not wanting to take on the additional labor of explaining something I did not think she would understand. Her comment created a significant point of disconnection for me, one that did not feel possible to repair.

Exercise: Think about what you would say to a client about your ethnic bias. What specific words would you use? How might it differ for a client of a similar ethnicity to your own compared to one of another ethnic group?

As a therapist myself, I am also not exempt from making mistakes about race or being influenced by internalized racism. My work with a client I will call Kate is an example. Kate was a first-year graduate student in literature. Her primary concern was the racism she was experiencing in her department. As someone who identified as biracial White and Chinese American, she was the only person of color in her student cohort. Nor were there any BIPOC faculty in the department. As she described, whenever someone had a question about Asians or Asian Americans in a departmental meeting, all eyes would turn to her. "I keep telling them that I don't represent all Asian Americans," Kate said, exasperated. However, no one appeared to hear her. Kate was furious.

I could also perceive a sense of loneliness and hurt. I responded to her as a "pretty good White therapist" would, reflecting her emotions back to her and helping her name them.

However, what I did not do was the very thing I believe Kate was looking for, which was to name the racism she was experiencing, not just her feelings. This would have shown solidarity with her. Nor did I join her in her outrage. Doing these two things would have validated her perspective and helped her feel less alone. At the time, I simply did not feel any anger, in part due to having become inured to the racial microaggressions I had experienced myself while in academia (see chapter 7 for a critical examination of the ubiquity of racism in psychology training programs). This lack of awareness of my own internalized racism is in keeping with betrayal trauma theory (Freyd, 1996), and led to my inability to see Kate's situation more objectively. In another attempt to seek support, Kate again shared how she felt pressured to be the "Asian voice" in the room. Again, I failed to acknowledge that the department was behaving in a racist manner, although I empathized with how stressful the situation sounded for her. Kate never returned to therapy after that first session.

Kate's intake session and my own experience as a client demonstrate how being a "pretty good White therapist" is wholly inadequate. When a therapist does not actively cultivate self-awareness of internalized racism and racist beliefs, and other forms of bias, the therapist is likely to do harm. Additional examples of client experiences of racial harm can be found in chapter 6, which includes testimonios offered by Asian American clients.

I next introduce a tool I developed, the Rings of Betrayal Inventory, which can be used for developing counselor self-awareness and for understanding client worldviews in the assessment of trauma.

RINGS OF BETRAYAL INVENTORY

A thorough trauma assessment with Asian Americans can be complex. As the first three chapters of this book demonstrate, Asian Americans not only experience a high rate of family betrayal trauma, but also cultural betrayal trauma, institutional betrayal trauma, racism, intergenerational trauma, and historical trauma. I developed the Rings of Betrayal Model presented in chapter 2 to show how these forms of betrayal trauma co-exist in various social spheres across time. In order to translate that theoretical model into practice, I created the Rings of Betrayal Inventory. It represents a unique approach to assessing trauma by:

1. Emphasizing the relational and contextual nature of trauma
2. Identifying different spheres of influence within which traumas can occur

3. Highlighting that family and cultural betrayal traumas can co-occur in time with those stemming from dominant culture and institutions, and offering a visual representation of how historical and intergenerational betrayal traumas intersect in the present.

The Rings of Betrayal Inventory presents a description of each sphere of social influence from the Rings of Betrayal Model and provides examples as prompts. I acknowledge that these examples are far from inclusive, and that some experiences may fall under more than one category. For example, trauma related to international adoption can be associated with both family betrayal trauma (e.g., a birth mother being forced to give up a child) and institutional betrayal trauma (e.g., falsification of paperwork by an adoption agency). It is all right to highlight both. The main idea of using the inventory is to gain an understanding of the multifaceted social context of trauma.

I developed two versions of the Rings of Betrayal Inventory: one specifically for Asian Americans (worksheet 4.1) and another adapted for the general population (worksheet 4.2). Both versions of the Rings of Betrayal Inventory can be found on the website https://shinshintang.com/, and can be downloaded for personal and educational use. Each version begins with the outermost layer of the Rings of Betrayal Model that encompasses history and time. This is to emphasize the broad context in which all trauma occurs, as well as the collective nature of Asian cultures. This outermost level is also the most often neglected in trauma assessment. However, it is essential for gaining a complete understanding of our own and the client's current areas of privilege and oppression. It is a place to record intergenerational and historical traumas, which frequently involve institutional betrayal. Examples include parent, grandparent, and ancestral trauma; war; famine; and racialized violence in the United States.

The next level, Dominant White Culture, refers to current prevalent biases that shape US culture, including White supremacy, oppression, racism, sexism, homophobia, transphobia, ableism, etc. These manifest as the steep rise in hate crimes against BIPOC and LGBTQIA+ communities; the idealization of White, thin bodies in the media; and racial stereotypes, such as the model minority myth. Institutional betrayal trauma also occurs at this level, such as in the increased state legislation against gender-affirming care for transgender youth.

Biases from the dominant White culture inform the development of neighborhoods and systems that comprise the level of Dominant Culture Community and Institutions, such as cities, schools, workplaces, and the health-care system. Examples include the neglect of Asian Americans in COVID-19 counts, and the denial of high rates of ACEs among Asian Americans by scholars (see chapter 3). These constitute a failure by institutions and those in power to protect those with less privilege.

Interactions between oppressed communities and the broader community at large comprise the next sphere of influence on an individual. Racism and other forms of discrimination in workplaces and institutions dominate this category. Examples include a college professor telling Asian American students that they do not count as people of color, a doctor failing to recognize signs of sexual abuse in an Asian American child, or a family member being suddenly deported due to a decades-old misdemeanor. Additionally, family and cultural betrayal trauma as well as institutional betrayal from Asian organizations can occur in this realm. For example, an abusive relative may lie to authorities when asked about their children's injuries, parents may side with an abusive teacher rather than their child, or an Asian American church might collude with other churches in the suppression of sexual abuse allegations.

In the Asian American version of the inventory (see worksheet 4.1), the last three levels comprise Asian community, other oppressed identities, and family members. In the general version (see worksheet 4.2), the Asian community level is omitted, but retains a category for other oppressed identities. These social spheres also include institutional betrayal trauma from within the oppressed groups, cultural betrayal trauma, and family betrayal trauma. Of note, the arena of family members for many Asian Americans includes both immediate and extended family. It can, at times, also include family friends.

The following instructions and self-reflection questions will help users gain the most value from the inventory. To provide a concrete example of how to use the inventory, I have completed one using my own story, and responded to the self-reflection questions (see worksheet 4.3).

Instructions for Using the Rings of Betrayal Inventory:

1. For each level of influence, write down the related traumas.
2. Label the traumas that are high in betrayal trauma.
3. Take time to respond to the self-reflection questions.

Self-Reflection Questions:

1. What patterns do you notice? For example, are the traumas you experienced concentrated in a particular sphere of influence, or are they located throughout the spheres?
2. What types of betrayal trauma are present?
3. Can you identify intergenerational trauma?
4. What does the pattern of trauma indicate about areas of oppression and areas of privilege in your life?

Worksheet 4.1. Rings of Betrayal Inventory: Asian American Version

Domain	Description	Experience
History and Time	• Ancestral trauma • Historical trauma • Institutional betrayal trauma	
Dominant White Culture	• White supremacy, oppression, racism, sexism, homophobia, transphobia, ableism, etc. • Institutional betrayal trauma	
Dominant Culture Community and Institutions	• Neighborhood, city, educational system, workplaces, health-care system • Institutional betrayal trauma	
Interactions with Dominant Culture	• Interactions between the dominant community and institutions with the Asian and Asian American community/individual • Institutional betrayal trauma from dominant culture • Institutional betrayal trauma from Asian organizations • Cultural betrayal trauma • Family betrayal trauma	
Asian and Asian American Community	• Asian American relatives, religious groups, Asian affinity organizations • Institutional betrayal trauma from Asian organizations • Cultural betrayal trauma • Family betrayal trauma	
Additional Oppressed Communities	• e.g., other BIPOC, LGBTQIA+, disabled people, women, neurodiverse people • Institutional betrayal trauma from oppressed communities • Cultural betrayal trauma • Family betrayal trauma	
Family Members	• Immediate and extended family members • Institutional betrayal trauma from oppressed communities • Intergenerational trauma • Cultural betrayal trauma • Family betrayal trauma	

Worksheet 4.2. Rings of Betrayal Inventory: General Version

Domain	Description	Experience
History and Time	• Ancestral trauma • Historical trauma • Institutional betrayal trauma	
Dominant White Culture	• White supremacy, oppression, racism, sexism, homophobia, transphobia, ableism, etc. • Institutional betrayal trauma	
Dominant Culture Community and Institutions	• Neighborhood, city, educational system, workplaces, health-care system • Institutional betrayal trauma	
Interactions with Dominant Culture	• Interactions between the dominant community and institutions with the individual • Institutional betrayal trauma from dominant culture • Institutional betrayal trauma from oppressed communities • Cultural betrayal trauma • Family betrayal trauma	
Oppressed Communities	• e.g., BIPOC, LGBTQIA+, disabled people, women, neurodiverse people • Institutional betrayal trauma from oppressed communities • Cultural betrayal trauma • Family betrayal trauma	
Family Members	• Immediate and extended family members • Institutional betrayal trauma from oppressed communities • Intergenerational trauma • Cultural betrayal trauma • Family betrayal trauma	

Worksheet 4.3. Rings of Betrayal Inventory: Shin Shin's Example

Domain	Description	Experiences
History and Time	• Ancestral trauma • Historical trauma • Institutional betrayal trauma	• Communist revolution, forced migration of grandparents, extreme poverty on mother's side, persecution of father's family in China
Dominant White Culture	• White supremacy, oppression of marginalized people, racism, sexism, homophobia, transphobia, ableism, etc. • Institutional betrayal trauma	• Rise in anti-Asian hate crimes, bias in media, idealization of white, thin bodies, model minority lie
Dominant Culture Community and Institutions	• Neighborhood, city, educational system, workplaces, health-care system • Institutional betrayal trauma	• Neglect of Asian Americans in COVID-19 counts, denial of ACEs among Asian Americans
Interactions with Dominant Culture	• Interactions between the dominant community and institutions with the Asian and Asian American community/individual • Institutional betrayal trauma	• Microaggressions at most places I have worked by colleagues and clients • Racial trauma from orthodontist's office when assistant caused undue physical pain • Discrimination by teachers • Racial bullying at school • Sexual harassment by babysitter's husband • Racism and sexism in graduate school
Asian and Asian American Community	• Asian American relatives, religious groups, Asian affinity organizations • Institutional betrayal trauma • Cultural betrayal trauma	• Internalized racism of model minority lie • Adults neglecting to intervene with childhood abuse
Asian and Asian American Family Members	• Asian and non-Asian family members and extended family • Intergenerational trauma • Cultural betrayal trauma • Family betrayal trauma	• Physical and emotional abuse, witnessing domestic violence, pressure to excel academically, patriarchal norms

Shin Shin's Responses to Self-Reflection Questions:

1. What patterns do you notice? For example, are the traumas you experienced concentrated in a particular sphere of influence, or are they located throughout the spheres?

   I notice a link between the historical trauma of the first level experienced by my grandparents and parents, and the intergenerational trauma that occurred in the last level. I also notice a pattern of institutional betrayal trauma occurring at nearly all levels.

2. What types of betrayal trauma are present?

   Institutional, cultural, and family betrayal traumas are all present in my history.

3. What does the pattern of trauma indicate about areas of oppression and areas of privilege in your life?

   In my case, I notice the presence of institutional, cultural, and family betrayal traumas. At the same time, my privilege is indicated by the absence of queerphobia, police brutality, or poverty.

4. What feelings arise as you review your completed inventory?

   I feel a mixture of sorrow, anger, and horror. Also, when I acknowledge all the external betrayals that I have experienced, I feel some relief from the shame and guilt that I carry for feeling depressed and exhausted at times— essentially for not always being okay.

UNDERSTANDING THE CLIENT'S WORLDVIEW

The second domain of the MSJCC focuses on the client. It urges privileged and marginalized counselors to be "aware, knowledgeable, skilled, and action-oriented in understanding clients' worldview" (Ratts et al., 2015, p. 6). Working on cultural competence may feel overwhelming at times. Indeed, questioning one's assumptions and beliefs, identifying areas of bias, and acknowledging racial wounds is an ongoing and, at times, arduous process. Beginning therapists and trainees in particular often worry about "messing up" and harming their clients. I want to offer encouragement that simply acknowledging your limitations and trying to educate yourself will mean a great deal to your clients. It is like learning a few phrases of a local language when traveling; it demonstrates effort, respect, and a willingness to be vulnerable, typically resulting in a warmer reception. The same applies to therapy.

The following stories illustrate the importance of understanding trauma and culture in working with Asian Americans. They are based on interviews with people who were courageously willing to share their stories with me, including their trauma histories.

The first is of Shreya (a pseudonym), an Indian American woman in her late twenties who is a 1.5-generation immigrant, meaning she was born in India and immigrated to the United States as a child (personal communication, July 26, 2021).

I also share the stories of two adoptees, Cam Lee Small (personal communication, November 29, 2021) and Kira Omans (personal communication, November 12, 2021). Asian international adoptees occupy a unique space among Asian Americans. While they experience the racial discrimination of being Asian American, they can also face discrimination from within Asian American communities, who deem them "not Asian enough." Their stories also illustrate how the adoption industry perpetrates institutional betrayal trauma.

Shreya's Story

Shreya is a woman in her late twenties who identifies as Indian American and neurodivergent. The following story is based on an interview I conducted with her. I have interspersed it with questions for therapists in training. These are opportunities to pause and reflect on your emotional reactions to her story, identify areas where you may want to increase your knowledge of her cultural history, and consider what questions or reflections you would ask Shreya.

On Being Indian American

Shreya's wide smile warmed the computer screen in our online meeting. Her wavy black hair was pulled back in a loose ponytail, and large, gold-rimmed glasses framed her dark eyes. Born in India, Shreya moved to Los Angeles, California, at the age of two with her mother and father. She quickly clarified that her family is from Northeast India, which sets them apart from many other Indian immigrants in the United States who more commonly emigrate from the more affluent northwestern or southern regions. Shreya's parents were also born in rural villages rather than cities, further differentiating them from many other Indian immigrants. There was affection in her voice when she described her family's northeastern Indian American community as small and tightly knit. Shreya is also trilingual; though English is her first language, she also speaks Hindi and Oriya, the language specific to her family's origins. It was clear she is proud of her ancestry and the Oriya community.

Shreya described growing up with several identities: one at home with her family, one in public with the Indian American community, and one with everyone else. She said her parents wanted her to be able to be a part of different groups of people, and expressly taught her there would be different cultural values and expectations in each group. At home, she would eat Oriya food and speak Oriya, switch to Hindi when she was with other Indian communities, and then revert to English and American culture at school.

Discussion: What questions as a therapist would you have for Shreya in hearing about her multiple cultural identities?

Intergenerational Trauma

Shreya's father was raised in extreme poverty. A math prodigy, his family depended upon his prize money from math competitions to be able to afford food. As a result, they required him to study every night. Shreya recounted that his mother beat him severely when he stayed out with friends one night. She described her father as easily angered, and he has physically and verbally abused her and her brother.

To give historical context to Shreya's story, famines and deaths multiplied during the 200 years of British colonial rule in India (Siddiqui, 2017). One such famine occurred in 1866, when a million people died in a single year in Odisha, the state her family is from. An additional 4 to 5 million died in surrounding areas. Historians have linked these catastrophes to British policies of pressuring farmers to export the reserve grains they usually stored as a safeguard against drought (Bhatia, 1991; Sen, 1982; Siddiqui, 2020). The reigning government also practiced a "laissez-faire" policy toward the famine, refusing to interfere with market supply (Siddiqui, 2020). These forms of institutional betrayal make the likelihood of intergenerational transmission of trauma high among Shreya's ancestors.

Discussion: What is your knowledge of British colonial history in India? In addition to increased famines, what institutional betrayals occurred there that could have influenced prior generations of Shreya's family? Take some time to research this information if needed.

Racism

Amid escalating anti-Asian violence during the pandemic, Shreya has become increasingly frightened for the safety of her Asian American friends. She shares, "A few of them are going on a trip to Las Vegas, and I worry it will be the last time I see them. I feel like the mother of the group, that I need to protect them."

On Being Asian and Disabled

Shreya also identifies as neurodivergent, having been diagnosed with ADHD (attention-deficit / hyperactivity disorder) in college. At first, her parents did not want to believe she had ADHD, and her mother did not want her to take the medication Shreya's doctor had prescribed. Her father said she was simply not trying hard enough. Her parents' reaction triggered memories of her father becoming enraged when she was a child, calling her lazy when she did not understand the math he was trying to teach her. He would become even angrier when she cried, accusing her of being manipulative by trying to make him feel guilty.

This narrative of being lazy or not trying hard enough is a common theme among children with undiagnosed ADHD. However, it is perhaps even more intense among Asian American families, many of whom view academic success as depending more on effort than talent (Lee & Zhou, 2015). ADHD and other neurodivergent disorders are also poorly understood among Asian cultures. Shreya recounted her parents constantly comparing her to the nine other Asian Americans she attended high school with. As Shreya shared, "My dad would point out the best attributes of other Asian Americans and compare them to my worst ones, saying things like, 'Karen is a valedictorian; she's probably going to go to medical school and be very successful. What are you going to do? You can't even study for an hour!'"

Discussion: What emotions are you having in response to Shreya's story so far?

Indian Patriarchy

Shreya described her mother as being much more protective of her brother, who is also neurodivergent. According to Shreya, her mother said he deserves more patience and understanding because of his diagnosis. Shreya attributed the differential treatment of her brother to a cultural norm of Indian families generally favoring boys. Amin and Bansal (2023) identify patriarchy, in addition to racism and the Indian caste system, as a critical systemic influence that shapes experiences of marginalization and privilege in Asian Indian communities. The effects of this patriarchy can be viewed as a form of cultural betrayal trauma. However, Shreya was quick to note that favoritism does not translate to immunity, pointing out that her father was abused as a child, and he, in turn, abused her brother.

Sexual Assault

When she was 10 years old, Shreya was raped by an older cousin. In recent years, Shreya has considered speaking to her extended family about the assault, but both of her parents have discouraged her, saying, "He's changed, he's married now," and "We don't talk about sex." Shreya said of this cultural betrayal, "I have to keep him in my Facebook group, or other cousins would notice he was not there and ask questions." At the time of the interview, Shreya was engaged and planning to have a wedding ceremony in India. She told me, "I asked my mother whether I have to include him . . . and she said yes." She recounted the following conversation:

Her mother said, "We would have to explain why he is not invited. Didn't you tell your aunt about it? And what did she say?"

"She told me I was lying," Shreya responded.

"Do you want to go through all of that again?" her mother asked.

"No," said Shreya.

"I don't want to see him at my wedding," explained Shreya, "but I have to invite him. My parents are so concerned about keeping up appearances." (Shreya repeatedly noted with irritation that appearances are very important to her parents, something that is common in Asian cultures.)

"So, neither of them said, 'I'm so sorry that happened to you?'" I asked her.

"No," she replied.

Shreya also witnessed her mother being sexually assaulted when a White male stranger groped her mother's breasts on a city bus and then quickly walked away. Her mother told her that she did not say or do anything because nothing could be done about it, but the incident left Shreya feeling shaken, and she sounded distressed even as she described it.

Mental Health and Therapy

Shreya excelled in high school and was accepted into UC Irvine, where she double-majored in biology and sociology. As a freshman, she was diagnosed with ADHD, and the family conflict that ensued led to her becoming severely depressed. She sought therapy at her college's counseling center, which she continued for the next four years.

Shreya described the therapy as helpful, and that she liked her counselor, though she also hesitates. "But he was . . . well . . . White," she says. She explained that her counselor often did not understand her family's culture. "When I shared that my father yelled at me and beat me on the back with a rope, [the counselor] looked shocked. 'Where was your mother?' he asked. 'Why didn't she call the police?'" Shreya rolled her eyes and laughed at the thought of an Asian American calling the police on their own family member. She also explained how physical abuse is viewed differently in her family. When, as an adult, she shared with her mother that she felt her father had abused her, she recalls her mother saying, "Abuse is a White term—we call it discipline." After hearing how important saving face was to her family, I suggested Shreya allow me to alter her name for this book. She agreed, saying softly, "I don't mind sharing my story, but I have to think of my family."

Discussion: How could Shreya's therapist have responded to her story of family betrayal trauma differently? How might his response indicate areas of his privilege?

Cam's Story

Cam Lee Small is a Korean American who was adopted when he was three and a half years old by a White couple from rural Wisconsin. He is also a therapist who specializes in working with adoptees. Cam's birth father died when he was about three years old. His mother tried to raise him on her own, but was pressured by members of her family to relinquish him for adoption. This may have been because single mothers are often stigmatized in South Korea, as are their children.

Finding His Birth Mother

Most international adoptees are adopted into White families, often in suburban, largely White communities. During his childhood, Cam described not being interested in exploring his ethnic identity or in finding his birth mother. But in his mid-20s, he began to be curious about the meaning of being Asian. "There's probably a reason I've been treated a certain way throughout my life," he remembered thinking. Around the same time, he also started to search for his birth mother and, unlike most international adoptees, was able to locate her.

Cam traveled to South Korea to meet his birth mother, but once he arrived, she called to cancel their meeting. As he described, "It was too much for her to bear, and I think that opened up a window for me to begin grieving actually. I didn't realize what was happening, but when I look back in hindsight, [I was] really starting to put words and a name to the sense of loss of culture, of family, of ancestry, of my connection to Korea, and what that all meant." Several days after canceling, Cam's birth mother changed her mind and did meet with him. But in the interim, he had "gone through a few days of kind of just very dark places, of Why did this happen to me? Why is this happening to me? And really questioning all of that." As Cam shared, "My understanding, I guess, evolved in terms of going beyond just that one-dimensional 'Your mom was poor, she loved you so much, so she gave you up for adoption.' I realized it's much more complicated than that."

On Being Christian

Cam found a way to connect to Asian culture through religion, becoming involved with a Korean American Christian church while in college. He realized, "Christianity is more than just what my White parents do with their White community. All of a sudden, I'm sort of like meeting and becoming friends with this . . . vibrant Asian community on campus. You know, students, professors, teachers, parents, all these amazing people sharing meals daily, just hanging out searching for truth . . . living and existing beyond the stereotypes that I had in my mind."

On Parenting and Adoption Trauma

Cam shared how becoming a father has affected his feelings about being adopted.

> My youngest daughter is three and a half, and that's the age [I was] when I was adopted. And she is verbal, she's so smart, she loves to give us hugs and just be so close to us. It makes me wonder about the experience I must have had, having to say good-bye to my family, and I just can't imagine what that would be like, and that's where some of that trauma work comes in.

Cam thinks of the trauma of leaving Korea and being separated from his mother as related to

> my nervous system developing when I was three and a half years old, [and it] was stunted or derailed or compromised or assaulted in some way by that over-whelming, fearful event of not knowing why am I getting on this airplane, not knowing I'm getting off this airplane and there are these grown-ups taking me [away] . . . I was crying "Umma! Umma!"* That was overwhelming for a little three-and-a-half-year-old [boy who doesn't] speak English. There's no Korean food here, [and he's] literally in a completely different world.

The pressure on Cam's mother to relinquish her child may be considered a form of cultural betrayal trauma. I want to clarify that this is my interpretation and not Cam's. However, as a therapist, it is an issue that I may raise with a client upon hearing a story like his.

Discussion: During the interview, Cam posed a couple of thoughtful questions for therapists: 1) How could a therapist "help this little kiddo feel safe if the environment actually is safe"; and 2) How could a therapist validate his experience of not feeling safe due to being taken from his family, home, and country?

Kira's Story

An actor, martial artist, model, and dancer from Los Angeles, Kira Omans is also an outspoken advocate for adoptees. She was adopted from China when she was ten months old. Kira also has a younger brother whom her parents adopted from Korea, and a younger sister who is a biological child of her parents.

Umma means "Mom" in Korean.

Ethnic Identity

Kira began our meeting by sharing, "I love my parents. I attended a predominantly White Catholic elementary and middle school which was not very diverse, so going to school I was not surrounded by a lot of diversity. [My parents] definitely did their best to make sure that I had other outlets to explore my culture. I started Chinese dance when I was four years old and joined martial arts when I was six, but . . . school . . . definitely wasn't the most conducive environment to me having a good relationship with my identity as a Chinese American, let alone Chinese American adoptee. I experienced a lot of racism at school and bullying . . . as did my brother, who definitely got [an even] shorter end of the stick because he's also gay . . . I think that that also added another layer of complexity to his experience. But for me, I think my parents did their best to deal with it as they could, but they are White, and so they just would never truly understand what we were going through . . . I felt like, at that time, with the resources available to them, . . . they did do their best. But yeah, growing up was not the easiest in terms of exploring my identity as an Asian American and having parents that just were trying to be supportive but didn't really understand what I was going through . . . They put my brother and I in counseling, but when the counselor is also White and doesn't really know, it's kind of a never-ending cycle."

Advocating for Adoptees

Kira explained that adoptive parents dominate conversations about adoption, while adoptees "are incredibly underrepresented in conversations about adoption and in adoption legislation." She continued, "My goal is very much just to raise awareness for adoptees' stories and experiences, and to add more nuance to the narrative that adoption is not just [about] love, and it's not just a family coming together; it's also loss and grief, and a child losing their family, and for transracial adoptees and international adoptees, it's losing a culture and other aspects of the adoptee experience that aren't really discussed in the wider conversation."

Kira explained some of the challenges she faces with advocacy, saying, "Right now it's just very difficult for adoptees to even have any kind of, like, open-minded response from the public. . . . Anytime an adoptee makes the criticism about the adoption system or any aspect of the negative parts of being adopted, we are so often met with just an overwhelming amount of people going, 'You should be grateful, like, you were rescued from a horrible situation and you should just be happy,' like your parents are saints. [You're] very much eating into the White savior complex and, like, the White savior mentality of a lot of adoptive parents, unfortunately, and so . . . I just do my best to combat that . . . I think that education is the best way to do that."

Adoption as Trauma

I asked Kira whether she felt adoption was a trauma. She replied, "I personally do believe that it is trauma, and I would not have said that a couple of years ago. I think that the more that I have really delved into my relationship with my adoption and how it has affected so many different areas of my life, and my relationships and my happiness, and how I think about the world and how I cope with different problems . . . even at infancy I think that losing that connection has such an impact on how adoptees form relationships, form bonds, and, like, in those very formative months of just existing for the first couple of months or years of your life."

Kira shared that she struggled with separation anxiety for much of her life. A breakthrough for her came in therapy when her therapist pointed out that her experience as an infant of being left alone on a bridge for strangers to find her was a traumatic event that her body would remember, even if she consciously did not. "That was kind of a turning point for me in the way I began to think of adoption . . . I do think that I would call it a trauma," said Kira.

As Kira stated, international adoptees are often told they should be grateful to have been rescued. This attitude toward them makes it difficult to acknowledge the racial trauma they experience in the United States. Similarly, adoptees are also discouraged from acknowledging family betrayal trauma, either by their birth parents or by their adopted parents. Though none of the adoptees interviewed for this book reported being abused by their birth parents, there is ample anecdotal evidence that such abuse does occur. However, to date, no empirical research has been conducted on rates of child maltreatment among international adoptees.

ADOPTION AND INSTITUTIONAL BETRAYAL TRAUMA

The international adoption industry has its roots in the historical trauma of the Korean War. American soldiers left behind tens of thousands of mixed-race children they had fathered with Korean women, many of whom had been forced into sex work to support a postwar economy dependent upon the United States. Their adoption to people in the United States and Europe formed the basis of what would become a lucrative industry in South Korea over the next several decades, bringing millions of dollars to adoption agencies. These agencies would sometimes tell pregnant unwed women that they would be selfish to keep their baby when instead it could be adopted by a wealthy, two-parent household in the United States (Jones, 2015). Additionally, some adoption paperwork was also fraudulent, as when a relative gave up a baby without the mother's consent because they thought it would be better for her. Agency workers often did not verify whether the mother had truly consented to the adoption (Jones, 2015). Stories of fraud and even child trafficking have surrounded adoptions from China (Lelund, 2011). Therefore, for some international adoptees, institutional betrayal trauma may play a role in their story, even though many may not be able to determine if this was the case for them.

Side by Side by Glenn and Julie Morey (https://sidebysideproject.com/) is a documentary project that features 100 interviews of South Korean transnational adoptees living in seven countries, including the United States. The interviewees are not identified by name. In one interview, a woman with a wavy bob haircut and white blouse describes the moment she realized she was leaving Korea at age six with her new adopted family as a "major trauma." She recounts, "I started screaming and wailing at the top of my lungs." She continued screaming and crying for hours, making her new parents question their decision to adopt. She describes having little memory of the first few years in her new home, but she does remember trying to teach her adoptive parents Korean songs and games. "Everything about me I would try to pass on," she says. She also describes how she became the "little maid" of the family. Her mother would say to her friends, "I told Henry I wanted a little maid, and he got me a girl from Korea." The adoptee also discloses that Henry, her adoptive father, began sexually abusing her when she was nine years old.

MOVING TOWARD LIBERATION

In summary, a liberation approach to therapy with Asian Americans begins with the therapist developing self-awareness and identifying their racial biases. There are many ways to do this, including exploring one's trauma history via the Rings of Betrayal Inventory. Doing so helps therapists understand how their own trauma likely has systemic and intergenerational roots. It will also help identify areas of privilege and oppression. In becoming more self-aware as therapists, we move ourselves toward liberation, allowing us to better help our clients.

The Rings of Betrayal Inventory can also be used as a framework for case conceptualization and assessment to better understand Asian and Asian American clients. The distance in the relationship between clients and their therapists caused by the therapist's lack of cultural understanding is often not something clients will mention. Respect for authority figures and older adults is a common value in Asian cultures. Correcting them or causing them to feel embarrassment is therefore deemed unacceptable. Additionally, BIPOC clients may feel there is little point in trying to educate someone outside of their culture, or feel it is a burden to do this additional labor. Finally, a history of betrayal trauma creates a tendency for many to silence themselves for the sake of preserving a needed relationship. As a result, clients often settle for therapy that is a mixture of help and harm. Obviously, it is a problem when therapy exacerbates the feeling of being alienated and hopeless. And it is an enormous lost opportunity for clients to heal from racism.

Chapter 5 extends the incorporation of context to the next domain of the MSJCC: the therapeutic relationship. It explains how the decontextualization of trauma by Western psychology, rooted in empiricism, behaviorism, and the eugenics movement, has harmed Asian Americans and other marginalized communities. The liberation of psychotherapy requires a relational approach, one that addresses the power imbalance in the therapeutic relationship, especially when the therapist holds more social privilege than the client. Relational-cultural therapy (RCT) is one such approach that promotes power-sharing and mutual empathy as active ingredients for healing.

ADDITIONAL RESOURCES

- Singh, A. A. (2019). *The racial healing handbook: Practical activities to help you challenge privilege, confront systemic racism, and engage in collective healing.* New Harbinger Publications.

    The Racial Healing Handbook helps guide BIPOC and White people alike toward a greater understanding of themselves and others.
- The following videos can be used to practice trauma assessment using the Rings of Betrayal Inventory:
    - The University of Minnesota's Immigration History Research Center hosts a free online library of hundreds of oral history videos that can be searched by ethnicity and country of origin. https://tinyurl.com/UM OralHistory

SCAN ME

One of the videos in the collection tells the story of Manichan Xiong, a Hmong Laotian refugee (Xiong, 2014). Her family had aided a wounded American pilot during the "Secret War," a clandestine conflict waged in Laos by the US government at the same time as the Vietnam War. In retaliation, communist soldiers killed her grandfather. The Secret War resulted in the deaths of tens of thousands of Hmong soldiers recruited by the CIA and ended with the victory of the Laotian communist party in 1975.

Xiong, M. (Creator). (2014). *Southeast Asian Refugee Stories: Manichan Xiong*. University of Minnesota, Immigration History Research Center. https://tinyurl.com/Manichan

◦ Morey, G., & Morey, J. (Directors and Producers). (2013–2015). *Side by Side* [Documentary video and film series]. https://sidebysideproject.com/

The Side by Side Project features 100 interviews of Korean transnational adoptees living in seven WEIRD (Western, educated, industrialized, rich, and democratic) countries. The story of the adoptee described above can be found at https://sidebysideproject.com/stories/dc6874

Chapter Five

Decolonizing Therapy with Asian Americans: A Relational-Cultural Approach

Seeking therapy poses an enormous risk for anyone. In a sense, it is like putting one's head in a guillotine where the therapist controls the rope. Indeed, the therapist has the power to confirm what a client already suspects about themselves or has been told by others—that they are "mental" or "crazy." This belief is understandable given the medicalization of mental health that pathologizes trauma and locates mental illness within individuals rather than relationships and society. Within this model, therapists are upheld as experts, and the client is reduced to a diagnosis, a generalized other with "no feelings, no face, and no voice" (Birrell, 2006, p. 104). Thus, the client risks everything, while the therapist can choose to risk nothing. This dynamic creates an enormous power differential in the therapeutic relationship, even before it has begun.

This chapter provides a critical examination of the dualistic roots of Western psychology that promote a power-over dynamic. This dualistic framework leads to the endorsement of practices that can be considered in opposition to the values of liberation psychology. In most cases, therapists are trying to help clients, but unawareness of racial and cultural power dynamics can still cause harm. Using a case example, I show how dynamics of oppression can arise in the therapy room even when the therapist—myself, in this case—is well-intended.

I then introduce relational-cultural therapy (RCT), which Singh et al. (2020) describe as one of the only approaches that help a therapist implement liberation psychology values. They observe that "classical theories focusing on individuals and/or families were not created with the goal of dismantling systems of oppression" (p. 261). RCT tackles oppression in the therapeutic relationship by providing a feminist-oriented framework for dismantling unhealthy power dynamics. This framework acknowledges the importance of historical and social context, as well as relational harm. As the first several chapters of this book have demonstrated, the majority of Asian Americans have experienced betrayal traumas, from the historical and institutional to the intergenerational and intracultural. Thus, RCT is particularly pertinent to Asian Americans. A case study demonstrates how RCT may be used to address various topics relevant to Asian Americans, such as betrayal trauma, ethnic identity, and intersectionality.

ASIAN AMERICANS, PSYCHOTHERAPY, AND RISK

For Asian and Asian American clients, additional factors make seeking therapy especially risky, widening the asymmetric therapist–client power differential. Two of these are cultural barriers and histories of betrayal traumas. The introduction in this book outlines multiple cultural barriers to therapy that many Asians and Asian Americans contend with. These include a taboo on discussing mental health issues, and cultural values of relational harmony and saving face. As a result, attending therapy sessions can trigger both internal shame and shaming from family members. Psychologist Jyothsna Bhat (2021) describes the way one of her South Asian clients ended therapy:

> "I don't think I can do this after today," she said, in clear distress and palpable shame. "My mom told me she will disown me if I ever think of doing something like this." She saw herself as weak and felt she was neglecting her mother's advice to "stop being negative" and "pray more."

At the same time, it is important to recognize the diversity of Asians and Asian Americans and not overgeneralize. Many are more open to therapy than before, regardless of whether they are first-, second-, or later-generation. For example, a first-generation Korean American father, concerned about his teenage daughter's depression, once contacted me on her behalf. He also attended her first appointment with her. It was apparent that she took comfort in his presence, as she sat closely next to him, leaning into his side at times. The following story of Aranya, a first-generation immigrant, demonstrates how attitudes toward therapy can change when a client has a positive experience.

Aranya's Story

Aranya began by describing how her parents taught her to "keep problems in the family." She felt ashamed to tell others that her mother, who lived in Thailand, had Alzheimer's disease. "We're supposed to take care of our own problems . . . like, you keep them in the family, and it's like when my mom was first diagnosed, I couldn't tell anyone because I thought it was kind of a shame . . . I mean, it's so common now, but still, it's like there's a lot of stigma, so it's embarrassing. . . . I noticed that my mom's friends and family, I mean, they kinda stayed away." However, after spending a month in Thailand caring for her mother, Aranya returned depressed and angry. "I was just, you know, yelling at my husband and yelling at [my daughter]."

Aranya's family urged her to seek therapy, but it was not until after a second trip to Thailand left her "a mess" that she contacted her primary care provider for a referral. However, her doctor did not respond for several weeks. Aranya eventually found a therapist herself, and expressed gratitude that the therapist taught her skills for managing her anger. Aranya is now an advocate among her friends for seeking therapy.

Regardless of a client's readiness for therapy, the enormous risk that attending therapy poses for many Asians and Asian Americans means that the ones who do come exhibit immeasurable courage. Therefore, a great deal of damage can occur when a therapist is unaware of, dismisses, or abuses their power. As Haddock-Lazala observes (2020), "When therapists do not readily offer power to be negotiated, clients find themselves reactively asserting their wills by putting up resistance in hopes of reclaiming freedom and justice" (p. 160). Further, clients who have experienced betrayal traumas often have highly honed instincts for disingenuousness or condescension (i.e., "bullshit meters"), and may feel justifiably angry or hurt in response. Paradoxically, according to betrayal trauma theory, the same clients may also have a heightened need to preserve the relationship due to a conditioned response to prior betrayal (e.g., Freyd, 1996; Freyd, 1997; Freyd & Birrell, 2013). As a result, they may overlook oppressive behavior. The therapy room then becomes yet another venue for fragmentation as opposed to integration and for oppression versus liberation.

SHAME, BETRAYAL, AND ASIAN AMERICANS

The first three chapters of this book detail the multiple forms of betrayal trauma that many Asians and Asian Americans have experienced, from the historical and institutional to the intergenerational and intracultural. Betrayal traumas, being complex in nature, have correspondingly complex sequelae, including but not limited to addiction, dissociation, depression, anxiety, panic, rage, and alienation. Herman (2011, 2018) has proposed that these states of distress are driven by shame. Indeed, research has found that traumas high in betrayal are more strongly associated with shame than those with less betrayal (Platt & Freyd, 2015; Platt et al., 2016). Platt and Freyd (2015) propose that shame arises as a self-protective mechanism to preserve relationships—in other words, blaming oneself can be psychologically and physically safer than blaming the perpetrator. This theory has been supported by empirical research that included participants from India, the United States, and Israel, demonstrating a linear relationship between shame and devaluation in all three countries (Sznycer et al., 2016). That is, as the potential for being devaluated increased, so, too, did shame.

Shame, in turn, breeds fragmentation of the psyche, as parts of oneself deemed unacceptable become suppressed (Herman, 1992). Lorenz and Watkins (2001) have described this fragmentation as "silenced knowings," the

> understandings that we each carry that take refuge in silence, as it feels dangerous to speak them to ourselves and to others. The sanctions against them in the family, community, or wider culture render them mute and increasingly inaccessible. Once silenced, these knowings are no longer available to inform our lives, to strengthen our moral discernment. Once pushed to the side, these knowings require our energy to sustain their dissociation, and our numbing to evade their pain. (pp. 1–2)

"Shame is always implicitly a relational experience" (Herman, 2018, p. 161). Therefore, healing from shame is necessarily relational (Birrell & Freyd, 2006). Shame pervades all cultures as an innate human emotion and one of the "primary regulators of social relations" (Herman, 2018, p. 157). It is an oversimplification to characterize Asian cultures as "shame-based," with the implication that Western cultures are not. However, culture does influence how shame is perceived and enacted. For example, Stadter and Jun (2020) describe Chinese culture as viewing shame more positively than in the United States, and using it "more to motivate prosocial behaviour by families and authorities." They also note that Chinese people are more likely to feel vicarious shame or guilt when someone they are connected to commits a shameful act. In India, shame intersects with identity in the hierarchical caste system (Kumar, 2014).

Thus, dismantling the power dynamic in a therapeutic relationship is necessarily an issue of ethics (Birrell & Freyd, 2006). By dismantling, I do not presume that it can be made to disappear altogether. Rather, I mean that therapists must continually challenge themselves to break from the colonial foundations of psychology and psychotherapy, as Martín-Baró (1996) urged. The previous chapter described how to begin this process by conducting a self-assessment of privileged and marginalized statuses using the Rings of Betrayal worksheet. It also recommended doing the same for the client. These two steps mirror the first two domains of the Multicultural and Social Justice Counseling Competencies (MSJCC; Ratts et al., 2016). The third domain of the MSJCC urges therapists to apply this awareness to the counseling relationship. To do so, therapists must adopt power-sharing as their primary approach, guiding the relationship toward equality by taking risks of their own.

THE CARTESIAN CART: COLONIALISM IN COUNSELING

In one of the first classes I took in my doctoral program in clinical psychology, the professor described therapy using a metaphor of a horse pulling a cart full of apples. The apples represent the intervention, and the horse cart, the therapy relationship. The sole purpose of the cart is to deliver the intervention. "But can't the cart also be the intervention and not just the vehicle?" I wondered. Two decades later, a wealth of research shows this to be true—that the therapy relationship itself is therapeutic. Not only are the cart and apples inexorably linked, but the cart itself accounts for the bulk of growth and change in therapy (e.g., Flückiger et al., 2018; Wampold & Imel, 2015).

The separation of horse from cart is rooted in the dualism promoted by 17th-century French philosopher-scientist René Descartes (Damasio, 1994), who argued that a complex system could be understood by examining its individual parts. This led to the belief that the workings of the mind are separate from the body and emotions. This reductionist paradigm was furthered by Newton in his development of classical physics, which emphasized the primary separateness of objects (Jordan, 2000). The ontological implication of reductionism is that all phenomena, including the mind and emotions, are ultimately made of matter (Heylighen, 2006).

From its inception, psychology sought to establish itself as a "hard science," aligning itself with reductionism and Newtonian physics (Jordan, 2000). In doing so, it was "strongly influenced by and closely affiliated with eugenics, defined by its originators as the 'science of racial betterment'" (Yakushko, 2019, p. 1). American psychologists were the strongest proponents of eugenics, focusing on developing intelligence and personality tests to establish the inferiority of racial minorities and women. A lasting influence of eugenics on psychology is the emphasis on behaviorism, first developed by John B. Watson (Yakushko, 2019). A leader in the American eugenics movement, Watson used eugenics values and language to promote the use of empiricism to reduce human psychological factors to biology and invalidate the role of social context (Watson, 1914, 1919, 1928, as cited in Yakushko, 2019).

A colonial and eugenic bias continues to influence research and practice in psychology. Behaviorism, empirical research, and empirically supported therapies are considered the "gold standard," while, in the ultimate irony, human emotion and connection are devalued. Even psychodynamic theories, which are not empirically driven, have historically emphasized analysis of the individual, the intrapsychic, and movement toward independence as the path of development (Jordan, 2001). This Western point of view runs counter to the fact that emotion and reason are inseparable (Damasio, 1994), something Asian philosophies, healing systems, and spiritual practices have understood for millennia.

As one example of a nondual indigenous framework, Advaita Vedanta teaches that all beings are interconnected, each a manifestation of *Ishvara*, or God. According to the Vedas, the ancient texts upon which Vedanta is based, the egoic sense of individuality, the *ahankara*, is an illusion perpetuated by ignorance of the self as whole, complete, and free. The Vedas elaborate on the connection between mind and environment by describing psychological processes such as *pratibhāsika*, or the ability of the mind to subconsciously project its interpretations onto other objects or people. The projections are based upon *vāsana*s, unconscious impressions of the mind based on prior learning. *Pratibhāsika* is essentially what is now known in modern psychology as top-down cognitive processing, a 20th-century "discovery" that revolutionized how scientists understand the workings of the brain.

Asian systems of medicine, likewise, are based on understanding the nondual nature of mind and body. For example, there is no term such as "mind–body connection" in Ayurveda because mind and body are already understood as inseparable. Therefore, there is no need for a "connection." It is also understood that relationships are rooted in the physical body, where humans (and most other living beings) are neurologically wired for social connection.

An individual's psychology and well-being cannot be accurately understood outside the context of relationships (Martín-Baró, 1996). However, the Cartesian paradigm still dominates in the mechanistic application of evidence-based therapies (EBTs) and empirically supported treatments (ESTs), which are much easier to quantify and research due to their standardization. Most approaches for trauma (and other diagnoses) are singularly focused on symptom reduction. However, the harm of complex trauma and betrayal trauma extends beyond symptoms, into issues of one's very identity and relationships.

In the past two decades, new varieties of "apples" have been developed to address symptoms of post-traumatic stress. Some of the most well-known are EMDR (eye movement desensitization and reprocessing), PE (prolonged exposure), and CPT (cognitive processing therapy), all of which are highly prescriptive and manualized. Others that are less manualized but also prescriptive include somatic-oriented and psychodynamic therapies, such as accelerated experiential dynamic psychotherapy (AEDP).

Western psychology is entrenched in a patriarchal medical model that amplifies the therapist's power over the client with a neoliberal focus on productivity. Thus, quick fixes are extremely attractive, as are directive therapies that can be standardized like a franchise. (Indeed, many lucrative psychotherapy franchises exist today.) The promotion of manualized therapies for trauma is a direct result of their promise of brief, 8- to 12-week "treatments" that have at best moderate support in empirical research.

The belief that the therapist acts upon the client by delivering an intervention without regard to the human relationship is oppressive and misinformed. It is oppressive because it assumes that the therapist as expert knows better than the client what is good for them. While therapists do have specialized training and can suggest skills, it is dehumanizing to assume we know better, as though therapists are working on car engines rather than people. I have seen this repeatedly occur in the (mis) application of manualized therapy. For example, one of my former supervisors would tell her clients who wanted to quit doing prolonged exposure, because they were feeling overwhelmed with distress, that they were making a big mistake. She would even inform them that their baseline of mental health would be worse than when they started, although there is no evidence to support this claim. I suppose she was doing what she thought was best, but at least one of her clients became extremely angry and never returned.

Prolonged exposure is a particularly grueling protocol that requires clients to repeatedly recount their trauma at each therapy session and listen to recordings of those accounts daily as homework. I feel deep regret for the instances in which I used my power to push clients to participate in this protocol, when they clearly expressed that it made them feel terrible. What can happen as a result is a reenactment of victimhood dynamics in the therapy relationship, whereby the client is essentially coerced into doing something they feel is bad for them.

In contrast, approaches consistent with liberation psychology seek to dismantle power and privilege in therapy. In a liberation approach, the therapist seeks to share power with the client, increasing the client's capacity to connect with their own power and feel comfortable wielding it. I do continue to use prolonged exposure sparingly. However, the client's volition will always take precedence over the protocol.

The following case illustrates how an anti-oppressive approach can—and must—inform therapy.

Irfan's Story: The Ethics of Compassion

Irfan left me a voicemail, saying he wanted to start therapy because he was having panic attacks for the first time in his life. They began a couple of months ago after an accident at a café where another customer walked into him, spilling hot coffee on them both. Neither party was injured beyond minor burns, but Irfan said the incident was extremely upsetting because the other person began to yell at him, and used a racist slur.

At our first meeting, Irfan explained that he was a visiting professor from Indonesia. Another faculty member who witnessed the incident at the café had repeatedly encouraged him to seek therapy. Irfan seemed very ill at ease, stating more than once that he was not crazy, an expression of the shame he felt for being there.

"I don't think you are either," I replied. "What you went through was pretty awful, though."

"In Indonesia, nobody goes to therapy," he explained. "My wife is really worried other people will find out."

"Are you worried other people will find out, too?" I asked.

"Well . . ." He shrugged and nodded. "You won't tell anyone, will you?"

I spent more time than usual explaining the terms of confidentiality and the legal consequences to my practice if I should break them. This seemed to reassure him. We also discussed what he would like to do should we happen to cross paths in public, which would not be unusual in the small university town we were in. I also explained that therapy could be like talking to a friend who is not emotionally involved in your life, so they can be more objective. I encouraged him to continue asking any other questions he might have.

In response to this invitation, Irfan asked, "Do you have a family? Are you married?" With Asian and Asian American clients, I operate with more fluid boundaries, mirroring cultural norms and working to mitigate the shame that some may feel about being in therapy. On the surface, it seemed Irfan wanted to gain a sense of my life experience and qualifications. But I also saw his asking personal questions as a way to normalize our conversation. Assuming this was true, trying to process the reasons for his questions in a classically psychodynamic manner rather than answering them would have been inhumane. Instead, I told Irfan that, yes, I was married, and had children.

Irfan responded with a smile, saying, "Ah! My wife and I hope to have children as soon as we return to Indonesia." We talked about how he wanted to raise his children in Jakarta, near where his parents live. It was important to him that they be connected to their extended family and cultural heritage. I viewed this time making small talk as a necessary investment in developing our relationship and mitigating shame.

He began to share how his relationship with his wife had become strained since the incident at the café. She could not understand why he could not just "forget about it," and why he was much more withdrawn and irritable than usual.

Irfan then turned to the story of the event at the café. When the accident happened, Irfan recalled immediately apologizing to the person who ran into him, even though Irfan did not think he was at fault. The other person, whom Irfan described as a young White man, began to yell and swear at him, blaming Irfan for burning him, and not caring that Irfan was also hurt. He also hurled a racial slur that referred to a non-Asian ethnic group before storming off. "I had to ask one of my colleagues later what it meant," Irfan said. He expressed feeling humiliated in front of the many other people who witnessed the incident. One person asked if he was all right, and gave him some napkins to dry himself.

I suggested we try PE. On the rare occasions that I use PE, I choose cases where the identified trauma appears to be associated with a single discrete event, as Irfan's was. After explaining the protocol to Irfan, he agreed to try it, and we began the first session.

Part of the PE intervention is called imaginal exposure, in which the client closes their eyes and tells the story of a traumatic event repeatedly over the span of about 45 minutes. I asked Irfan to close his eyes and recount his story, starting from when he entered the café to just after the accident. He began to recount the incident in the present tense, as if it were happening at the moment, per the PE protocol. However, during the second retelling, he shared, "I don't feel too comfortable—I can't see you. It's hard to feel you're still there."

"I'm here, listening," I said, attempting to reassure him, as I was trained to do when implementing PE. "Can you try to continue?" *[In retrospect, I recognize that even this nudging was a form of exerting power over him rather than connecting with him. I missed an opportunity to let him know his distress mattered—that he mattered.]*

With each retelling, Irfan's story became more coherent and his memory clearer concerning what had happened, and its sequence in time, which is typical with PE sessions. However, as soon as Irfan opened his eyes at the end of the imaginal exposure, he again reiterated his distress at not being able to see me and not feeling a connection with me. He said that while he understood better what had happened during the incident, the process of retelling it made him feel very alone. Irfan shook his head from side to side as if to rid himself of his fear. Looking at me, he pleaded, "Please, I can't do this anymore."

This is the fork in the road that a therapist must navigate over and over again within each session. Does one veer right or left? Cart or apples? Or is the cart also the apples? With the therapeutic relationship and a liberation approach as my clear priorities, I chose to honor Irfan's wishes. Not because I let compassion interfere with what is best for the client, but because what is best for the client is compassion. This is no mere intellectual debate, but one of the utmost ethical importance (Birrell & Freyd, 2006). If compassion is cast aside for the sake of a protocol, then immeasurable harm is being done. The therapist assumes the role of a perpetrator, using their power to override the client's will, while the client becomes a dehumanized object that is acted upon. The client learns once again that their voice does not matter, that no one will hear them, no matter how loudly they protest. On the other hand, if the therapist demonstrates that they can be moved by the client, then there is an opportunity for healing through mutual empathy (Jordan, 2000). The client becomes a human being with agency in the relationship, learns to trust their own judgment, and knows they have the right to protect themselves. Healing from relational trauma cannot occur in the absence of compassion (Birrell & Freyd, 2006).

The dynamic of insisting a client complete a therapy protocol against their will mirrors the racism and oppression of the macrosystem of the Rings of Betrayal Model, especially between a White therapist and a BIPOC client. Finally, it reenacts the dynamic of betrayal traumas experienced in the microsystem and mesosystem. These reasons may explain the exceedingly high dropout rates for PE and CPT, whereby three-fourths of people offered these protocols either do not want to start them, or do not complete them if they do start (Miles & Thompson, 2016). The reenactment of oppressive dynamics may also explain why BIPOC are significantly more likely to drop out of PE and CPT protocols than their White counterparts (73% vs. 45%; Lester et al., 2010).

Lester et al. (2010) attempted to minimize this finding by saying "there are no differences in treatment outcome," as Black Americans had equivalent PTSD symptom score reductions as Whites. However, *this result excludes the 73% of Black Americans who could not tolerate the protocols*. Discounting most of the sample cannot be considered sound science. Furthermore, this high dropout rate does not include those whom clinicians did not deem good candidates for these therapies, or those who declined the offer to participate in them. In my own experience at two VA clinics, where we were required to offer all veterans exposure therapy, the majority declined and/or never returned.

Finally, the authors did not measure the potential long-term harm that a poor therapy experience engenders, such as increased feelings of isolation, failure, and shame. As the authors acknowledged, not establishing sufficient trust in the therapy setting creates a barrier for Black clients' willingness to disclose trauma to someone who is perceived as an outsider of their community (Boyd-Franklin, 2003, as cited in Lester et al., 2010). Though no studies on PE and CPT have been conducted specifically with Asian Americans, the same need for establishing trust holds true for them, especially for those in first- and second-generation households who often are taught not to discuss mental health or disclose personal problems with others outside the family.

Inattention to the social context of race and culture is a critical flaw of most manualized treatments that can exacerbate the stress and trauma of racism. Had I insisted on continuing with PE, Irfan might well have complied out of the cultural respect accorded to medical providers, but at what cost to him?

Alternatively, he may have discontinued therapy immediately. If so, it would be highly unlikely he would try therapy again after such a negative experience, considering the cultural hurdles he had to overcome just to try it the first time. Unfortunately, in my clinical training, I had to work with multiple Irfans before identifying these patterns, upon which my conclusions are based.

Irfan and I continued to explore his emotions related to the incident in the café using a relational-cultural therapy approach, which shares similarities with psychodynamic therapy in its incorporation of emotional processing (Frey, 2013). He was able to identify feeling ashamed that he apologized to the other man. He wished he had not been so "weak." I suggested that his apologizing was a self-protective response in a situation where he already felt unsure of himself due to being in a foreign country. We also traced his automatic response of apologizing to a childhood in which he was frequently bullied by both his peers and teachers because his family was impoverished. Irfan also experienced physical abuse at home. He began to recognize how his sense of shame was in part caused by corporal punishment being normalized in his culture. Understanding how his response to the present incident could be traced to past trauma and cultural beliefs helped him relinquish his shame. He felt freer to share more of what he was feeling with his wife, which helped resolve the tension between them and brought them closer to each other. Irfan's course of therapy was relatively brief. He stopped experiencing panic attacks after about two months; at three months, he was ready to end therapy. Though RCT lends itself to long-term therapy, it can also be used for short-term treatment (Jordan, 2010).

RELATIONAL-CULTURAL THERAPY: GROWING THROUGH AND TOWARD CONNECTION

RCT was developed in the 1970s by psychiatrist Jean Baker Miller and psychologists Judith V. Jordan, Janet Surrey, and Irene Stiver at the Stone Center at Wellesley College. Relational-cultural therapy distinguishes itself from traditional Western theories of psychology that emphasize movement from dependence to independence (Jordan, 2001). Where psychology historically assumed individuation to be a natural course of mature development, RCT posits that human beings grow toward and through relationships (Jordan, 2018). Our brains—and our bodies—are healthiest when we feel connected to others in a safe and nurturing environment (Siegel, 2006). As Jordan (2018) describes, RCT "seeks to lessen the suffering caused by chronic disconnection and isolation, whether at an individual or societal level, to increase capacity for relational resilience, and to foster social justice" (p. 23).

By centering relationships and connection, RCT also rejects the traditional view of the therapist as an immutable blank slate, leading to a more equal (or, more accurately, less unequal) balance of power. For example, in RCT, the therapist acknowledges any responsibility they may have for conflict or ruptures in the therapeutic relationship. As Jordan (2018) explains, RCT should not be "misconstrued as a compendium of harmonious and cozy relationships" (p. 8). Conflict is viewed as potentially therapeutic if the therapist can offer the client a new experience of it that leads to increased connection as opposed to disconnection. This can only occur if the therapist does not "withdraw into a position of power, distance, or all-knowing objectivity. Instead, the therapist must be present to the differences that arise and open to admitting and learning from [their] contribution to the conflict or disconnections that ensue from the interactions" (p. 8).

Movement toward mutuality and growth-fostering relationships is the overarching goal in RCT. RCT proposes that mutually growth-fostering relationships result in Five Good Things (Miller & Stiver, 1997):

1. a desire to move into more relationships, because of how a good relational experience feels;
2. a sense of zest or energy;
3. increased knowledge of oneself and the other person in the relationship;
4. a desire to take action both in the growth-fostering relationship and outside of it;
5. an overall increased sense of worth.

Mutual Empathy and Mutual Empowerment

According to RCT, mutuality forms the core of growth-fostering relationships. The relational process necessarily includes the therapist. As Jean Baker Miller has often been quoted, "In order for one person to grow in a relationship, both people must grow" (Jordan & Walker, 2004, p. 3). There are at least two processes through which mutuality occurs: mutual empathy and mutual empowerment.

Judith Jordan (2018) described mutual empathy as a

> dance of responsiveness: The therapist says to the client, in effect, "I empathize with you, with your experience and pain, and I'm letting you see that your pain has affected me and you matter to me." The client sees, knows, and feels the therapist's empathy and thereby begins to experience a sense of relational competence and efficacy. (p. 7)

Whereas empathy is a foundation of human connection, mutuality is a creative process. As Rothenberg (1987) writes, "This process is not the same as simply seeing things from another's viewpoint . . . empathic understanding in treatment is actively and creatively achieved in the context of a mutual creative process involving both therapist and [client]" (p. 445). To be clear, this mutuality does not mean that the therapist expects or demands empathy from the client; the therapist continues to maintain boundaries with the client, and encourages the client to do so as well. What mutual empathy does offer both therapist and client is an opportunity to grow in their capacity to trust each other, just as Irfan challenged me to trust him. This empathic extension of trust is inextricably linked to mutual empowerment.

Along with mutual empathy, a growth-fostering therapeutic relationship also requires an active effort by the therapist to share power with the client. Mutual empowerment "is built on a relationship of engagement, of being present and caring about the relationship as well as the individuals in it" (Jordan, 2018, p. 135). The result is "more aliveness, more clarity, and a greater sense of possibility and potential agency" (Jordan, 2018, p. 135). In Irfan's case, sharing with him the power to determine the course of therapy also resulted in my own empowerment; it liberated me from my own participation in an oppressive system in which the therapist is untouchable. Consistent with Miller's statement above, it was not possible to liberate one of us but not the other. A result of our mutual empowerment was my being able to be more emotionally present with him, have less anxiety about controlling the session, and facilitate the space for taking risks by bringing forth increasingly more of his own emotions. For Irfan, my trusting his judgment did three things: 1) It increased his sense of safety and made it more possible to trust me; 2) it humanized our relationship as one in which his feelings mattered; and 3) because his feelings mattered, it lessened the imbalance of power between us.

Empirical Support for RCT

Frey (2013) and Lenz (2016) have conducted detailed reviews of research concerning the theoretical constructs of RCT and its effectiveness. Both found strong support across numerous studies for the roles of mutuality, relational health, and connection–disconnection in mental health. Among these, Belford et al. (2012) found that relational health mediated the association between betrayal trauma and borderline personality disorder. A study by Tantillo and Sanftner (2010) focusing on women diagnosed with eating disorders randomly assigned participants to either a CBT (cognitive behavioral therapy) or an RCT group. Research on RCT typically includes measures of relational health in addition to symptom reduction. While RCT was found to be equally effective as CBT in symptom reduction, participants in the RCT group reported higher levels of mutuality with other group members. At the same time, if the effectiveness of RCT is to be evaluated at a purely empirical level, more randomized control studies are needed (Lenz, 2016).

Relational-Cultural Therapy with Asians and Asian Americans

RCT is a lens through which to explore the dynamics of a healthy relationship within the context of culture (Jordan, 2018; Walker & Rosen, 2004). The emphasis of RCT on sociocultural context, mutuality, and social justice makes it particularly relevant to those from Asian cultures for several reasons. First, the majority of Asian Americans have experienced various forms of betrayal traumas, from racial oppression and institutional betrayal to intracultural betrayal and family violence. As this chapter has argued, healing from betrayal trauma necessarily requires a relational approach to restore a capacity for trust, mitigate shame, and increase connections with others. Second, a relational approach directly maps onto collectivist aspects of Asian cultures (Desai, 1999; Ho, 1999; though it should be acknowledged that Asian cultures have individualist aspects as well).

Third, mutual empathy and mutual empowerment lend themselves to the practice of cultural humility, in which the therapist is open to seeing things from a different perspective and questions their own assumptions about what is deemed "normal." Lekas et al. (2020) describe cultural humility as "an orientation to care that is based on self-reflexivity, appreciation of patients' lay expertise, openness to sharing power with patients, and to continue learning from one's patients" (p. 1). This orientation is consistent with both RCT and the MSJCC (Ratts et al., 2016).

Thakore-Dunlap and Van Velsor (2014) described how the application of RCT in a therapy group for South Asian immigrant high school girls motivated them to grow toward relationships. "About midway through the group, the girls began socializing at school; and later, toward the end of the group, they continued to build relationships by spending time at each other's homes. Additionally, the girls' confidence showed at termination when they asked to form their own South Asian group" (p. 508).

Desai (1999) has described her work applying RCT with Indian college students who, like many Asian families, have complex social structures beyond the nuclear family that include other relatives and friends, with each relationship making empathic demands. According to Desai, working with Indian students "is about thinking like a family therapist when one is alone in the room with the student" (p. 5).

Intersecting Identities

Several scholars and therapists have written on the applicability of RCT to clients of color with multiple marginalized identities that compound a sense of disconnection. For example, Chan et al. (2021) observe that many older LGBTQIA+ adults of color are not only forced to contend with histories of racism, genderism, and heterosexism, but they additionally encounter ageism. The resulting grief and loss, isolation, and lack of social support mirror a hierarchy of power and privilege that impairs authentic connection and movement toward mutuality. Chan et al. (2021) offer multiple suggestions for using RCT with older LGBTQIA+ adults of color, including addressing the grief and loss associated with life transitions, such as retirement, the impacts of racism and sexual discrimination on health, and the role social identities play in power dynamics within relationships.

The following is a case of a younger client, Jesse, who identifies as nonbinary. I worked with them for several years using predominantly RCT, supplemented by mindfulness-based stress management skills. As with the other case examples in this book, Jesse is an amalgam of several clients.

Jesse's Story

Jesse's earliest memories include living in the family car and in shelters in Seattle, Washington. Their father had left suddenly, and their mother did not have any income of her own. As a result, Jesse and their mother had to move out of their rental home and into a shelter for the unhoused. They recalled frequently having to console their mother and reassure her that everything would be all right during this time. After a year, their father returned, and they all moved to rural Oregon together.

An aspiring writer with a sharp sense of humor, Jesse once quipped, "A week without therapy is a week that didn't happen." Jesse described their mother as overbearing and enmeshed; she forbade Jesse to close their bedroom door, read their journal multiple times despite it being hidden, and "wanted to do everything together." Jesse's biological father, a musician and mechanic, was in and out of their lives throughout their childhood. He would sometimes disappear for days or months at a time.

At the beginning of therapy, Jesse had been dating someone for several years. They lived in a van together with their two dogs. Jesse described this as a temporary situation they were choosing for the summer, so that they could save money to rent a home. They initially described their relationship as supportive, and spoke highly of their boyfriend's skills as an artist, though over time, Jesse began to view the relationship as restricting their freedom, as their boyfriend did not like them traveling without him, or the idea of them starting college.

Intergenerational Trauma

Jesse's paternal grandmother was from Japan, where she met Jesse's grandfather, an American serviceman stationed there during World War II. They had to wait for her to be able to immigrate to the United States. While the War Brides Act of 1945 was enacted by Congress to allow servicemembers to bring their spouses to the United States, the Act explicitly prohibited spouses from Asian countries, other than China (Chinese spouses were allowed after the Chinese Exclusion Act was repealed in 1943). The War Brides Act was not amended until five years later, in 1950, to allow Japanese and Korean spouses to immigrate on a non-quota basis. Tens of thousands of Japanese war brides immigrated to the United States at this time, the largest migration of Asian women in American history. These were typically not love matches; rather, many of the women, desperate to escape a defeated Japan, married near strangers who only a few years ago had been the enemy.

Jesse's grandparents settled in Seattle, where they raised their three children. Jesse does not know much about their grandfather other than he had a bad temper and was abusive toward their father. On the few occasions they spent time with their grandparents, they remember them arguing loudly. Their grandfather eventually committed suicide when he was in his 50s, which Jesse believed was traumatic for their father.

Listening, Shame, and the Need for a Witness

Listening relationally is often stereotyped as passively agreeing with the client. However, listening for the unspoken emotional truths within a client's narrative—the silenced knowings—is anything but passive. Rather, it demands constant vigilance and simultaneous awareness of one's own and the client's emotional state. It also requires the therapist to let go of all safety nets, such as protocol and preconceived frameworks of mental illness. Birrell (2006) cautions, "If we are not sufficiently open to listening in ways that challenge our own thinking, nothing is left us but the boredom of remaining in the same abstract frame, a state . . . [of] benumbment, or epistemic torpor" (p. 54).

Session after session with Jesse, I would panic inwardly at the depth of their despair caused by the crushing hegemony of poverty, discrimination, and generational trauma. Attempting to infuse some hope in them, and, in retrospect, for myself as well, I alternated between problem-solving and pointing out potential misconceptions, aka, "cognitive distortions." And time after time, they rebuffed my efforts, while feeling increasingly frustrated and alone. I wanted to make things better for them very badly, yet I would often make things worse. What the situation demanded was for me to jump off the cliff of control and into the emotional waters of relational therapy to meet them where they were. Each time this choice felt risky, as though we would both drown. Yet, almost miraculously, the tone of the session would abruptly shift as I focused on hearing Jesse's pain. Their anger would melt into vulnerable tears, and by the end of the session, they would arrive at a place of hope and express motivation to make some changes.

As an example of this dynamic, Jesse once described a situation where they did not feel good enough to hang out with friends who were all more financially well-off.

Jesse: They'll think I'm a loser. I mean, they all have jobs, and I'm not doing anything right now. I've got nothing, absolutely nothing to show for two years of the pandemic. I'm back to square one.

Me: Didn't you go to school? (*I say this because I want to convince them that they did do something worthwhile.*)

Jesse: Barely—I dropped my last class!

Me: But didn't you get credits for the others?

Jesse: Yeah, but here I am again, doing nothing. I'm such a loser. I have a '90s fear of success, like a Tony Robbins trope.

Me (*recognizing we are at an impasse, but still wanting to try to push through it—I want to "win" against their depression*): I think we all end up internalizing capitalism to some degree, to where our self-worth is based on how much we do or don't have.

Jesse (*impatiently*): I know it's internalized capitalism, but that doesn't make me feel any better. It's not like I'm going to hang out with them! I feel shitty, but what can I do about it?

Me (*aware that I just created distance between us with my intellectualizing*): It must feel so lonely.

Jesse: Yeah, and I can't tell anyone! (*softening*) Everyone either wants me to help them, or they tell me I'm too angry. I am so lonely!

Me: I can understand how tired you must be—you've tried really hard.

Jesse: Yeah, I have! I'm so exhausted. (*Jesse looks relieved that I finally hear them.*)

As I continued to empathize with them and allowed them to share their story, Jesse's "zest for life" gradually began to emerge. They brought up plans for re-enrolling in school and starting to write again. It was a stark contrast to the despair they began the session with, but we were not quite done yet. Even the closing can be therapeutic, as shame often emerges at the end of sessions like this one; it is another opportunity for them to have an experience of acceptance. "I'm so sorry I was so negative, and I was arguing with you," Jesse said, seeming embarrassed.

"There's nothing to be sorry for," I reassured them. "I like that you trust me enough to show when you're angry. It doesn't upset me."

"That really helps to hear," they responded. "All my friends tell me I'm too much when I get angry."

RCT helps the client believe there is someone they can trust, one person in the world who allows them to be themselves. I wanted Jesse to know they deserved a relationship where they could freely share their feelings. It was true that many of their friends disliked their anger and depression. But if I could offer at least one place where they could bring forth the parts of themself that they normally kept hidden, to integrate their silenced knowings, this would extend to other friendships over time. And it has. Over several years, they developed the courage to leave their relationship, published an e-zine of their short stories, and developed new, more balanced friendships.

The following is another example of helping move Jesse from the alienation of shame to connection. Once again, we touch on the topic of poverty, but this time, with empathy.

> *Jesse:* It was really stupid of me to spend so much money going out to eat. I just wanted to have breakfast with my friends. It was so much fun! But now I'm totally broke.

> *Me:* Wanting to be able to buy breakfast isn't asking for too much. Poverty really robs a person of their dignity, doesn't it? (*In focusing on poverty, I am pointing toward a form of external oppression and away from the client's internalization of shame.*)

> *Jesse:* It really does! (*They smile with the relief of being understood.*)

Using the Rings of Betrayal Model to Lessen Shame

Helping clients understand the link between various forms of betrayal trauma they experienced and their relational patterns can reduce the amount of shame they feel. The following is one of several discussions I had with Jesse about their difficulty with trusting others. The explanation I provided them is based on the Rings of Betrayal Model, which I always keep in mind when working with clients. Asking them to complete the Rings of Betrayal Inventory for themselves is another means of helping them process the many levels of betrayal they have experienced.

Jesse: "I do this thing where I always put all of my energy into one friend, and when that relationship ends, I'm all f***** up."

Me (*silent for a moment while I recognize how fearful they must be in relationships and how this realization increases my compassion toward them*): I wonder if it takes a lot to even trust one person.

Jesse: Yeah! It does! (*They light up with enthusiasm.*)

Me: Is that maybe why it's easier to focus on one person at a time?

Jesse: Yeah (*frowning*). Is that normal?

Me: I think when you've been through as much betrayal trauma as you have, like when all the adults around you betrayed your trust when you were a child, then it makes sense that it's hard to trust others. Add to that the racism you experience regularly. I think of that as betrayal, too.

Jesse: Wow, I never thought of it that way before. That makes total sense. So, a lot of people do this?

Me: Yes, this is actually a fairly common pattern for people who experience betrayal traumas.

Jesse: I feel better knowing it's not just me.

Ethnic Identity, Intersectionality, and Shame

Although Jesse identifies as biracial and often spoke of the sexualized racism they had experienced, they did not initially identify as Japanese American. Instead, they expressed a sense of shame around this identity. This struggle with not belonging and the associated sense of shame is common among Asian American survivors of family betrayal trauma.

"I don't know if I deserve to call myself Japanese American," they explained. "I've always been more comfortable identifying as Asian American. Asian American feels more like a community than an ethnic identity." The sense of not being "Asian enough" is one that many Asian American clients have expressed to me, though the reasons can vary. Seeking to understand Jesse's perspective (as well as to question it), I asked, "Why don't you think you're deserving of calling yourself Japanese American?"

"Well, it's not like I speak Japanese," Jesse responded. "And you know how Asians are about queer people—I don't feel like I fit in. I don't know anything about how to be Japanese American. I feel like a fraud!" (*There are many unspoken issues I heard Jesse bringing up here, including queerphobia in Asian cultures, which can compound a sense of marginalization and alien-*

ation. I made a mental note to circle back to these topics later. For the sake of completing our current line of discussion, I chose to ask about ethnic identity. At the same time, I wonder in retrospect if this is part of my own bias as a cisgendered, straight woman. Would a queer-identified therapist have made a different choice? Perhaps there was a way to weave all of these issues into a single conversation that I did not see at the time.)

"But who gets to define what it means to be Japanese American? Who owns that identity?" I asked.

Jesse was silent for a few moments as they considered this question. "I don't know," they said, with a shrug.

I took hope in this response as an indication that they were willing to consider the possibility that people outside themself did not have the sole authority in defining what it means to be Japanese American. Perhaps they, too, could have a say. I shared these thoughts with them.

"Maybe," they tentatively responded. I sensed this was far enough to push for the moment, and we moved on to other topics.

A few weeks later, Jesse referred to themself as Japanese American in passing.

"Wait!" I interrupted with a smile. "What was that you said?"

Jesse returned my smile. "Oh, I guess I'm more okay with calling myself Japanese American now. It's who I am, right?"

Ethnic identity is a very personal choice, and had Jesse decided they did not want to call themself Japanese American, I would have supported it. What I wanted to help them overcome was the sense of shame associated with feeling undeserving of the identity.

Several months later, Jesse shared that they were increasingly sure they were bisexual. However, they were hesitant to claim that identity because they had so far only been in relationships with men. We identified feelings of being undeserving and shame that underlay this uncertainty. We also explored how these feelings echoed their journey with ethnic identity, childhood trauma, and internalized oppression. I affirmed their right to claim their own sexual identity just as they had claimed their ethnic identity. Over the next few months, Jesse began to share being bi with their friends, which led to them feeling more accepted by them.

Growing through and toward Relationship

About four and a half years since we had first begun to work together, Jesse described an incident in which they attended a martial arts class led by a friend's mother, who unexpectedly began the class by talking about sexual assault. This triggered Jesse's history of trauma, and they left the class abruptly. Later, their friend's mother invited them to dinner. As Jesse described, "She wanted to know why I left her class and what she could do better. I told her

I was surprised she cared because I just assume that no one cares. She said she was really sad to hear that, and that she does care, but I don't believe her."

Me: "Really? Why not?" (*I am actually not surprised at Jesse's statement, as it is a theme we have covered before, but I want to explore this deep-seated belief and express my empathy for them.*)

Jesse: Because people *don't* care. Even if they're trying to be nice and say they care, they're not being honest with themselves. I'd rather they just not say that—it makes me angry.

Me: It makes you angry?

Jesse: You know, I can't trust them anymore if they're lying about caring about me. Look, everyone's just out for themselves. That's why it's easier for me to talk to you—it's not so complicated.

Me (*now, really surprised*): Do you think I don't care about you?

Jesse: Well, I imagine you're really good at compartmentalizing for your job. I mean, you have a family to take care of, so you need to go home and forget about work. (*They say this in a matter-of-fact tone of voice, as though they are trying to be diplomatic rather than give me a direct answer. However, in their response, I hear an unspoken self-protective belief—"You don't really care about me"—and underneath that, a question: "Do you care about me?"*)

Me (*resolved that they need to understand how I feel, but also worried they may become angry and tell me I'm full of crap*): What if I told you I *do* care about you? That I would feel really sad if anything happened to you? We've been through a lot together over the last few years, and I've actually grown to care about you a great deal. (*Rather than getting angry, Jesse begins to cry.*) After a while, Jesse says tearfully, "Okay, I know sometimes the way I think is bullshit, and I want to change my beliefs about people not caring."

In our next session, Jesse shared that they went to a local pub they used to go to before the pandemic and reconnected with friends they had not seen for two years. They said their friends kept asking where they had been. They were surprised to learn that their friends missed them. "When I get down, I tell myself nobody cares," they said.

"I suppose that makes sense, given how much betrayal trauma you've been through," I replied, wanting to validate their feelings, but also not disagree that this is a relational pattern.

"I'm going to go back to meet my friends every week. I feel a lot better after seeing them." (*I saw that the renewed sense of connection was motivating them to move toward more connection.*)

"That's great!" I said, smiling.

Over the next year, we revisited the theme of Jesse feeling that nobody cares repeatedly. They began to acknowledge that this was a self-protective default pattern. This awareness allowed them to consciously choose to take more risks rather than being dominated by an internalized sense of alienation and oppression. There is not a tidy ending to Jesse's story. They continued to struggle financially and had to withdraw from school in order to focus on their job. However, as we ended our work together, they reported feeling more confident in their relationships and have continued to publish their writing.

Combining RCT with CBT and Other Therapies

Relational-cultural therapy can be used in conjunction with more prescriptive forms of psychotherapy, such as cognitive behavioral therapy and approaches that are targeted toward symptoms of PTSD. By being nonprescriptive, RCT not only can accommodate prescriptive approaches, but mitigate their potential harm by upholding feminist and liberation values, as in Irfan's case. Adhering to RCT can shape the course of each encounter with a client to be more congruent with values of liberation psychology.

Several therapists have proposed ways to adapt CBT for use with Asians and Asian Americans (e.g., Iwamasa et al., 2019; Naeem et al., 2010; Shah & Tewari, 2019). However, while both CBT and RCT have a goal of changing beliefs, the former tries to do so without fully integrating the powerful tool of the therapeutic relationship. In CBT, the relationship is seen as the cart that brings the apples rather than also being the apples themselves. Had I challenged Jesse's belief that no one cared about them by labeling it a form of "cognitive distortion" (e.g., all-or-nothing thinking or overgeneralization), we would have stayed in the realm of intellectualizing their behavior. Additionally, Jesse would likely have argued that I didn't know what I was talking about. What appears as client resistance is often a reaction to a failure on the therapist's part to partake in mutual empathy and mutual power-sharing. Without connecting with Jesse emotionally, I would have missed what they wanted most but had left unspoken—the desire to know that somebody, anybody, cared about them and believed them.

Ma and Lan (2022) provide an example of how RCT established a safe frame from which to incorporate CBT in the case of a second-generation Chinese American early adolescent. Initially, there was difficulty implementing CBT to address symptoms of obsessive-compulsive disorder. According to the authors, "Relational-cultural theory (RCT) provided a means to foster connections, provide a safe environment, and validate the sociopolitical realities that lead to psychological distress." RCT was used over the course of two years to address multiple oppressed identities, such as being Chinese American, gay, and transgender, and how these identities impacted her self-worth, family relationships, and her place in the world. CBT was reintroduced more successfully later, "after the therapist had addressed the client's underlying concerns." The addition of monthly family sessions helped to improve the parent–child relationship. Ma and Lan emphasize that "this case highlights the importance of incorporating relational, contextual, and cultural factors when working with ethnic and gender minority youth."

MOVING PSYCHOTHERAPY TOWARD LIBERATION

The introduction in this book describes the two-fronted battle that the majority of Asian Americans face, with racism and discrimination on the one front and intergenerational trauma on the other. It addresses how betrayal is a key mechanism by which these relational traumas do harm, with shame being one of the most wounding and salient sequela. Shame, in turn, leads to silenced knowings, a process by which survivors learn to preserve needed relationships. Therefore, it is necessary to adopt a therapy frame that promotes the expression of silenced knowings, especially in the case of Asian Americans.

Historically, Western psychology has upheld the therapist as an untouchable expert. This frame predisposes the counseling relationship to reenacting dynamics of oppression. Therefore, the "healing power of any psychotherapeutic method depends on the dosage of its break with the dominant culture" (Martín-Baró, 1996, p. 120). Breaking with the dominant culture requires the therapist to liberate themselves from the hegemony of the current medical model. Only then can they facilitate the client's movement toward liberation. In other words, adopting a relational approach liberates both the client and the therapist. Therefore, relational-cultural therapy can serve as a framework for dismantling unhealthy power disparities in therapy. Its emphasis on power-sharing and mutual empathy combined with attention to historical, social, and cultural context provides a path forward. Empathic listening can be used to identify silenced knowings regarding the oppression of poverty, childhood abuse, and other forms of being marginalized.

However, moving toward liberation requires enormous courage on the therapist's part, for several reasons. First, as the opening quote to this chapter suggests, it means rejecting what is popular for the sake of what is just. This is much more difficult than it sounds. Normative ways of thinking about psychology are inculcated for years in traditional clinical and counseling graduate training programs, both in research and practice, as well as in larger institutions, such as the US Department of Veterans Affairs. For my own part, it took several years in private practice to deprogram myself from institutionalized approaches that I believe caused harm to my clients.

Second, adopting a decolonized and liberatory frame means relinquishing some of the emotional security and power over the client afforded by the "expert" status. While most therapists are not purposefully using their power to harm the client, inattention to this disparity in power can and does actively harm clients, especially when the therapist has much more privilege than the client. Dismantling power in the counseling relationship requires the therapist to match the risk the client takes. It means offering to share power with the client and be affected by them, to have the humility to learn from the client's lived experience.

Finally, and perhaps one of the most challenging steps, adopting a relational approach means prioritizing mutual empathy over following protocol. Prescriptive approaches that prioritize what to *do* to a client over how to *be* with them alleviate a sense of anxiety that many therapists share. It is common, especially among (but not by any means limited to) new trainees, to feel as though "merely" listening is inadequate. It feels relieving to point to a protocol that is ostensibly empirically supported, so that any failure falls on the shoulders of the client, and not the therapist. It is also painful to sit with someone in pain and not try to problem-solve it away. Trusting in the value of the therapeutic relationship in the absence of a protocol can be anxiety-provoking because it can feel as though one is not doing anything useful. This trust must be repeatedly renewed by the therapist taking risks that challenge this anxiety again and again. The following chapter offers an opportunity to do so by bearing witness to the experiences of dozens of Asian Americans and Asian Canadians in psychotherapy.

I conclude this chapter with a quote from Martín-Baró (1996), taking the liberty of replacing the words "Latin American" with "Asian American."

> It is not easy to figure out how to place ourselves within the process alongside the dominated rather than alongside the dominator. It is not even easy to leave our role of technocratic or professional superiority and to work hand in hand with community groups. But if we do not embark upon this new type of praxis that transforms ourselves as well as transforming reality, it will be hard indeed to develop [an Asian American] psychology that will contribute to the liberation of our peoples. (p. 29)

ADDITIONAL RESOURCES

• Craft, L., Kasmauski, K., & Tolbert, K. (Directors). (2015). *Fall seven times, get up eight: The Japanese war brides* [Documentary]. Blue Chalk Media. https://www.fallsevengetupeight.com/
  Fall Seven Times, Get Up Eight tells the story of three Japanese war brides, tackling issues they faced, such as being viewed as social outcasts in Japan for "marrying the enemy," and trying to assimilate into American culture.

SCAN ME

• Jordan, J. V. (2009). *Series VIII—Psychotherapy in six sessions: Relational-cultural therapy over time* [Video]. American Psychological Association; Alexander Street. https://tinyurl.com/JordanRCT
  Relational-Cultural Therapy Over Time features six sessions of psychotherapy led by Dr. Judith Jordan.

SCAN ME

Chapter Six

In Our Voices: Asian American Experiences in Therapy

Books on psychotherapy typically present case studies of a therapist's work, but these are chosen by the authors. Rarely do they include testimonios from people whom the authors normally would not encounter or whose voices the authors do not influence. Honoring the wisdom and expertise of clients can only benefit the practice of psychotherapy. Therefore, this chapter presents the feedback of 45 Asian Americans and Canadians who completed a brief, anonymous survey asking about their lived experiences in therapy.

Most of the people who provided feedback were from a Facebook page, Subtle Asian Mental Health, which includes a wide range of Asian identities among its 60,000 international members. All respondents were from the United States or Canada, self-identified as Asian or Asian American, and either currently or previously attended therapy. Ages ranged from 18 to over 60, with the majority being between 25 and 40 years old. There was also representation among nonbinary, nongendered, and cisgendered people. The survey asked about positive and negative experiences in therapy, whether or not they had discussed racism in their sessions, and what advice they had for therapists working with Asian Americans. This chapter presents what they shared, organized into general themes. I have kept grammar and spelling edits minimal, making changes only for clarity, so that the comments maintain their original voice as much as possible. The clients offered numerous suggestions for decolonizing therapy when working with Asians, Asian Americans, and Asian Canadians.

WORKING WITH A BIPOC THERAPIST

Nearly all respondents commented on the importance of ethnic match to them. As one shared broadly, their therapist "being Asian and having lived it, too" was beneficial. Many respondents had sought Asian American (47.7%) and other BIPOC (36.4%) therapists. Considering that only 5% of therapists in the United States identify as Asian and 10% as other BIPOC (Lin et al., 2018), these responses indicate a concerted effort to find them. As one respondent shared,

> My therapists have been very understanding about my Asian-American culture because they were either Black or Filipina-American (my ethnicity). I actively seek out therapists who are non-White through the Psychology Today database.

This sentiment is consistent with research on ethnic matching in therapy that finds people of color tend to prefer therapists of their own ethnic group (e.g., Cabral & Smith, 2011), and that this holds true for Asians and Asian Americans (Lee et al., 2014). Research also indicates that a therapist's ethnic similarity is positively associated with establishing a positive working alliance and therapist credibility (Meyer et al., 2011). Indeed, respondents described a sense of comfort and understanding when there was a shared ethnic background. For example, one stated that their therapist "is Asian herself, and it made it so much easier for me to talk about my experiences as an Asian American because the therapist was able to relate to me."

Specifically, understanding family dynamics was the most commonly perceived benefit of having an Asian therapist, as these responses indicate:

- I don't have to explain or elaborate on family traditions or ties. I don't have to explain why I can't just completely cut my family off.
- When I had an Asian therapist, they could relate to my experiences with my family.
- My current therapist is Asian, so she understands the nuances of growing up with Asian parents and their expectations, I think.
- He (the therapist) also came from being raised in an Asian and multiracial culture (specifically in Singapore), which we discuss [when we talk] about the hardships of growing up and living in that family setting.
- She relates to my childhood because she said she grew up with Asian immigrant parents as well.
- My therapist is Korean American (like me), so I did not have an issue with microaggressions or lack of understanding of my culture. She was able to understand language/culture specific stuff. I think we're both very familiar with Korean culture, which made me feel comfortable. An example is, I am estranged from my father, [for] six years [now], and I think Korean culture really forces filial piety and encourages family connection, to look past and forgive toxic people no matter what. I believe in some circumstances, going no contact may not be appropriate for the situation, but it was appropriate for mine. I have been a lot happier

without contacting my father and having his presence in my life, and I'm glad [my therapist] was able to ascertain my situation and not make me feel uncomfortable/guilty for cutting my father off.

Related to family dynamics, an Asian therapist personally being "able to relate to [inter]generational trauma" was also described as helpful by two respondents.

Though people generally described positive experiences with Asian therapists, this was not always the case. As one lamented,

> I had one therapist who was actually Asian herself but was the worst. She basically blamed me for my issues. It felt like her opinions were coming from her old Asian perspective/biases.

Another woman whose therapist was East Asian described how he had difficulty understanding

> how different types of Asians observe some topics differently despite being from that category. I had to explain to him about my partner's background (half White / half Indian) and their background several times.

Asian American therapy clients also gave examples of how they felt understood by their non-Asian BIPOC therapists. One person wrote,

> My precious therapists were Black and Latino, so while they didn't have firsthand insight into [the] AAPI experience, I really appreciated that they understood or seemed to understand the immigrant experience, or growing up non-White in a White world.

Practicing cultural sensitivity with diagnosing was another benefit that one person found. She wrote,

> I had an Arab psychiatrist that didn't formally diagnose me with Bipolar II (especially due to the hostility my family had toward [mental illness]).

WORKING WITH A WHITE THERAPIST

Despite many Asian American clients seeking Asian and BIPOC therapists, more than half (56.8%) reported having worked with a White therapist (the total reported therapist ethnicity is greater than 100 percent, because some respondents had worked with more than one therapist). These clients and former clients shared a mixture of helpful and hurtful experiences.

Positive Experiences

Things that they appreciated included their therapist asking for more information about their culture, and their therapist having even a small amount of cultural knowledge. Some examples of how White therapists understood Asian or Asian American cultures follow.

Understanding Asian Culture and Family Dynamics

- He completely understood why I had so many barriers to dealing productively with my mental health, seeing as how I was raised to just keep my negative feelings inside.
- She understood that mental health was taboo in Asian cultures and that it might be harder to talk about issues of alcoholism.
- Understood family obligations, pressures of being second-generation.
- Understood Asian parenting vs. White parenting, and was considerate of cultural differences.
- [Understood that my] not looking into her eyes was not disrespectful or lying. She knew it was just part of my culture.
- She recognized that in a lot of Asian cultures, a more collectivistic ideal prevails, and that the pressure/ties to family and honor play a big role in how we react to things.
- When discussing my Indian heritage and [the] ways my grandma's heritage impacts some ways she sees things.
- Parental expectations in terms of [earning a] degree, career, family honor.
- She was aware that many Asian cultures lean toward collectivism as opposed to [the] individualism [often found] in Western countries.
- She had some awareness of Vietnamese refugees.

Addressing Discrimination

Even when a therapist did not understand Asian culture, they were able to help by acknowledging historic racism, as these clients shared:

- [She understood] what it feels like to be "othered," since she is a Jewish woman, and how it feels to fight tradition sometimes.
- [She did] not necessarily [understand] culturally, but she did acknowledge the damage White supremacy has done to BIPOC communities. On other counts she's made an effort to listen.

Processing Intergenerational Trauma

One person offered an example of how their therapist helped them to better understand their father's behavior by linking it to intergenerational trauma:

> My parents are refugees—I was talking about my dad's tendency to buy a lot of things and then never use them, and his disdain towards selling or getting rid of things. My therapist made a connection between this tendency now and when he was a refugee, fighting to survive with nothing.

Asking Clarifying Questions

Clients expressed appreciation that therapists asked them about their culture in order to gain a better understanding of their worldview, saying:

- Most of my therapists were Asian American, but the few that weren't always asked [me] to clarify, which any good therapist should be doing anyway.
- Both therapists didn't assume anything and asked clarifying questions to better understand my upbringing.

Supporting Client Sharing

Some clients pointed to ways their White therapists made space for their sharing and were responsive and insightful.

- He didn't say much, he just let me talk.
- When I talk about my narcissistic mother, she helps me understand what could be cultural and what is just a trait of being a narcissist.
- When I say something is important to me, they recognize, empathize [with] it, and talk with me more about it, instead of dismiss[ing] it, or chang[ing] the topic.

Negative Experiences

Racial Microaggressions

Asian American clients shared numerous ways in which they felt hurt or othered by their White therapists. Their responses exemplify the fact that "when clinician and client differ from one another along racial lines . . . the relationship may serve as a microcosm for the troubled race relations in the United States" (Sue et al., 2007, p. 280).

Devaluing Culture

Several replied that they did not think there was any cultural understanding or consideration of intersectional identities. For example, one respondent wrote that their therapist had "absolutely no understanding of Buddhism, Asian family dynamics, and what it is to be biracial and fat in the culture," and another described their therapist as not racist but "ignorant." Others remarked on therapists not recognizing that there are numerous cultures under the umbrella of "Asian." One client shared how the lack of cultural understanding limited their ability to explore culture and ethnic identity in therapy, saying,

> Both therapists were non-Asian, so certain dynamics of my ethnicity weren't delved into deeper than they could've been because they lacked an understanding of how much of an influence some factors were (e.g., how common it is in my ethnicity for men to have more than one wife).

Another felt the lack of cultural understanding resulted in having "a harder time unpacking past childhood issues."

Many Asian American therapy clients reported that their therapist did not seem to place any importance on cultural context, though one wrote that they did not want to discuss culture anyhow.

- She never addressed the culture difference being an issue.
- My therapist didn't show any interest, nor was I interested [in] discuss[ing] cultural stuff.
- My cultural status or standard didn't matter during my counseling.
- She didn't acknowledge that some of my hardship trying to fit in to this country was due to cultural difference.

Devaluing Family: Transposing White Culture onto Asian Culture

Therapists "making implicit assumptions," as one respondent described, was problematic for many Asian American clients. Not understanding Asian family dynamics was the most cited issue. Assuming the dominant culture is the standard leads therapists to make culturally inappropriate interpretations and suggestions. Ruptures in the therapeutic relationship arise as a result, with one client sharing that their therapist "sometimes [made] me feel judged or [like I] have abnormal parents."

Regarding family dynamics, respondents shared the following:

- My White therapist did not understand how confrontation does not work for Asian households.

- They tried suggesting ideas or things to do that I really feel I couldn't do with my parents. One had suggested having a "family meeting" and having a discussion where everyone is heard. I thought it was a ridiculous idea and lost all trust and confidence in that therapist. I was of undergraduate age then, and I knew that the power dynamic between me and my parents wouldn't allow for such a thing to happen.
- [Not understanding] the dynamic/expectations of traditional Asian parents.
- They have never been able to address the family issues of alcoholism.
- [Not understanding] diverse family structure, how the line between codependency and interdependency is just different from other cultures.
- Filial piety is a hard thing to explain, and creating [boundaries with] my parents is more difficult than it should be because of my upbringing.
- I told her my mom spanked me as a kid. She thought my mom was abusive, but that's just a standard thing Asian parents do. At least most do. This kind of action is not okay, but I wouldn't go as far as using the word "abuse."
- She made a comment about challenges I was having with my family dynamic, saying, "You're 18—why don't you just do what you want?"
- I brought up things about my parents and she identified them through a very clinical, Caucasian-American viewpoint. There was no connection, just a cold identification of terminology. It made me feel like I wasn't sure if she truly understood or could help me with my experiences.

One nonbinary client shared that they wished therapists would understand that for some Asian Americans, "family bonds are a burden. We can't escape it so easily. It's so hard to just 'tell our family/parents' how we feel, because 'it's our feelings and we can't control theirs.'" The same client also shared:

> I do think it's important for therapists to understand the high-achieving standards of immigrant parents and the pressures that can be put on their kids, even if to other cultures, it's not a big deal.

Another client added, "There are generational issues to deal with; respect for elders makes addressing family issues so hard."

Educating the Therapist

Related to the therapist asking clarifying questions, several Asian American clients found themselves in the position of educating their therapists. Sometimes educating the therapist is additional labor that the client shoulders disproportionately, although the first comment implies that the client appreciated their therapist asking about culture.

- When I had my first session with my White therapist, she made sure to ask me if culturally, there was anything she needed to know.
- I would tell my therapist how my family had certain expectations and I was going into a nontraditional field, therefore they were less supportive of me. I was a woman, and my parents tend to favor my brother more than me.
- I think the biggest help for my therapist was explaining what I know about Asian culture, to the best of my ability, to her, with the knowledge I have.

Additional Forms of Racism

Five of the respondents (11%) explicitly reported experiencing a racial microaggression from their therapist. This statistic is much lower than the rates found in research, which range from 53% at a university counseling center (Owen et al., 2014) to as high as 81% in a large-scale study of 2,200 people (Hook et al., 2016). The lower rate in the current survey is likely due to respondents not naming or recognizing other experiences as microaggressions, such as in the examples above, where clients describe therapists giving culturally tone-deaf advice and dismissing cultural context. The research studies, on the other hand, explicitly named these behaviors as microaggressions.

The following are some experiences of racism Asian American clients shared:

- Due to the model minority myth (I assume), "not being able to believe that" I would need support, not only was I not given an ADHD diagnosis, but the (older White [male] psychologist hypothesized in my formal assessment report about whether I had histrionic personality disorder, which every mental health provider I've worked with has vehemently denied, and said was unprofessional and potentially unethical (but not illegal / not bad enough to go through the board), for the way the report was written up. This especially when I refused getting tested and medication because I didn't believe I deserved it (due to all the sociocultural messaging I received as an Indian woman about mental health) for years, and finally had gotten the courage to access services. A decade later all my current providers have validated and acknowledged how I should have received an ADHD diagnosis; I wonder how my life would be had I had a culturally informed provider that very actively harmed (suicide attempts, panic attacks, hypo-manic episodes from undiagnosed Bipolar II comorbidity) the trajectory of my life and treatment by this lack of / misdiagnosis.

  The same client continued: I had a psychiatrist call me a different Indian name and/or pronunciation of my name the entire time we worked together (a year). It was honestly quite impressive how creative she got with my name, which is a very simple and phonetic four-letter word! She also minimized my experiences and discounted certain symptoms due to "my culture," which she knew about because her husband worked with an Indian man at one point (not even currently). As a mental health provider, I'm clearly able to identify and advocate for myself and still felt defeated, and knew I was receiving subpar services, but needed some medication, rather than none—though the medication itself didn't work and led to some not great repercussions as well. Gosh, I have so many more [examples] . . .

- I don't remember exactly, but it was something along the lines of being told that my country was poor after I went into reasons why I want to do the career I'm doing.
- The White therapist I was matched with during my intake appointment told me I was a model minority after I explained that I do research on Asian American stereotypes and how they impact mental health.
- The current therapist's response to me feeling disconnected from the Asian community because I'm mixed was to suggest I need to examine my internalized racism against White people . . . and I never mentioned White people. There have also been a number of clumsy responses to cultural things because of viewing situations through the lens of Whiteness, which didn't seem intentional, but felt awkward. A former therapist said that we didn't know the true motive behind the Georgia shootings or other hate crimes in response to my distress about the rise in anti-Asian sentiment, in an attempt to comfort me, I think? But it instead made me feel as if the community's collective trauma was being erased.

These testimonios exemplify how hurtful and costly these microaggressions can be. Research has found that 76% of therapist racial microaggressions are not addressed in therapy (Owen et al., 2014). Owen et al. (2018) investigated whether this was because therapists do not recognize racial–ethnic microaggressions when they occur, or if they feel anxiety about the process of addressing them. It appears both cases are likely true. In a controlled study, they showed therapists a video of a therapy session that contained three microaggressions. Therapists were able to identify microaggressions about 38% to 52% of the time (Owen et al., 2018). That these proportions are greater than the 24% of the time that therapists *do* address microaggressions indicates that at least some of the time, therapists are both aware that they have committed a microaggression and are avoiding discussing them. Owen et al. (2014) found that those clients who experienced a microaggression that the therapist did not discuss rated their therapeutic alliance lower than clients who did not experience a microaggression, or who experienced a microaggression but discussed it. Therefore, it is ethically necessary for therapists to exercise moral courage when they recognize they have committed a microaggression, by acknowledging having done so, apologizing to the client, and helping the client process their experience of the microaggression.

HOW TO DECOLONIZE THERAPY: ADVICE FROM ASIAN AMERICAN CLIENTS

A psychology of liberation for Asian Americans requires centering not only our voices but our histories. As Millner et al. (2021) observe, "Mental health concerns among Asian Americans constitute complex phenomena that cannot be extricated from history and context." They also outline a roadmap "to decolonize and reconstruct the existing mental health practice framework through a social justice lens of postcolonialism" (p. 333). They recommend centering

> Asian experiences by responding to cultural mistrust, dissonance, and conflict, examining the matrix of domination through the lens of intersectionality, and shifting the therapist's positionality to prevent further perpetuation of neocolonial invalidation and trauma. [They] also propose an Asian-centric reconstruction of mental health practices that prioritize collectivistic values, (re)integrate religion and spirituality, and elevate recovery, resilience, and resistance. (p. 333)

Consistent with these recommendations, Asian American clients themselves offered suggestions for moving from an individualistic focus sanitized of historical context toward one rooted in generational and sociocultural relationships. I also provide an example of how relational-cultural therapy (RCT) facilitates addressing microaggressions.

Center Family

As the survey responses demonstrate, considering the role of the family is of primary importance. Clients expressed a desire for therapists to understand:

- Our upbringing—Asian parents and our childhoods are very different from non-Asians. Sometimes our social rules in regards to our families are a little different (especially if they're not super-Americanized), so finding solutions that work might take a little time. And please don't downplay anti-Asian violence.
- How important family is to us; the "honor your elder" [toxicity exists]. We are trained to hide our emotions [and] model minority norms; [there is also] racial trauma for immigrants.
- [Intergenerational] culture clashes.

- Multiple cross-intersectional issues of culture that you have to consider: Traditional Asian in the parents' home; liv[ing] in Western society; mixed culture in my own home; cross-generational issues; negotiating the past and present times; consider [that] some people, old and young, change, and some don't.
- The emphasis of collectivism in [Asian] family structure.
- Importance of family and values.
- That a lot of the reason why we're here in the first place is because of trauma from families, and we have diverse interests that aren't pertaining to academics.
- (Maybe applies to immigrant families in general) Many of us can have personal or family history of trauma and struggles. Therefore, our perceptions and values may seem pretty different from non-immigrants / non–people of color. Be open to the different experiences each person holds.

Respondents also cautioned against stereotyping Asian American families. For example, one observed, "Asian parenting is different, but it doesn't mean Asian parents don't love their kids." Of note: Asian families can learn to adapt and change stigmatized views on mental health, though it may take time. According to one client:

> [I sought therapy] a decade ago because of undiagnosed mental health issues that also had [included] multiple suicide attempts. None of this was addressed due to a traditional Indian parent mentality [of] not believing in therapy/medication and believing family can solve and repair harm (caused within families, too). However, I want to note that over the years, my parents have come a long way, and did the work; they read and watched shows around mental health, and now they actively support therapy, and when I'm with them, [they] will be the ones doing daily reminders about taking my medication and encourag[ing] others to access it.

Address Client Experiences of Racism Directly

Though racism is a near-universal experience among Asian Americans, only a slight majority (56.8%) raised the issue in therapy. Of those clients who did not raise the issue of racism, 63.2% said it just did not occur to them. As one respondent shared, "Genuinely it didn't even occur to me to talk about racism in my session, because I'm so used to bottling things up and downplaying things. There are many layers to us, I think." Being used to bottling things up, including racism, is an example of containing the silenced knowings discussed in the previous chapter, a form of fragmentation in which parts of oneself deemed unacceptable are suppressed.

Other clients who were conscious of the impact of racism on their lives nonetheless did not raise the issue in therapy, due to not believing the therapist could help (21.1%), or not believing their therapist would understand (18.5%). Therefore, it is often necessary for the therapist to initiate a conversation about racism to demonstrate their willingness to talk about it, and to help the client reintegrate these silenced knowings. The therapist naming racism for the client is akin to assisting a sexual assault victim name that they were raped. According to clients' reports, a minority of therapists (29.5%) did ask them about their experiences of racism. One person cited "not recognizing the negative impact of racial stereotyping" as a form of not understanding Asian American culture.

Addressing Microaggressions: Apologize and Repair

Most people prefer to avoid discussing race, with therapists being no different. White therapists in particular may be afraid that anything they say about race will make them appear biased and racist, or they may discover internalized biases that evoke shame (Sue, 2015). However, therapists have a moral and ethical duty to strive to be different. Inflicting a microaggression in therapy is a betrayal of trust that must be repaired lest lasting harm is done. According to Sue (2015), "Research . . . shows that while racial microaggressions might seem to be micro acts or small slights, they oftentimes have devastating macro harmful consequences (Sue et al., 2007; Zou & Dickter, 2013)." A common response to microaggressions is confusion and self-blame, including wondering if one is being "too sensitive," a belief their peers often reinforce (Sue, 2015). Immobilization and a sense of increased isolation follow (Jordan, 2010).

When a microaggression occurs in therapy, it can disempower the client and reinforce the therapist's dominance (Hutton, 2011). Therefore, "the rewriting of a psychological paradigm becomes an act of social justice" (Jordan, 2010, p. 26). As discussed in the previous chapter, relational-cultural therapy (RCT) views disconnections as potentially therapeutic if the therapist can offer the client a new experience of repair that leads to increased connection. Practicing mutual empathy and mutual power-sharing can repair the disconnection caused by microaggressions.

However, if an attempt at repair is not made,

> if the target person is not allowed or encouraged to voice her or his hurt or anger, that person will learn to suppress that aspect of her or his experience. Thus, she or he learns to hide aspects of themselves, mold themselves to fit in, and present to others (especially those holding more power) with inauthenticity in

order to stay in relationship. This can lead to the less powerful person feeling "profoundly disempowered and unseen." (Jordan, 2010, p. 26; Hutton, 2011, pp. 39–40)

Repairing the relational rupture caused by therapist microaggressions benefits both the client and therapist. The client is liberated from having to hold yet another silenced knowing, this time on behalf of their therapist. Connection is not only restored, but strengthened and made more authentic (Sackett and Jenkins, 2019). For the therapist, addressing microaggressions with RCT can help them to 1) recognize their areas of privilege and internalized biases; 2) reject the dominant culture's narrative that race does not matter; 3) avoid being complicit in re-creating a dynamic of oppression within therapy; 4) become more relationally and culturally competent; and 5) learn about the emotional pain that a microaggression can cause. Although it is beyond the scope of the survey, it should be noted that microaggressions also regularly occur in the context of clinical supervision (Proctor et al., 2016) and by clients toward therapists (Sackett and Jenkins, 2019).

Moksh's Story

Sometimes, biases about race and sexual orientation can intersect, as in a microaggression I committed when working with Moksh, an international student from India. During the intake appointment, I wanted to know about his social relationships, but instead of asking him if he had a partner, which I normally would do, I asked him if he had a girlfriend. With a wry smile, he replied, "I'm actually gay." I was instantly horrified by my mistake, realizing it was based upon a stereotype I held of first-generation Asians being homophobic. "I am so sorry!" I responded. "It's okay; I'm used to it," he replied.

Exercise: *Imagine how you would respond to Moksh at this point. If this is not a microaggression you think you would typically commit, you can imagine another one for this exercise.*

"I feel sad hearing that you're 'used to it,'" I said, wanting to show him that his response affected me. "At the same time, I am guessing you probably do have some feelings about it. I wonder how it feels to have me assume you're straight. I mean, you're taking a risk by coming here for help. You even mentioned you wanted an Asian therapist. But here I am, making a wrong assumption about you that is probably hurtful, and part of the homophobia currently in Asian cultures."

"Well, I know you didn't mean it," Moksh replied. "But yeah, I guess it feels weird."

"Weird how?" I asked, making a mental note of his repeated attempts to assuage my feelings. Perhaps this was a protective mechanism in relation to being gay and Asian? And/or perhaps he had been raised to take care of others in his family. Regardless of its origin, I did not want to perpetuate the dynamic of deferring to power in therapy.

To practice mutual power-sharing, I continued to encourage Moksh to tell me how he felt about my microaggression. He admitted he felt frustrated and disappointed, and that he wanted to feel like he was in a safe space that was different from the one he was raised in. He shared that none of his family, including cousins, uncles, and aunts, knew he was gay. His parents especially wanted him to get married soon, and were sending him prospective matches of Indian women.

I also asked Moksh how he felt about telling me he was angry and disappointed with me. This led to a deeper discussion on how it was usually not possible for him to share his feelings about his family members' homophobia with them. Working to repair the rupture was also an opportunity to demonstrate that I welcomed all his feelings in our work together, and that I wanted to facilitate an empowering experience of voicing his silenced knowings.

Consider the Legacy of Colonialism

Although the survey did not ask specifically about decolonizing therapy, many of the responses were consistent with a decolonial perspective. For example, they pointed to the need to understand the history of colonialism and its association with the current biased practice of ahistoricism, which is endemic to psychotherapy:

- I think [my therapist] has not quite grasped the lasting impact that colonialism and White supremacy have [had] in the Asian American community, with fetishization, the Vietnam War as a source of trauma for Viet American families, stuff like that.
- Have some understanding of [religions] outside of Christianity. Understand Christianity as colonization. Do not reinforce [a] model citizen narrative.

Appreciate the Diversity of Asian Americans

Many of the survey respondents expressed a wish that therapists view Asian Americans as a diverse group. Comments included:

- We are not a monolith.
- We're not all the same.
- There's no such thing as "Asian." It's such a spectrum of cultures and traditions and history. Can't generalize it all.
- Not all Asians and Asian Americans are going to have the same reaction or response to racist remarks. The same goes for Asian adoptees—no two adoptees are going to view their story the same way.

Another gave an example of how the model minority myth can create bias in diagnosing, saying "Attention deficit disorder is not commonly diagnosed in Asian American women. I was not diagnosed until I was 38 years old."

Finally, one client expressed a desire for therapists to understand the complexity of Asian American identity:

I wish they could understand the feelings of belonging and not belonging at the same time. We identify uniquely with being Asian and American, but not 100% with both. It causes a lot of identity issues, because we are neither a "here nor there," and struggle often, being torn between two cultures that demand very different things from us.

Understand the Stigma of Mental Illness

Many Asian American clients recommended that therapists give serious consideration to how difficult it can be for Asians and Asian Americans to talk about mental health. As a couple shared:

- The stigma related to mental illness . . . prevents people from taking it seriously and seeking professional help. This means that a lot of us don't seek out therapy until adulthood, after years of inventing our own coping mechanisms.
- Mental health within Asians and Asian Americans is stigmatized, and it will take a while for them to build trust to talk about their feelings, because they grew up not feeling validated.

Develop a Unique Racial Justice Lens for Asian Americans

Another recommendation was to avoid indiscriminately applying what one knows about one ethnic group to another. For example, one client said:

The main microaggression that I wish could be addressed by therapists is using a racial justice lens (that was very importantly created to understand and provide a framework for Black race-based experiences) that doesn't map onto Asian American experiences. For example, I acknowledge and recognize my privilege in not having the same fear of the police as my Black/[Latinx] community members, but mine stems from "alien" or "terrorist threat" due to being a dark-skinned Brown South Asian immigrant.

Along with the fear of the authorities that stems from othering/tokenizing of Asian identities, here's another example of how we need a racial justice–informed mental health framework that maps on other and differing racial [identity] experiences. How due to the issues with [the] model minority myth, and diasporic Asian cultures around perseverance and hard work, receiving a label and diagnosis was validating for me, and I needed it as an intervention for me to start healing, because I and my family now could acknowledge there was actually something wrong and build a toolkit that worked for me specifically. Whereas when I hear about how to be racially competent in treatment, due to the weaponizing of diagnoses toward Black and Brown boys (and girls), there's a push to not provide diagnoses. We need a spectrum of solutions for the spectrum of race and racial violence.

Just Ask

One client cautioned therapists not to make assumptions about Asian American clients, saying "Do not project your own experiences into us because that will not allow you to completely understand us." Others encouraged therapists to ask questions about race, culture, and family. Two such comments were:

- Don't be afraid to just ask if and how an experience may align with our upbringing as Asians. We might not even see it as part of that experience, because we're so deeply entrenched in it that we just see it as the norm. We might not even consider the possibility of what patterns our experiences have [to do] with being Asian.
- Understanding that every person has a different relationship with their culture; I think it's better to ask more questions rather than less, if culture seems like a big factor in a client's [symptoms/behaviors].
- Never assume. Always be curious.

Sometimes people feel awkward about asking questions concerning culture or race. However, it is crucial to do so, for several reasons:

- It signals [that it's] safe to talk about these topics.
- You are willing to learn what you do not know.
- You will increase your understanding of your client as an individual, rather than assuming Asian American clients have the same concerns as White clients, or that all Asian American clients are alike.

Although lived experience is irreplaceable, some things that clients appreciated about their Asian American therapists can also be adopted by non-Asian therapists. For example, learning about Asian family dynamics and Asian American histories would help greatly with understanding the perspectives of Asian American clients, and making them feel more at ease. Topics clients wanted therapists to understand better, in addition to the ones named above, included transracial adoption trauma; and intersecting identities, such as disability, gender, body size, internalized White supremacy, and somatization (the physical manifestation of emotional distress).

Be an Advocate

Advocacy is a core component of cultural competence according to the Multicultural and Social Justice Counseling Competencies (MSJCC; Ratts et al., 2015). In this domain of competence, "Privileged and marginalized counselors intervene with, and on behalf of, clients at the intrapersonal, interpersonal, institutional, community, public policy, and international/global levels" (p. 11). Advocacy can take many forms and can be woven into daily practice. For example, a former client and Chinese international student wanted a companion animal in her university apartment. She was required to meet with a housing administrator, and was told beforehand that it would be a "casual meeting." Therefore, she was shocked when the interviewer asked her to describe her mental health issues in detail. She gave me permission to speak with the interviewer on her behalf to explain that asking an Asian or Asian American person to disclose mental health issues is something that should be treated with care, due to it being a stigmatized topic in Asian cultures. Further, many Asian students have experienced racism on campus, including by the administration, and are wary of sharing personal information with them. The interviewer was fortunately very receptive and planned on conducting trainings for her staff on cultural sensitivity.

Advocacy also includes reexamining one's internalized biases. My training in documenting trauma symptoms according to the medical model is an ongoing source of my own subconscious bias. Recently, when completing the "Symptoms" portion of a progress note for a Chinese American client, I initially wrote "difficulty trusting others." However, the reality was that the client was experiencing racism from her supervisor and other colleagues at work. She was still able to maintain close relationships with friends and family. Therefore, I amended my note to reflect this important context, saying "workplace racism leaves the client with few they can trust there." One might even argue that this is no longer an individual symptom, which is part of my point.

One respondent who had worked with multiple therapists offered hope that therapist training is improving in its efforts to consider culture, stating,

> Seemed like the [therapists] I had many years ago were the ones who tended to just have no idea about Asian culture . . . In some ways, my more recent non-Asian therapists were sensitive to issues of Asian culture . . . so it seems like . . . they had better training/education.

I share the above client's hope that therapists are increasing in cultural competence. At the same time, many of the testimonios offered by the survey respondents point to ongoing systemic racism and the devaluation of culture among therapists, which is consistent with the literature. Training programs play a fundamental role in determining the degree to which future therapists will value and practice cultural competence and social justice. However, the curricula for these programs typically center White scholarship and paradigms (Carrero Pinedo et al., 2022). More egregiously, psychology programs often perpetrate institutional betrayal trauma in the form of racism and other forms of discrimination against their graduate students (Clark et al., 2012; Yamazaki-Jones, 2023). Beyond directly harming BIPOC students, this practice models oppression as the norm for future therapists. Therefore, the next chapter is a call for institutional courage to decolonize both the curricula and the climates of clinical and counseling psychology programs.

ADDITIONAL RESOURCES

Rather than videos, this chapter features podcast resources. Both come from the podcast *The Thoughtful Counselor*, produced by Dr. Dèsa Karye Daniel.

- Daniel, D. K. (Host & Producer). (2021, May 5). Racial healing: Understanding racism, meaningful allyship, and reclaiming your whole self (No. 203) [Audio podcast episode]. In *The Thoughtful Counselor*. Palo Alto University. https://tinyurl.com/ThoughtfulCounselor
  In this episode, Dr. Dèsa Karye Daniel talks to Dr. Annelise Singh about the power of racial healing, the importance of exploring racial identity, and how to advocate for social justice.

SCAN ME

- Tyler, J. (Host & Producer). (2021, December 15). Decolonizing counseling practice (No. 218) [Audio podcast episode]. In *The Thoughtful Counselor*. Palo Alto University. https://tinyurl.com/Decolonizingcounselingpractice

    In this episode, Dr. Jessica Tyler speaks with Dr. Brandee Appling, who shares strategies about how counselors can enact social justice in sessions and decolonize their therapy work.

Chapter Seven

Liberating Psychology Training Programs: A Call to Institutional Courage

What Leong observed in 1986 remains true today: "Therapists' or counselors' bias toward Asian-Americans and other minorities comes from at least two sources: their own cultural and personal backgrounds and their professional training" (p. 196). While a trainee's cultural and personal background is largely formed by the time they enter graduate school, professional training programs can be altered and improved.

In this chapter, I argue that psychology training programs have a crisis of racism and sexism that harms students and leads to a lack of preparation for working with diverse populations. The testimonios offered by Asian American and Asian Canadian clients in the previous chapter and throughout this book highlight the need for increased cultural competence and cultural humility on the part of psychotherapists.

Therefore, I call on psychology departments to embrace institutional courage by 1) decolonizing their curricula, and 2) protecting graduate students by dismantling departmental racism and sexual harassment. The American Psychological Association (APA) also has a duty to protect these students, especially those who attend APA-accredited programs. Although this chapter focuses on racism and sexual harassment, additional forms of harm, such as ableism, homophobia, and transphobia, have also impacted students' mental health and their ability to matriculate.

Drawing from scholarship on institutional courage (e.g., Freyd, 2018; Smith & Freyd, 2013; Smith & Freyd, 2017), I offer concrete steps that psychology departments and other training programs can take to accomplish these goals and model social justice for all of their students. Graduate students in other types of training programs, such as social work, also experience institutional discrimination (e.g., Johnson et al., 2021). Thus, many of the criticisms and recommendations in this chapter are applicable to their programs as well.

139

I focus primarily on psychology doctoral programs among the many mental health degrees for three main reasons. First, they are seen as the flagships of the field, occupying a position of the highest prestige (with the exception of psychiatry). Even within the various types of psychology doctoral programs, there are levels of stature. As I discuss in chapter 5, psychology, from its inception, has sought to establish itself as a "hard science," aligning itself with behaviorism, eugenics, and measurement (Helms, 2012; Yakushko, 2019). It is, therefore, no surprise that the most empirically oriented of the degrees, the clinical psychology PhD, is generally the most respected.

The second reason for focusing on psychology doctoral programs is that they require the most extended immersion in the academy, with an average of seven years to degree completion (National Science Foundation, National Center for Science and Engineering Statistics, n.d.). In my clinical experience, seven years of chronic exposure to oppression is long enough to effect personality change through internalized shame. Indeed, research has found that the mental health of graduate students tends to deteriorate over time, with fifth-year students faring significantly worse than first-year students (Bolotnyy et al., 2021). Overall, rates of depression and anxiety are three times higher among graduate students than the population average, with 1 in 10 reporting suicidal ideation (Bolotnyy et al., 2021; Garcia-Williams et al., 2014).

Finally, psychology doctoral students are particularly vulnerable in their reliance on faculty to provide strong letters of recommendation for clinical internships, which are extremely competitive and are a prerequisite for graduation. This vulnerability extends beyond the typical pressures that all graduate students face, of needing their advisors to assist with conducting and publishing research, approving dissertations, and helping with professional networking.

Of particular concern to psychology graduate students is a deficit of internships accredited by the American Psychological Association (Keilin et al., 2022), a situation that has remained unresolved for the past two decades. Having an accredited internship is a requirement for future employment at the Veterans Administration, the largest employer of psychologists in the United States. It is also a prerequisite for some postdoctoral fellowships and university teaching positions. Failure to obtain an accredited internship can mean having to extend one's graduate studies another year, which results in accruing more tuition fees and increasing student loan debt. Therefore, the internship requirement is a source of stress from the moment prospective psychologists begin their graduate training. As a result, many psychology graduate students feel powerless to complain openly about discrimination or to advocate for more inclusive curricula.

DECOLONIZE CURRICULUM CONTENT
AND TRAINING MODELS

A paradigm shift is needed in the curricula of graduate training programs, which center White academics and a decontextualized, neoliberal perspective (Carrero Pinedo et al., 2022). Palmer and Parish (2008) observe that

> toward this aim, counseling models and contemporary paradigms must be deconstructed and the profession redefined in order to move away from a Euro-American-centric individualist outlook, which does not acknowledge its own social, cultural, economic, and political contexts and ramifications. (Bemak, 1998)

While many programs now offer a course on multicultural counseling, integration of cultural responsiveness is seen as adjunctive (Carrero Pinedo et al., 2022). However, liberation psychology and critical race theory can be used as frameworks to reshape the content of training programs (Carrero Pinedo et al., 2022; Singh et al., 2020). Detailed, concrete roadmaps for disrupting the influence of White supremacy in psychology have already been developed. For example, Neville et al. (2021) have created a training model called public psychology for liberation (PPL) that "reflects a science, a pedagogical commitment, and practice of, by, and with the people who have been most marginalized in society" (p. 1248). The model is based on core tenets of liberation psychology, including social justice, intersectionality, radical healing, and sense of connection. The model also includes a call for curriculum decolonization that rejects the premise of academic psychologists being the sole source of knowledge in the field. Rather, it advocates for the indigenization of psychology and interrogation of the very notion of "evidence." The PPL model can be incorporated with other social-justice-oriented training models, such as the scientist-practitioner-advocate (SPA) model (Miles & Fassinger, 2021), which argues for the need to integrate advocacy into education, research, and practice.

As an example of training consistent with the PPL model, my graduate advisor, Dr. Jennifer Freyd, taught seminars that upended my understanding of mental illness and its treatment. My classmates and I learned about how Western psychology, since its inception, has been closely affiliated with eugenics, the pseudoscience of racial betterment that led to unethical experiments on Black Americans, women, and those with severe mental illness (Lombardo & Dorr, 2006; Yakushko, 2019). We read scholarship critical of the medical model of mental illness, about how arbitrarily most of the diagnostic criteria for psychiatric disorders were developed, and about how the profound effect of relational trauma on mental illness is often dismissed due to the bias in psychology that favors biological explanations, a legacy of eugenics (Read et al., 2004; Yakushko, 2019). We learned how drug companies capitalized upon the now-debunked chemical imbalance theory of the brain to boost antidepressant sales, while suppressing data that showed their therapeutic effect was largely due to placebo (e.g., Kirsch et al., 2008; Kirsch, 2009). Perhaps most importantly, we learned to use scholarship in the service of social justice for trauma survivors.

Complementing the liberation-oriented curriculum was clinical training in relational-cultural theory (RCT), a feminist framework for contextualizing trauma (see chapter 5) led by Dr. Pam Birrell. Although I have since received training in a wide variety of therapy approaches for post-traumatic stress, my work is anchored in the lessons I learned from Dr. Birrell about the importance of listening, bearing witness, and power-sharing. Ironically, this training was over the protest of the clinical psychology department, which championed cognitive behavioral therapy to the exclusion of non-manualized approaches. However, relational-cultural therapy has since been acknowledged as one of the only approaches that support the values of liberation psychology (Hutton, 2011; Singh et al., 2020).

INSTITUTIONAL BETRAYAL OF PSYCHOLOGY GRADUATE STUDENTS

As essential as it is to reenvision graduate training, the climate of the departments needs to change as well. Racial discrimination and sexual harassment pervade academia, with graduate students as some of its most vulnerable targets (e.g., Brunsma et al., 2017; Rosenthal et al., 2016). If these practices are not dismantled, psychology departments will continue to perpetuate oppression regardless of how much they incorporate liberation values in their courses. To offer an analogy, imagine a workplace cafeteria that does not follow basic hygiene practices, such as hand-washing and proper refrigeration. As a result, the cafeteria serves contaminated meals that consistently cause food poisoning, and the employees no longer want to eat there. Rather than address the lack of hygiene, the company's solution is to add different ethnic foods to its menu to make it more appealing to its diverse workforce. Doing so also has the benefit of improving the company's public image. However, the root causes of worker illness remain unresolved.

Little attention has been paid to fixing the underlying causes of harm toward students enrolled in psychology training programs (or, for that matter, in any graduate programs). Research has found that approximately 40% of female and 25% of male graduate students (Rosenthal et al., 2016), as well as 33% of nonbinary and genderqueer graduate students (Cantor et al., 2015), have been sexually harassed by faculty and staff. One study focusing on psychology doctoral students found even higher rates when including harassment by other students, with 75% of female and 68% of male graduates reporting sexual harassment during graduate school (Schneider et al., 2002). Only cisgender identities were included in this study.

Racism is an equally ubiquitous experience among graduate students of color. As Brunsma et al. (2017, p. 5) write, "The literature makes one thing very clear: Graduate students of color face racism, discrimination, and daily microaggressions within their departments." Psychology departments are no exception to this phenomenon (Clark et al., 2012; Maton et al., 2011; Yamazaki-Jones, 2023). BIPOC psychology graduate students consistently report significantly more negative race-related experiences than White graduate students (Clark et al., 2012; Maton et al., 2011). Yamazaki-Jones (2023) found that Asian American psychology graduate students across the country regularly experience racial microaggressions, such as being made to feel that one represents "cultural diversity," being assumed to be quiet, and being made to feel invisible in a group setting. Of the over 100 participants of the study, *100% reported experiencing at least one form of microaggression in their programs* (J. Yamazaki-Jones, personal communication, December 18, 2022).

Graduate students have a reasonable expectation of protection from their professors and departments. Further, they often have few courses of action available to them. In the cafeteria analogy above, workers can opt to eat elsewhere or prepare their own lunches. However, the only option for graduate students typically is to leave their programs and forfeit their aspirations of becoming psychologists. It follows, then, that discrimination in graduate school is a form of institutional betrayal trauma, defined as "wrongdoings perpetrated by an institution upon those dependent upon that institution" (Freyd, 2020). This betrayal exacerbates the harm of racism and sexism (Gómez, 2015). In addition to having a negative impact on mental health, sexual harassment for female graduate students has been found to be significantly associated with additional forms of institutional betrayal (Rosenthal et al., 2016). Commonly reported forms of institutional betrayal included "creating an environment where this type of experience seemed more likely to occur," "not doing enough to prevent this type of experience," and "making it difficult to report the experience."

Not surprisingly, BIPOC graduate students in general (Clark et al., 2012; O'Meara et al., 2017), and BIPOC psychology students in particular (Syropoulos et al., 2021), report a significantly lower sense of belonging than White students. Racial microaggressions are also associated with racism-related stress (Yamazaki-Jones, 2023). As Carrero Pinedo (2022, p. 143) observes, when discrimination is not addressed, BIPOC trainees will continue to be placed in predicaments in which they must

> work to critically engage in their education and training while simultaneously having to deconstruct the structural inadequacies that further perpetuate White supremacy and colonialism. These situations can materialize into moments wherein they have to confront microaggressions and educate their peers, faculty, and staff as a means of both addressing systemic racism and survival, even when doing so can result in having less social support and feeling disconnected from others around them. (Sturgis et al., 2020)

The following is a testimonio based on an interview with Victoria (a pseudonym), a Filipina American psychologist who volunteered to share some of her experiences as a graduate student. She described multiple forms of institutional betrayal trauma that created a departmental climate hostile to women and BIPOC graduate students.

Victoria's Story

When Victoria started her doctoral program and began meeting with members of the outgoing class, she was struck by the poor state of their mental health. "I mean, these are people who went through hell and back just to get into the program," she said. "What happened to them? Was this an 'us' problem, as in we need to have better time management?" she recalled wondering at the time. However, Victoria, unfortunately, learned through personal experience why the majority of psychology graduate students in the United States develop symptoms of anxiety, depression, and chronic physical illnesses (Rummell, 2015). "Some of my colleagues are now being medicated for high-level anxiety and depression and panic attacks, and all of these other things, and it's, like, that was not what they were experiencing before this program," she said.

One of her earliest experiences began with an ethics instructor who had exhibited preferential treatment of students and other problematic behavior, a pattern that had continued for years. Only when students from a different counselor training program on campus organized themselves and wrote a letter to the dean, complaining about the instructor's behavior, was she dismissed.

Cultural Betrayal

Institutional betrayal is exacerbated by cultural betrayal trauma when the offenders are faculty of color. Victoria described challenging interactions with a BIPOC faculty member while organizing a departmental event. "She was especially unkind to me, and I didn't understand why. I tried every possible way to just communicate and figure it out with her and navigate it, and it just wasn't a good fit." (At this point in our conversation, I felt the need to interject, as I would with one of my clients, and said, "Not a good fit? This was not your fault—it's not that you were not a good fit. When someone is bullying you, we don't say it was 'not a good fit.'")

Victoria continued by saying, "What bothered me the most about [it] is that she didn't speak to me directly. She went to my advisor . . . and told her [she] needed to speak to me because I was 'really unprofessional' . . . I'm also not used to people not telling me things directly either, so that was hard for me."

Sexual Harassment and Racism

Victoria next encountered a clinical supervisor who, as she described, "was notorious for being inappropriate with female students." Graduate students who had worked with this faculty member warned Victoria and her class-mates not to be alone with him and to look out for each other. "From what the students that were impacted shared with me, it was always the type of touch that could be . . . misconstrued . . . where it was just like a hand to the back, or a hand would end up on the thigh or something like that, and, like, demonstrating appropriate ways to touch children versus not . . . and that sort of thing," she said. Victoria recalled the warnings from students "also came with a lesson of, like, 'Hey, you can report [it] if you want, but nothing's go-ing to change.' Sure enough, the students ahead of me had reported, and they talked to the [department heads, and they] did nothing."

For Victoria, making sure she and her classmates were never alone with the supervisor was a constant source of stress. She describes her worry for a friend, also a student of color, saying, "she really struggled to set boundaries with him, and he took advantage of that." Victoria described how he would be "needlessly nitpicky" about her friend's clinical work in order to spend more time with her. According to Victoria, this supervisor was allowed to work with students for several years and was never punished for his behavior. She explained, "He was a friend of [a faculty member], and because he had experience with the rural community, [the department was] unwilling to let his expertise go."

Victoria further described how the director of a university mental health clinic she worked at repeatedly targeted an Asian international student during group supervision. "[The student] was doing a fine job. I've seen her [video]tape . . . But for whatever reason [the supervisor] took a dislik-ing to her and made it her role to just absolutely berate and mistreat this poor . . . woman. . . . She actively humiliated her by ripping apart her tape in front of the class . . . [She made] comments about her language ability . . . and some obviously cultural pieces like [needing to make more] eye contact, and basically the same stupid stereotypical stuff. . . . A big part of the issue here is [the supervisor] doesn't see a problem with this."

Research has found that vicarious exposure to racism, such as what Victoria witnessed, can be just as harmful to the physical (Martz et al., 2019) and mental health (Heard-Garris et al., 2018) of BIPOC as being the direct target. Studies of Asian Americans conducted amid the rise of anti-Asian racism during the COVID-19 pandemic found a direct association between exposure to vicarious racism and depression and anxiety (Chae et al., 2021) and sleep disturbance (Yip et al., 2022).

According to Victoria, tensions in the department grew so great due to the above issues that a university ombudsperson intervened to mediate between students and faculty. Students recounted personal experiences of harassment and requested a plan to address their mental health concerns. However, little change ensued. While the department chairs announced their imminent retirement, they promoted the clinic supervisor. The other supervisor also announced plans to retire, although the department website still lists him as an active faculty member.

THE SILENCING EFFECTS OF BETRAYAL

Faculty members are often unaware of the full extent to which students experience discrimination and betrayal within their departments. For example, in chapter 2, I described the case of Shizuko, an international student from Japan who was refused service at a campus dining hall. She was quite distraught when she raised the issue in therapy with me soon after the incident. After some processing of her emotions, she chose to file a report with the university, as well as with Stop AAPI Hate (https://stopaapihate.org/). However, she did not want to disclose the incident to her department. As she explained, several faculty members, including her advisor, had a reputation among the BIPOC students for being unsympathetic to complaints of racism, and she did not want to risk retaliation for complaining.

Self-blame and shame that arise from institutional and cultural betrayal trauma also lead to silencing the victim. As cultural betrayal trauma theory predicts (Gómez, 2017), it is often safer to do so than to risk disbelief, rejection, or castigation by one's own marginalized community. A victim can also feel a duty to protect the offender. For all of these reasons, I did not share for years my own experience of oppression in graduate school by a BIPOC faculty member. Like Victoria, I instead blamed myself for not being a good fit.

INSTITUTIONAL COWARDICE

Brown (2021) coined the term "institutional cowardice" to describe the failure to respond to problematic behavior. Institutional cowardice is a form of institutional betrayal distinguished by neglect, such as "not trying hard enough because it was inconvenient, [or] not being willing to stick out one's neck in case that neck, too, became caught in the maw of whatever more malevolent stuff was going on" (p. 2). Unfortunately, institutional cowardice was a hallmark of my experience of graduate school, just as Victoria's was.

As one example, the ethics class I took was taught by a White male professor who verbally bullied the students, most of whom were women of color. My classmates and I lobbied the director of clinical training to have him removed from teaching, but she declined, despite knowing his reputation for being sexist and racist. Ostensibly, this professor had promised to donate a large sum of money to the department's clinic. It was not until the following year, when he made several remarks that were so egregiously offensive they could not be easily dismissed, that he was no longer allowed to teach.

THE NEED FOR INSTITUTIONAL COURAGE

The time for change is long past due. Psychology graduate students should not have to fear for their emotional or physical safety to attend classes, receive clinical supervision, or participate in any other aspects of their education. There is no justification for faculty, staff, clinical supervisors, departments, and universities to be perpetrating institutional betrayal against those who have the least amount of power, either through direct abuse or the neglect of cowardice. Year after year, psychology graduate students of color arrive at my practice traumatized by the very people who should have protected them. Together, we begin the arduous work of disentangling the tentacles of racism and sexism that have become internalized in their psyches. We address panic attacks, exhaustion, nightmares, shame, and shattered self-esteem. However, I provide a caveat that they will not be able to recover fully until they leave their toxic environments. Even then, emotional recovery can require years, especially if the stress led to a chronic physical illness, as it often does.

Discriminatory practices harm all students and the departments themselves (Carrero Pinedo et al., 2022; Slay et al., 2019), beyond the devastating impact on the mental health of its victims. A program that behaves unethically not only violates various codes of conduct for psychology but models such standards for its students. In other words, unethical behavior becomes an integral part of the education and training of future psychologists. While I believe most psychologists enter the field to help others, being immersed in toxic training programs, at the very least, reinforces implicit biases that affect their approach to research and practice. At worst, it promotes predatory behavior by showing there are no consequences for it.

Another negative outcome of discrimination is student attrition. Despite no differences in qualifications, such as grade point average or graduate record examination scores, BIPOC and disabled psychology graduate students are more likely to drop out of their programs than their White and nondisabled peers (Callahan et al., 2018; Trent et al., 2020). This attrition results in a loss of labor to support faculty research and teach courses, as well as a loss of creativity in developing ways of understanding the world.

Finally, the loss of BIPOC graduate students has a profound impact on society. Now more than ever, every mental health professional matters if we are to meet the escalating crisis of anxiety and depression in the United States, especially those from underrepresented groups. BIPOC and disabled psychologists provide more services to the disenfranchised, such as the unemployed and the working poor, at a much higher rate than White or nondisabled psychologists (American Psychological Association, 2017a; American Psychological Association, 2017b).

Moving psychology programs toward social justice requires altering "social *structures*, not solely *individuals*" (Palmer & Parish, 2008, p. 280). Given the entrenched patriarchal and colonial nature of academia, change will not come easily or without a struggle. Therefore, institutional courage is needed (Freyd, 2014). Freyd defines institutional courage as:

> an institution's commitment to seek the truth and engage in moral action, despite unpleasantness, risk, and short-term cost. It is a pledge to protect and care for those who depend on the institution. It is a compass oriented to the common good of individuals, the institution, and the world. It is a force that transforms institutions into more accountable, equitable, effective places for everyone. (Center for Institutional Courage, n.d.)

A growing body of literature shows that institutional courage buffers against institutional betrayal by mitigating the association between institutional betrayal and trauma symptoms (Adams-Clark et al., under review). Institutional courage also fosters organizational commitment following workplace sexual harassment (Smidt et al., 2023). It is reasonable to believe that it can also foster organizational commitment to workplace racism.

HOW TO PRACTICE INSTITUTIONAL COURAGE

Freyd (2018) offers some general principles for implementing institutional courage to prevent and address institutional betrayal, which I have adapted for psychology departments.

1. **Comply with the Ethical Principles of Psychologists and Code of Conduct (American Psychological Association, 2017c).**

   Section 3 of the American Psychological Association (APA) ethics code, Human Relations, is particularly relevant, as it clearly condones unfair discrimination, sexual harassment, and other forms of harassment. It also states that psychologists should take reasonable steps to avoid harming others, including students and supervisees.

   Additionally, Freyd urges institutions to "Go beyond mere compliance. Avoid a check-box approach by stretching beyond minimal standards of compliance and reach for excellence in non-violence and equity." Toward this end, the Race and Ethnicity Guidelines in Psychology, published by the American Psychological Association, APA Task Force on Race and Ethnicity Guidelines in Psychology (2019), encourages increasing self-awareness of one's positionality, privilege, and biases. It also explicitly calls on psychologists to act against "bias, prejudice, and discrimination within institutions and professional groups." Social work programs can refer to the National Association of Social Workers Code of Ethics (National Association of Social Workers, 2021).

2. **Respond sensitively to student disclosures.**

   As Bowden and Buie (2021) write of racism in the academy, "Assume you and your institution have a problem" (p. 761). Starting with this assumption increases the likelihood of taking student complaints seriously. Freyd also recommends "[avoiding] cruel responses that blame and attack the victim. Even well-meaning responses can be harmful by, for instance, taking control away from the victim, or by minimizing the harm. Better listening skills can also help institutions respond sensitively."

3. **Bear witness, be accountable, and apologize.**

   Freyd advises, "Create ways for individuals to discuss what happened to them. This includes being accountable for mistakes and apologizing when appropriate." A sincere apology comprises an acknowledgment of wrongdoing, an expression of remorse, and includes a commitment to make amends.

4. **Cherish the whistleblower.**

   Graduate students and faculty who raise uncomfortable truths are potentially the best friends of the department. They offer the opportunity to move toward social justice and can help avoid potential legal consequences associated with perpetrating institutional betrayal. By cultivating trust in the institution and protecting whistleblowers, psychology departments can increase the likelihood of whistleblowing (Nicholls et al., 2021).

5. Conduct anonymous surveys and disseminate results.

According to Freyd, "Well-done anonymous surveys are a powerful tool for disrupting institutional betrayal. . . . This will inspire trust and repair." The Institutional Betrayal Questionnaire (IBQ) (Smith & Freyd, 2013; Smith & Freyd, 2017) is a tool by which psychology departments can assess their "vulnerability to potential problems, the ease or difficulty of reporting such issues, and how complaints are processed and handled." Graduate students, faculty, and staff can all complete the questionnaire. Share aggregated results to respect individual privacy and to demonstrate transparency.

6. Have clinicians teach clinical training courses.

Often, training courses on psychotherapy are taught by faculty who are primarily researchers. Some have not conducted therapy since their own graduate education. The perception that non-clinicians are qualified to teach clinical skills stems from the misperceptions that 1) psychotherapy can be reduced to a series of brief and predictable action steps—in other words, universally manualized; and 2) that manualized therapies are more empirically supported than other forms of therapy (Flückiger et al., 2012; Shedler, 2020). Decolonizing the training of future psychologists means valuing the professional experience of those whose primary focus is clinical practice. At the same time, all instructors, regardless of whether they are primarily clinicians or researchers, should be strictly held to ethical standards of conduct.

7. Commit resources to steps 1–6.

"Good intentions are a good starting place, but staff, money, and time need to be dedicated to make this happen," says Freyd. Addressing problematic behavior can be financially costly for departments. For example, removing an instructor may require additional outlay in paying adjunct faculty to take over. Confronting a colleague about problematic behavior can be awkward and stressful. But these costs are minute compared to the harm BIPOC, and other, graduate students continue to endure.

I believe that, with enough commitment and courage, these recommendations are achievable goals. Still, I also recognize that institutional courage is the exception rather than the norm. Therefore, greater oversight of psychology programs is also needed by the APA.

THE ROLE OF THE AMERICAN
PSYCHOLOGICAL ASSOCIATION

As the accrediting body for psychology training programs, the APA has a duty to help ensure the well-being of psychology graduate students. Accreditation by the APA signifies to prospective students that a program has been rigorously reviewed and can be trusted to deliver a high quality of mentorship and education. Therefore, the APA should take immediate measures to require that psychology programs address the current and ongoing internal pandemic of racism and sexism.

Suggestions for doing so include integrating internal climate surveys, such as the Institutional Betrayal Questionnaire, into the accreditation process, as well as interim reviews of accreditation. The APA also should convene a task force on the well-being of psychology graduate students that focuses on the frequency of discrimination and its effect on students; recommends solutions, including disciplinary action; and sets milestone targets for the reduction of discrimination.

A great deal of institutional courage and leadership will be required to increase social justice in training programs. But the call to do so is growing louder, and the need for change has never been more urgent than at present. Decolonizing the curriculum is necessary, though insufficient, if racism, sexism, ableism, transphobia, homophobia, anti-Semitism, and other forms of discrimination are not also addressed. May we all exercise courage, take risks, and move ourselves and those who depend on us toward liberation.

ADDITIONAL RESOURCES

- WRAL. (2022, September 1). *Former UNC grad student suing university for discrimination* [Video]. YouTube. https://tinyurl.com/UNClawsuit
  Graduate students are advocating for themselves and for their unions against racism, harassment, and bullying by professors. This news story features the story of Rose Brown, a Black graduate student who filed a lawsuit against her university for racial discrimination.

SCAN ME

- Hope, H. (2022, July 28). *Some UC San Diego grad researchers claim they were bullied by their supervisors.* CBS8. https://tinyurl.com/UCSDbullying
  Graduate students at the University of California, San Diego, joined forces to negotiate for better working conditions with their university after there was no official response to their individual complaints of workplace bullying.

SCAN ME

- Polaski, D. (2015, April 24). *Walking the line of Blackness* [Video]. YouTube. https://tinyurl.com/walkingthelineofBlackness
  Walking the Line of Blackness is a twenty-minute video featuring the stories of sixteen Black graduate students at the University of Michigan. They share the struggles they face, being Black in America, and in academia.

SCAN ME

- Palumbo-Liu, D. (Host). (2023, January 13). *Giving universities, and people, the courage to address sexual harassment and violence: Interview with Jennifer Freyd* (No. 7) [Audio podcast episode]. In Speaking Out of Place. Player FM. https://tinyurl.com/Freydpodcastinterview
  In this episode from the podcast Speaking Out of Place, Dr. David Palumbo-Liu interviews Dr. Jennifer Freyd about individual and institutional cowardice and courage in universities and other institutions. At approximately minute 35, Dr. Freyd provides an example of institutional courage by a university in handling a prior sexual assault perpetrated by university athletes.

SCAN ME

References

Acevedo, N. (2021, April 17). *Sikh community mourns the loss of four in Indianapolis FedEx mass shooting.* NBC News. https://www.nbcnews.com/news/us-news/sikh-community-mourns-loss-four-indianapolis-fedex-mass-shooting-n1264413

Adams, G., Dobles, I., Gómez, L. H., Kurtiş, T., & Molina, L. E. (2015). Decolonizing psychological science: Introduction to the special thematic section. *Journal of Social and Political Psychology, 3*(1), 213–238. https://doi.org/10.5964/jspp.v3i1.564

Adams-Clark, A. A., Barnes, M. L., Lind, M. N., Smidt, A. M., & Freyd, J. J. (under review). High institutional courage buffers against the association between institutional betrayal and trauma symptoms among undergraduate students experiencing campus sexual violence. Submitted to *Journal of Interpersonal Violence.*

Aguinaldo, E., & Pacis, V. A. (1957). *A second look at America.* Robert Speller and Sons.

American Psychological Association. (2017a). *CWS Factsheet Series: Psychologists providing services to the unemployed.* https://www.apa.org/workforce/factsheets/unemployed.pdf

American Psychological Association. (2017b). *CWS Factsheet Series: Psychologists providing services to the working poor.* https://www.apa.org/workforce/factsheets/working-poor.pdf

American Psychological Association. (2017c). *Ethical principles of psychologists and code of conduct* (2002, amended effective June 1, 2010, and January 1, 2017). https://www.apa.org/ethics/code/

American Psychological Association, APA Task Force on Race and Ethnicity Guidelines in Psychology. (2019). *Race and ethnicity guidelines in psychology: Promoting responsiveness and equity.* Retrieved from http://www.apa.org/about/policy/race-and-ethnicity-in-psychology.pdf

Amin, S. & Bansal, P. (2023). *Understanding the Asian Indian diaspora and mental health: Liberation from Western frameworks.* Cognella.

Andersen, J. P., & Blosnich, J. (2013). Disparities in adverse childhood experiences among sexual minority and heterosexual adults: Results from a multi-state proba-bility-based sample. *PLoS One, 8*(1): e54691. doi: 10.1371/journal.pone.0054691

Annesse, J. (2021, April 22). Pakistani college student, 21, blinded and disfigured in "heinous" acid attack outside her Long Island home. *New York Daily News.* https://www.nydailynews.com/new-york/ny-acid-attack-asian-hate-crime-20210422-ttqd-mi4zubc6nc3youd5j27yii-story.html

Associated Press. (2021, May 5). *San Francisco women stabbed amid wave of attacks on Asians.* ABC News. https://abcnews.go.com/US/wireStory/asian-american-women-stabbed-san-francisco-attack-77497315

Austin, A. (2013). *The impact of geography on Asian American poverty.* Economic Policy Institute. https://www.epi.org/publication/impact-geography-asian-ameri-can-poverty/

Bang, M. (2021, May 18). *Athenaeum Symposia artist Misoo Bang: The journey of the giantess* [Video]. YouTube. https://www.youtube.com/watch?v=8MC9piS7IJ0

Bang, S. H., Huang, Y. C., Kuo, H. J., Cho, E. S., & García, A. A. (2023). Health status and healthcare access of Southeast Asian refugees in the United States: An integrative review. *Public Health Nursing, 40*(2), 324–337.

Belford, B., Kaehler, L., & Birrell, P. (2012). Relational health as a mediator between betrayal trauma and borderline personality disorder. *Journal of Trauma & Disso-ciation, 13,* 244–257.

Beltrán, P., & Leung, J. (Directors). (2020). *Mu and the vanishing world* [Film]. DosVelas Pictures.

Berkman, L. F., & Syme, L. (1979). Social networks, host resistance, and mortality: A nine-year follow-up study of Alameda County residents. *American Journal of Epidemiology, 117,* 1003–1009.

Bernard, D. L., Calhoun, C. D., Banks, D. E., Halliday, C. A., Hughes-Halbert, C., & Danielson, C. K. (2020). Making the "C-ACE" for a culturally-informed adverse childhood experiences framework to understand the pervasive mental health im-pact of racism on Black youth. *Journal of Child and Adolescent Trauma.* https://doi.org/10.1007/s40653-020-00319-9

Bhat, J. (2021, December 16). The South Asian mental health journey. *Psychology To-day.* https://www.psychologytoday.com/us/blog/the-psychology-the-south-asian-diaspora/202112/the-south-asian-mental-health-journey

Bhatia, B. M. (1991). *Famines in India.* Konark Publishers.

Bhatia, S. (2017). *Decolonizing psychology: Globalization, social justice, and Indian youth identities.* Oxford University Press.

Bhatia, S. (2018). *Decolonizing psychology: Globalization, social justice, and Indian identities.* Oxford University Press.

Bhatia, S. (2020). Decolonizing psychology: Power, citizenship and identity. *Psycho-analysis, Self and Context, 15*(3), 257–266, https://doi.org/10.1080/24720038.2020.1772266

Birrell, P. J. (2006). An ethic of possibility: Relationship, risk, and presence. *Ethics & Behavior, 16*(2), 95–115. https://doi.org/10.1207/s15327019eb1602_2

Birrell, P. J., & Freyd, J. J. (2006). Betrayal trauma: Relational models of harm and healing. *Journal of Trauma Practice, 5*(1), 49–63.

Blow, C. (2012, September 19*).* I know why the caged bird shrieks. *The New York Times.* https://campaignstops.blogs.nytimes.com/2012/09/19/blow-i-know-why-the-caged-bird-shrieks

Bolotnyy, V., Basilico, M., & Barreira, P. (2021). Graduate student mental health: Lessons from American economics departments. *Journal of Economic Literature.*

Bowden, A. K., & Buie, C. R. (2021). Anti-Black racism in academia and what you can do about it. *Nature Reviews Materials, 6*(9), 760–761.

Boyd-Franklin, N. (2003). *Black families in therapy* (2nd ed.). Guilford Press.

Bronfenbrenner, U. (1977). Toward an experimental ecology of human development. *American Psychologist, 32*(7), 513.

Brown, A. (2018, January 9). *"Least desirable"? How racial discrimination plays out in online dating.* NPR. https://www.npr.org/2018/01/09/575352051/least-desirable-how-racial-discrimination-plays-out-in-online-dating

Brown, L. S. (2021). Institutional cowardice: A powerful, often invisible manifestation of institutional betrayal. *Journal of Trauma & Dissociation, 22*(3), 241–248.

Brunsma, D. L., Embrick, D. G., & Shin, J. H. (2017). Graduate students of color: Race, racism, and mentoring in the white waters of academia. *Sociology of Race and Ethnicity, 3*(1), 1–13.

Budiman, A., & Ruiz, N. G. (2021). *Key facts about Asian Americans, a diverse and growing population.* Pew Research Center. https://www.pewresearch.org/fact-tank/2021/04/29/key-facts-about-asian-americans/

Bui, T. (2017). *The best we could do: An illustrated memoir.* Abrams.

Cabral, R. R., & Smith, T. B. (2011). Racial/ethnic matching of clients and therapists in mental health services: A meta-analytic review of preferences, perceptions, and outcomes. *Journal of Counseling Psychology, 58*, 537–554. https://doi.org/10.1037/a0025266

Callahan, J. L., Smotherman, J. M., Dziurzynski, K. E., Love, P. K., Kilmer, E. D., Niemann, Y. F., & Ruggero, C. J. (2018). Diversity in the professional psychology training-to-workforce pipeline: Results from doctoral psychology student population data. *Training and Education in Professional Psychology, 12*(4), 273.

Campbell, R., Dworkin, E., & Cabral, G. (2009). An ecological model of the impact of sexual assault on women's mental health. *Trauma, Violence, & Abuse, 10*(3), 225–246.

Cantor, D., Fisher, B., Chibnall, S., Bruce, C., Townsend, R., Thomas, G., & Lee, H. (2015). *Report on the AAU campus climate survey on sexual assault and misconduct.* The Association of American Universities.

Capps, R., Gelatt, J., Ruiz Soto, A. G., & Van Hook, J. (2020). *Unauthorized immigrants in the United States: Stable numbers changing origins.* Migration Policy Institute.

Carrero Pinedo, A., Caso, T. J., Rivera, R. M., Carballea, D., & Louis, E. F. (2022). Black, indigenous, and trainees of color stress and resilience: The role of training and education in decolonizing psychology. *Psychological Trauma: Theory,*

Research, Practice, and Policy, 14(S1), S140–S147. https://doi.org/10.1037/tra0001187

Cash, S. J., & Bridge, J. A. (2009). Epidemiology of youth suicide and suicidal behavior. *Current Opinion in Pediatrics, 21*(5), 613.

Center for Institutional Courage (n.d.). Retrieved March 27, 2023, from https://www.institutionalcourage.org

Centers for Disease Control and Prevention (2010). *Adverse childhood experiences reported by adults—Five states, 2009.* https://www.cdc.gov/mmwr/preview/mmwrhtml/mm5949a1.htm

Centers for Disease Control and Prevention (2014). *Child maltreatment: Facts at a glance.* Retrieved from https://www.cdc.gov/violenceprevention/pdf/childmaltreatment-facts-at-a-glance.pdf

Centers for Disease Control and Prevention (2019). *Preventing adverse childhood experiences: Leveraging the best available evidence.* National Center for Injury Prevention and Control: Centers for Disease Control and Prevention.

Cervantes, A., Flores Carmona, J., & Torres Fernández, I. (2021). Testimonios and liberation psychology as praxis: Informing educators in the borderlands. *Journal of Latinos and Education, 20*(1), 20–31.

Chae, D. H., Clouston, S., Hatzenbuehler, M. L., Kramer, M. R., Cooper, H. L., Wilson, S. M., Stephens-Davidowitz, S. I., Gold, R. S., & Link, B. G. (2015). Association between an internet-based measure of area racism and Black mortality. *PloS One, 10*(4), e0122963.

Chae, D. H., Yip, T., Martz, C. D., Chung, K., Richeson, J. A., Hajat, A., Curtis, D. S., Rogers, L. O., & LaVeist, T. A. (2021). Vicarious racism and vigilance during the COVID-19 pandemic: Mental health implications among Asian and Black Americans. *Public Health Reports* (Washington, DC: 1974), *136*(4), 508–517. https://doi.org/10.1177/00333549211018675

Chan, C. D., Frank, C. D., DeMeyer, M., Joshi, A., Vargas, E. A., & Silverio, N. (2021). Counseling older LGBTQ+ adults of color: Relational-cultural theory in practice. *Professional Counselor, 11*(3), 370–382.

Chang, M. J. (2011). Battle hymn of the model minority myth. *Amerasia Journal, 37*(2), 137–143.

Chen, J. K., Pan, Z., & Wang, L. C. (2021). Parental beliefs and actual use of corporal punishment, school violence and bullying, and depression in early adolescence. *International Journal of Environmental Research and Public Health, 18*(12), 6270. https://doi.org/10.3390/ijerph18126270

Cheng, A. W., Chang, J., O'Brien, J., Budgazad, M. S., & Tsai, J. (2017). Model minority stereotype: Influence on perceived mental health needs of Asian Americans. *Journal of Immigrant and Minority Health, 19*(3), 572–581.

Chun, J. (n.d.). A reflection on Asian intergenerational trauma. *Asian Mental Health Collective.* Retrieved January 4, 2023, from https://www.asianmhc.org/a-reflection-on-asian-intergenerational-trauma/

Clark, C. R., Mercer, S. H., Zeigler-Hill, V., & Dufrene, B. A. (2012). Barriers to the success of ethnic minority students in school psychology graduate programs. *School Psychology Review, 41*(2), 176–192.

Cohn, D., & Passel, J. S. (2018). *A record 64 million Americans live in multigenerational households*. Pew Research Center. https://www.pewresearch.org/fact-tank/2018/04/05/a-record-64-million-americans-live-in-multigenerational-households/

Cole, N. (2006). Trauma and the American Indian. In T. M. Witko (Ed.), *Mental health care for urban Indians: Clinical insights from Native practitioners* (pp. 115–130). American Psychological Association. https://doi.org/10.1037/11422-006

Comas-Díaz, L. E., & Rivera, T. (2020). *Liberation psychology: Theory, method, practice, and social justice* (pp. xx–314). American Psychological Association.

Comstock, D. L., Hammer, T. R., Strentzsch, J., Cannon, K., Parsons, J., & Salazar II, G. (2008). Relational–cultural theory: A framework for bridging relational, multicultural, and social justice competencies. *Journal of Counseling & Development, 86*(3), 279–287.

Constantine, M. G., & Sue, G. W. (2007). Perceptions of racial microaggressions among Black supervisees in cross-racial dyads. *Journal of Counseling Psychology, 54*, 142–153. doi:10.1037/0022-0167.54.2.142

Cotton, E. (2021, April 4). *Artist Misoo Bang's giant Asian girl series challenges "vulnerable" stereotype*. Vermont Digger. https://vtdigger.org/2021/04/04/artist-misoo-bangs-giant-asian-girl-series-challenges-vulnerable-stereotype/

Cromer, L. D., Gray, M. E., Vasquez, L., & Freyd, J. J. (2018). The relationship of acculturation to historical loss awareness, institutional betrayal, and the intergenerational transmission of trauma in the American Indian experience. *Journal of Cross-Cultural Psychology, 49*(1), 99–114. https://doi.org/10.1177/0022022117738749

Dalaker, J. (2005). *Alternative poverty estimates in the United States: 2003*. US Census Bureau, Current Population Reports. https://www2.census.gov/library/publications/2005/demo/p60-227.pdf

Damasio, A. R. (1994). *Descartes' Error*. Random House.

Davenport, H. (1902, May 5). *"Kill everyone over ten."—Gen. Jacob H. Smith*. Theodore Roosevelt Papers. Library of Congress Manuscript Division. Retrieved from https://www.theodorerooseveltcenter.org/Research/Digital-Library/Record?libID=o274576

Delker, B. C., Smith, C. P., Rosenthal, M. N., Bernstein, R. E., & Freyd, J. J. (2018). When home is where the harm is: Family betrayal and posttraumatic outcomes in young adulthood. *Journal of Aggression, Maltreatment & Trauma, 27*(7), 720–743.

DeNavas-Walt, C., Proctor, B. D., & Smith, J. C. (2012). *Income, poverty, and health insurance coverage in the United States: 2011* (Current Population Reports no. P60–243). US Census Bureau.

DePrince, A. P., & Freyd, J. J. (1999). Dissociative tendencies, attention, and memory. *Psychological Science, 10*, 449–452.

DePrince, A. P., & Freyd, J. J. (2002). The harm of trauma: Pathological fear, shattered assumptions, or betrayal? In J. Kauffman (Ed.), *Loss of the assumptive world: A theory of traumatic loss* (pp. 71–82). Brunner-Routledge.

Desai, L. (1999). Relational theory in a South Asian context: An example of the dynamics of identity development, Paper No. 86. Jean Baker Miller Training Institute at the Wellesley Centers for Women. https://www.wcwonline.org/vmfiles/86sc.pdf

Devers, K., Gray, B., Ramos, C., Shah, A., Blavin, F., & Waidmann, T. (2013). *The feasibility of using electronic health records (EHRs) and other electronic health data for research on small populations*. The Urban Institute. https://aspe.hhs.gov/system/files/pdf/107231/rpt_ehealthdata.pdf

Dewan, S. (2021, March 18). How racism and sexism intertwine to torment Asian American women. *The New York Times*. https://www.nytimes.com/2021/03/18/us/racism-sexism-atlanta-spa-shooting.html

DisOrient screening World Refugee Day: Q&A: Mu and the vanishing world [Video]. (2021). Eventive. https://muandvw_at_disorientfilm.eventive.org/resources#!

Đoàn, L. N., Takata, Y., Sakuma, K. K., & Irvin, V. L. (2019). Trends in clinical research including Asian American, Native Hawaiian, and Pacific Islander participants funded by the US National Institutes of Health, 1992 to 2018. *JAMA network open*, *2*(7), e197432. https://doi.org/10.1001/jamanetworkopen.2019.7432

Dorahy, M. J., Schultz, A., Wooller, M., Clearwater, K., & Yogeeswaran, K. (2021). Acute shame in response to dissociative detachment: Evidence from non-clinical and traumatised samples. *Cognition and Emotion*, 1–13.

DRUM—Desis Rising Up & Moving and the Community Development Project of the Urban Justice Center (2012). *Workers' rights are human rights: South Asian immigrant workers in New York City*. http://www.drumnyc.org/wp-content/themes/wpaid/images/wc-report.pdf

Dunn, D. S., & Andrews, E. E. (2015). Person-first and identity-first language: Developing psychologists' cultural competence using disability language. *American Psychologist*, *70*(3), 255.

Edwards, V. J., Freyd, J. J., Dube, S. R., Anda, R. F., & Felitti, V. J. (2012). Health outcomes by closeness of sexual abuse perpetrator: A test of betrayal trauma theory. *Journal of Aggression, Maltreatment & Trauma*, *21*, 133–148.

Eftekhari, A., Ruzek, J. I., Crowley, J. J., Rosen, C. S., Greenbaum, M. A., & Karlin, B. E. (2013). Effectiveness of national implementation of prolonged exposure therapy in veterans affairs care. *JAMA Psychiatry*, *70*(9), 949–955.

Ertel, K. A., Glymour, M. M., & Berkman, L. F. (2009). Social networks and health: A life course perspective integrating observational and experimental evidence. *Journal of Social and Personal Relationships*, *26*(1), 73–92.

Evans-Campbell, T. (2008). Historical trauma in American Indian / Native Alaska communities: A multilevel framework for exploring impacts on individuals, families, and communities. *Journal of Interpersonal Violence*, *23*(3), 316–338. https://doi.org/10.1177/0886260507312290

Everson-Rose, S. A., & Lewis, T. T. (2005). Psychosocial factors and cardiovascular diseases. *Annual Review of Public Health*, *26*, 469–500.

Felitti, V. J., Anda, R. F., Nordenberg, D., Williamson, D. F., Spitz, A. M., Edwards, V., Koss, M. P., & Marks, J. S. (1998). Relationship of childhood abuse and household dysfunction to many of the leading causes of death in adults. The Adverse Childhood Experiences (ACE) study. *American Journal of Preventive Medicine*, *14*(4), 245–258. https://doi.org/10.1016/s0749-3797(98)00017-8

Finkelhor, D., Turner, H. A., Shattuck, A., & Hamby, S. L. (2015). Prevalence of childhood exposure to violence, crime, and abuse: Results from the National Survey of Children's Exposure to Violence. *JAMA Pediatrics, 169*(8), 746–754.

Flückiger, C., Del Re, A. C., Wampold, B. E., & Horvath, A. O. (2018). The alliance in adult psychotherapy: A meta-analytic synthesis. *Psychotherapy, 55*(4), 316.

Flückiger, C., Del Re, A. C., Wampold, B. E., Symonds, D., & Horvath, A. O. (2012). How central is the alliance in psychotherapy? A multilevel longitudinal meta-analysis. *Journal of Counseling Psychology, 59*(1), 10.

Foynes, M. M., Murakami, J. M., Hall, G. C. N., & Freyd, J. J. (2007, August). *Trauma, ethnicity and psychopathology* [Conference presentation poster]. The 115th Annual Convention of the American Psychological Association, San Francisco, California, United States.

Foynes, M. M., Platt, M., Hall, G. C. N., & Freyd, J. J. (2014). The impact of Asian values and victim–perpetrator closeness on the disclosure of emotional, physical, and sexual abuse. *Psychological Trauma: Theory, Research, Practice, and Policy, 6*, 134–141.

Frey, L. L. (2013). Relational-cultural therapy: Theory, research, and application to counseling competencies. *Professional Psychology: Research and Practice, 44*(3), 177.

Freyd, J. J. (1996). *Betrayal trauma: The logic of forgetting childhood abuse.* Harvard University Press.

Freyd, J. J. (1997). Violations of power, adaptive blindness, and betrayal trauma theory. *Feminism and Psychology, 7*, 22–32.

Freyd, J. J. (2014). *Official campus statistics for sexual violence mislead* [Op-Ed]. Al Jazeera America. http://america.aljazeera.com/opinions/2014/7/college-campus-sexualassaultsafetydatawhitehousegender.html

Freyd, J. J. (2018, January 11). *When sexual assault victims speak out, their institutions often betray them.* The Conversation. https://theconversation.com/when-sexual-assault-victims-speak-out-their-institutions-often-betray-them-87050

Freyd, J. J. (2020). *What is a betrayal trauma? What is betrayal trauma theory?* Retrieved January 10, 2023 from http://pages.uoregon.edu/dynamic/jjf/defineBT.html

Freyd, J. J., & Birrell, P. (2013). *Blind to betrayal: Why we fool ourselves we aren't being fooled.* Wiley.

Freyd, J. J., DePrince, A. P., & Zurbriggen, E. L. (2001). Self-reported memory for abuse depends upon victim–perpetrator relationship. *Journal of Trauma & Dissociation, 2*(3), 5–17.

Freyd, J. J., Klest, B., & Allard, C. B. (2005). Betrayal trauma: Relationship to physical health, psychological distress, and a written disclosure intervention. *Journal of Trauma & Dissociation, 6*(3), 83–104.

Friedman, M. S., Marshal, M. P., Guadamuz, T. E., Wei, C., Wong, C. F., Saewyc, E. M., & Stall., R. (2011). A meta-analysis of disparities in childhood sexual abuse, parental physical abuse, and peer victimization among sexual minority and sexual nonminority individuals. *American Journal of Public Health, 101*(8), 1481–1494. doi: 10.2105/AJPH.2009.190009

Futa, K. T., Hsu, E., & Hansen, D. J. (2001). Child sexual abuse in Asian American families: An examination of cultural factors that influence prevalence, identification, and treatment. *Clinical Psychology, 8*, 189–209.

Gamache Martin, C., Van Ryzin, M. J., & Dishion, T. J. (2016). Profiles of childhood trauma: Betrayal, frequency, and psychological distress in late adolescence. *Psychological Trauma: Theory, Research, Practice, and Policy, 8*(2), 206.

Gao, G. (2016). *The challenges of polling Asian Americans.* Pew Research Center. https://www.pewresearch.org/fact-tank/2016/05/11/the-challenges-of-polling-asian-americans/

Garcia-Williams, A. G., Moffitt, L., & Kaslow, N. J. (2014). Mental health and suicidal behavior among graduate students. *Academic psychiatry, 38*(5), 554–560.

Geschwind, N., & Galaburda, A. M. (1987). *Cerebral lateralization: Biological mechanisms, associations, and pathology.* MIT Press.

Ghosh, A., & Pasupathi, M. (2016). Perceptions of students and parents on the use of corporal punishment at schools in India. *Rupkatha Journal on Interdisciplinary Studies in Humanities, 8*, 269–280. 10.21659/rupkatha.v8n3.28.

Giano, Z., Wheeler, D. L., & Hubach, R. D. (2020). The frequencies and disparities of adverse childhood experiences in the US. *BMC Public Health, 20*(1), 1–12.

Goldsmith, R. E., Barlow, M. R., & Freyd, J. J. (2004). Knowing and not knowing about trauma: Implications for therapy. *Psychotherapy: Theory, Research, Practice, Training, 41*, 448–463.

Goldsmith, R. E., Freyd, J. J., & DePrince, A. P. (2012). Betrayal trauma: Associations with psychological and physical symptoms in young adults. *Journal of Interpersonal Violence, 27*(3), 547–567.

Goldstein, E., Topitzes, J., Miller-Cribbs, J., & Brown, R. L. (2020). Influence of race/ethnicity and income on the link between adverse childhood experiences and child flourishing. *Pediatric Research, 89*, 1861–1869. https://doi.org/10.1038/s41390-020-01188-6

Gómez, J. M. (2012). *Cultural betrayal trauma theory: The impact of culture on the effects of trauma.* Retrieved from https://sites.google.com/site/betrayalbook/betrayal-research-news/cultural-betrayal

Gómez, J. M. (2015). Microaggressions and the enduring mental health disparity: Black Americans at risk for institutional betrayal. *Journal of Black Psychology, 41*(2), 121–143. https://doi.org/10.1177/0095798413514608

Gómez, J. M. (2017). Does ethno-cultural betrayal in trauma affect Asian American / Pacific Islander college students' mental health outcomes? An exploratory study. *Journal of American College Health, 65,* 432–436. doi: 10.1080/07448481.2017.1341896

Gómez, J. M. (2019). Group dynamics as a predictor of dissociation for Black victims of violence: An exploratory study of cultural betrayal trauma theory. *Transcultural Psychiatry, 56*(5), 878–894. https://doi.org/10.1177/1363461519847300

Gómez, J. M. (2021). Gendered sexual violence: Betrayal trauma, dissociation, and PTSD in diverse college students. *Journal of Aggression, Maltreatment & Trauma, 30*(5), 625–640.

Gómez, J. M., & Freyd, J. J. (2018). Psychological outcomes of within-group sexual violence: Evidence of cultural betrayal. *Journal of Immigrant & Minority Health, 20*, 1458–1467. https://doi.org/10.1007/s10903-017-0687-0

Gómez, J. M., & Freyd, J. J. (2019). *Betrayal trauma.* In J. J. Ponzetti (Ed.), *Macmillan encyclopedia of intimate and family relationships: An interdisciplinary approach* (pp. 79–82). Cengage Learning, Inc.

Gone, J. P. (2013). Redressing First Nations historical trauma: Theorizing mechanisms for indigenous culture as mental health treatment. *Transcultural Psychiatry, 50*(5), 683–706.

Gone, J. P. (2021). Decolonization as methodological innovation in counseling psychology: Method, power, and process in reclaiming American Indian therapeutic traditions. *Journal of Counseling Psychology, 68*(3), 259.

Haddock-Lazala, C. M. (2020). Urban liberation: Postcolonial intersectional feminism and developing a socially conscious therapeutic practice. In L. Comas-Díaz & E. Torres Rivera (Eds.), *Liberation psychology: Theory, method, practice, and social justice* (pp. 149–168). American Psychological Association. https://doi.org/10.1037/0000198-009

Harvey, M. R. (1996). An ecological view of psychological trauma and trauma recovery. *Journal of Traumatic Stress, 9*(1), 3–23.

Haynes, S. (2021, March 18). The Atlanta shooting highlights the painful reality of rising Anti-Asian violence around the world. *Time.* https://time.com/5947862/anti-asian-attacks-rising-worldwide/

Heard-Garris, N. J., Cale, M., Camaj, L., Hamati, M. C., & Dominguez, T. P. (2018). Transmitting trauma: A systematic review of vicarious racism and child health. *Social Science & Medicine, 199*, 230–240.

Helms, J. E. (2012). A legacy of eugenics underlies racial-group comparisons in intelligence testing. *Industrial and Organizational Psychology, 5*(2), 176–179.

Herman, J. (1992). Complex PTSD: A syndrome in survivors of prolonged and repeated trauma. *Journal of Traumatic Stress, 5*(3), 377–391.

Herman, J. (2015). *Trauma and recovery.* Basic Books. (Original work published in 1992.)

Herman, J. L. (2011). Posttraumatic stress disorder as a shame disorder. In R. L. Dearing & J. P. Tangney (Eds.), *Shame in the therapy hour* (pp. 261–275). American Psychological Association. https://doi.org/10.1037/12326-011

Herman, J. L. (2018). Shattered shame states and their repair. In J. Yellin & K. White (Eds.), *Shattered states* (pp. 157–170). Routledge.

Heylighen, F. (2006). *The Newtonian world view.* Principia Cybernetica Web. http://pespmc1.vub.ac.be/NEWTONWV.html#:~:text=The%20world%20view%20underlying%20traditional,reflection%2Dcorrespondence%20view%20of%20knowledge

Ho, D. Y. F. (1999). Relational counseling: An Asian perspective on therapeutic intervention. *Psychological Test and Assessment Modeling, 41*(1/2), 98.

Hong, C. P. (2020). *Minor feelings: An Asian American reckoning.* One World.

Hook, J. N., Farrell, J. E., Davis, D. E., DeBlaere, C., Van Tongeren, D. R., & Utsey, S. O. (2016). Cultural humility and racial microaggressions in counseling. *Journal of Counseling Psychology, 63*(3), 269–277. https://doi.org/10.1037/cou0000114

Human Rights Watch (2020). *COVID-19 fueling anti-Asian racism and xenophobia worldwide.* https://www.hrw.org/news/2020/05/12/covid-19-fueling-anti-asian-racism-and-xenophobia-worldwide#

Hutton, L. E. (2011). *A new praxis: Exploring class-based microaggressions and the application of relational-cultural theory and liberation psychology in social work practice and research* [Unpublished master's thesis]. Smith College School for Social Work. https://scholarworks.smith.edu/theses/1043

Ima, K., & Hohm, C. (1991). Child maltreatment among Asian and Pacific Islander refugees and immigrants. *Journal of Interpersonal Violence, 6,* 267–285.

Indersmitten, T., & Gur, R. C. (2003). Emotion processing in chimeric faces: Hemispheric asymmetries in expression and recognition of emotions. *The Journal of Neuroscience: The Official Journal of the Society for Neuroscience, 23*(9), 3820–3825. https://doi.org/10.1523/JNEUROSCI.23-09-03820.2003

Inside the numbers: How immigration shapes Asian American and Pacific Islanders communities (Report). (2019). Asian Americans Advancing Justice. https://www.advancingjustice-aajc.org/sites/default/files/2019-06/1153_AAJC_Immigration_Final_Pages_LR-compressed.pdf

Itin, B. (n.d.). *Statistically, Asians in the USA outperform Whites at every resolvable metrics . . .* [Comment on Facebook post by Róisín, F., *The not-so model minority.* The Juggernaut.]. *Facebook.* Retrieved August 25, 2021.

Iwamasa, G. Y., Hsia, C., & Hinton, D. (2019). Cognitive behavior therapy with Asian Americans. In G. Y. Iwamasa & P. A. Hays (Eds.), *Culturally responsive cognitive behavior therapy: Practice and supervision* (pp. 129–159). American Psychological Association. https://doi.org/10.1037/0000119-006

Izard, C. E., Libero, Z., Putnam, P., & Haynes, O. M. (1993). Stability of emotion experiences and their relations to traits of personality. *Journal of Personality and Social Psychology, 64,* 847–860.

Jackman, J. (2018, April 11). *The meme account hilariously exposing creepy Asian fetish guys on tinder.* Vice. https://www.vice.com/en/article/kzxpdn/fleshlight-chronicles-asian-fetish-tinder-memes

Jensen, B. T. (2007). Understanding immigration and psychological development: A multilevel ecological approach. *Journal of Immigrant & Refugee Studies, 5*(4), 27–48.

Jeung, R., Yellow Horse, A. J., Chen, T., Saw, A., Tang, B., Lo., A., Ro, M., Schweng, L., Krishnamurthy, S., Chan, W., Chu, & M., Cho, C. (2022). *Anti-Asian hate, social isolation, and mental health among Asian American elders during COVID-19.* Stop AAPI Hate. https://stopaapihate.org/wp-content/uploads/2022/05/SAH-Elder-Report-526.pdf

Johnson, N., Archibald, P., Estreet, A., & Morgan, A. (2021). The cost of being Black in social work practicum. *Advances in Social Work, 21*(2/3), 331–353.

Jones, G. (2012). *Honor in the dust.* Berkley.

Jones, M. (2015, January 14). Why a generation of adoptees is returning to South Korea. *New York Times Magazine*. https://www.nytimes.com/2015/01/18/magazine/why-a-generation-of-adoptees-is-returning-to-south-korea.html

Jordan, J. V. (2000). The role of mutual empathy in relational/cultural therapy. *Journal of Clinical Psychology*, *56*(8), 1005–1016.

Jordan, J. V. (2001). A relational-cultural model: Healing through mutual empathy. *Bulletin of the Menninger Clinic*, *65*(1: Special issue), 92–103.

Jordan, J. V. (2010). Relational-cultural therapy. In M. Kopala & M. Keitel (Eds.), *Handbook of counseling women* (pp. 63–73). SAGE Publications.

Jordan, J. V. (Ed.). (2013). *The power of connection: Recent developments in relational-cultural theory*. Routledge.

Jordan, J. V. (2018). *Relational-cultural therapy* (2nd ed.). American Psychological Association.

Jordan, J. V., & Walker, M. (2004). Introduction. In J. V. Jordan, L. M. Hartling, & M. Walker (Eds.). *The complexity of connection: Writings from the Stone Center's Jean Baker Miller training institute*. Guilford Press.

Kalton, G. (2009). Methods for oversampling rare subpopulations in social surveys. *Survey Methodology*, *35*(2), 125–141.

Kambhampaty, M. (2020, May 22). In 1968, these activists coined the term "Asian American"—and helped shape decades of advocacy. *Time*. https://time.com/5837805/asian-american-history/

Kang, J. C. (2021, February 3). The many lives of Steven Yeun. *The New York Times*. https://www.nytimes.com/2021/02/03/magazine/steven-yeun.html

Kaur, S. (2021, October 26). Part two of disabilities in focus: Punjabi and Sikh communities. *Baaz*. https://www.baaznews.org/p/accessibility-sikh-spaces-disabilities-in-focus

Keilin, W. G., Aosved, A. C., Ponce, A. N., & Self, M. M. (2022). Balancing the imbalance: An examination of recent changes in psychology doctoral internship supply and demand. *Training and Education in Professional Psychology*, *16*(1), 1–9. https://doi.org/10.1037/tep0000357

Keltner, D., & Harker, L. (1998). The forms and functions of the nonverbal signal of shame. In P. Gilbert & B. Andrews (Eds.), *Shame: Interpersonal behavior, psychopathology, and culture* (pp. 78–98). Oxford University Press.

Kenny, M. C., & McEachern, A. G. (2000). Racial, ethnic, and cultural factors of childhood sexual abuse: A selected review of the literature. *Clinical Psychology Review*, *20*(7), 905–922.

Khúc, M. (2021, June 18). *Decolonizing mental health: Diagnosing our collective unwellness* [Webinar]. Chicago Minds.

Kiecolt-Glaser, J. K., McGuire, L., Robles, T. F., & Glaser, R. (2002). Emotions, morbidity, and mortality: New perspectives from psychoneuroimmunology. *Annual Review of Psychology*, *53*, 83–107.

Kim, H. J., Park, E., Storr, C. L., Tran, K., & Juon, H-S. (2015). Depression among Asian-American Adults in the community: Systematic review and meta-analysis. *PLoS One 10*(6): e0127760. https://doi.org/10.1371/journal.pone.0127760

Kim, J. (January 15, 2023). *Indiana's Asian American community is grieving after a bus stabbing attack.* National Public Radio. https://www.npr.org/2023/01/14/1149273748/bus-stabbing-indiana-university-student-asian-hate-crimes

Kim, Y. (2021, November 10). *All eyes on Suni Lee.* POPSUGAR Fitness. https://www.popsugar.com/node/48564671

Kirsch, I. (2009). *The emperor's new drugs: Exploding the antidepressant myth.* Bodley Head.

Kirsch, I., Deacon, B. J., Huedo-Medina, T. B., Scoboria, A., Moore, T. J., & Johnson, B. T. (2008). Initial severity and antidepressant benefits: A meta-analysis of data submitted to the Food and Drug Administration. *PLoS Medicine, 5,* e45 doi: 10.1371/journal.pmed.0050045

Knoll, C. (2021, September 21). A family, a dream and a season of fear. *The New York Times.* https://www.nytimes.com/2021/09/21/nyregion/than-than-htwe-death.html

Kochnar, R., & Cilluffo, A. (2018, July 12). *Income inequality in the U.S. is rising most rapidly among Asians.* Pew Research Center. https://www.pewsocialtrends.org/2018/07/12/income-inequality-in-the-u-s-is-rising-most-rapidly-among-asians/

Kogawa, J. (1994). *Obasan.* Anchor.

Koreatown Immigrant Workers Alliance (n.d.). *A just economy for all.* https://kiwa.org/a-just-economy

Krieger, N., Rowley, D., Hermann, A. A., Avery, B., & Phillips, M. T. (1993). Racism, sexism and social class: Implications for studies of health, disease, and well-being. *American Journal of Preventive Medicine, 9,* 82–122.

Kumar, V. (2014). Inequality in India: Caste and Hindu social order. *Transcience, 5*(1) 36–52.

LAAUNCH (2021). *STAATUS Index report 2021.* https://uploads-ssl.webflow.com/5f629e7e013d961943d5cec9/6098a7be3d627168e03054da_staatus-index-2021.pdf

Lai, D. W., & Surood, S. (2008). Predictors of depression in aging South Asian Canadians. *Journal of Cross-Cultural Gerontology, 23*(1), 57–75.

Lee, E. (2015). *The making of Asian America: A history.* Simon & Schuster.

Lee, E. J., Chan, F., Ditchman, N., & Feigon, M. (2014). Factors influencing Korean international students' preferences for mental health professionals: A conjoint analysis. *Community Mental Health Journal, 50*(1), 104–110.

Lee, J. (2014, October 2). *Why Asian American parents don't spank their kids.* The Society Pages. https://thesocietypages.org/socimages/2014/10/02/why-asian-american-parents-dont-spank-their-kids/

Lee, J. (2021). Asian Americans, affirmative action & the rise in anti-Asian hate. *Daedalus, 150,* 180–198.

Lee, J. (2022, October 11). *Are Asian Americans people of color or the next in line to become White?* Brookings. https://www.brookings.edu/blog/how-we-rise/2022/10/11/are-asian-americans-people-of-color-or-the-next-in-line-to-become-white/

Lee, J., & Choi, M. J. (2018). Childhood shadows: Psychological distress of childhood maltreatment among Asian-American women. *Journal of Child and Family Studies, 27*(9), 2954–2965.

Lee, J., & Zhou, M. (2015). *The Asian American achievement paradox*. Russell Sage Foundation.

Lee, S., Juon, H. S., Martinez, G., Hsu, C. E., Robinson, E. S., Bawa, J., & Ma, G. X. (2009). Model minority at risk: Expressed needs of mental health by Asian American young adults. *Journal of community health, 34*, 144–152.

Lee, S., & Waters, S. F. (2021). Asians and Asian Americans' experiences of racial discrimination during the COVID-19 pandemic: Impacts on health outcomes and the buffering role of social support. *Stigma and Health, 6*(1), 70–78. https://doi.org/10.1037/sah0000275

Lekas, H. M., Pahl, K., & Fuller Lewis, C. (2020). Rethinking cultural competence: Shifting to cultural humility. *Health services insights, 13*, 1178632920970580. https://doi.org/10.1177/1178632920970580

Lelund, J. (2011, September 16). For adoptive parents, questions without answers. *The New York Times*. https://www.nytimes.com/2011/09/18/nyregion/chinas-adoption-scandal-sends-chills-through-families-in-united-states.html

Lenz, A. S. (2016). Relational-cultural theory: Fostering the growth of a paradigm through empirical research. *Journal of Counseling & Development, 94*(4), 415–428.

Leong, F. T. (1986). Counseling and psychotherapy with Asian-Americans: Review of the literature. *Journal of Counseling Psychology, 33*(2), 196.

Leong, F., Park, Y. S., & Kalibatseva, Z. (2013). Disentangling immigrant status in mental health: Psychological protective and risk factors among Latino and Asian American immigrants. *American Journal of Orthopsychiatry, 83*(2–3), 361–371. https://doi.org/10.1111/ajop.12020

Leskela, J., Dieperink, M., & Thuras, P. (2002). Shame and posttraumatic stress disorder. *Journal of Traumatic Stress: Official Publication of the International Society for Traumatic Stress Studies, 15*(3), 223–226.

Lester, K., Artz, C., Resick, P. A., & Young-Xu, Y. (2010). Impact of race on early treatment termination and outcomes in posttraumatic stress disorder treatment. *Journal of Consulting and Clinical Psychology, 78*(4), 480.

Levin, B. (2021). *Report to the nation: Anti-Asian prejudice & hate crime*. Center for the Study of Hate and Extremism CSUSB.

Lew, K. M. (2016). Incarceration, identity and resilience: understanding the long-term psychological impacts of racial trauma on Japanese Americans who were imprisoned during World War II. [Master's Thesis, Smith College]. https://scholarworks.smith.edu/theses/1756

Lewis, H. B. (1990). Shame, repression, field dependence, and psychopathology. In J. L. Singer (Ed.), *Repression and dissociation: Implications for personality theory, psychopathology and health* (pp. 233–257). University of Chicago Press.

Lew-Williams, B. (2018). *The Chinese must go*. Harvard University Press.

Lim, D. (2021, August 7). *Asian American runner dragged, bitten in San Francisco's Pacific Heights*. ABC7 San Francisco. https://abc7news.com/pacific-heights-woman-bitten-asian-attacked-sf-dragged-runner/10938084/

Lin, L., Stamm, K., & Christidis, P. (2018). How diverse is the psychology workforce? *Monitor on Psychology, 49*(2), 19.

Lin, R. (2020, December 31). Coronavirus has besieged Filipino, Vietnamese Americans in Bay area. *Los Angeles Times*. https://www.latimes.com/california/story/2020-12-31/filipino-vietnamese-americans-coronavirus-silicon-valley

Litam, S. D. A., & Oh, S. (2021). Effects of COVID-19–Related racial discrimination on depression and life satisfaction among young, middle, and older Chinese Americans. *Adultspan Journal, 20*(2), 70–84.

Liu, L. (2011). Social connections, diabetes mellitus, and risk of mortality among White and African-American adults aged 70 and older: An eight-year follow-up study. *Annals of epidemiology, 21*(1), 26–33. https://doi.org/10.1016/j.annepidem.2010.10.012

Liu, Y., Elliott, A., Strelnick, H., Aguilar-Gaxiola, S., & Cottler, L. B. (2019). Asian Americans are less willing than other racial groups to participate in health research. *Journal of Clinical and Translational Science, 3*(2–3), 90–96. https://doi.org/10.1017/cts.2019.372

Lombardo, P. A., & Dorr, G. M. (2006). Eugenics, medical education, and the public health service: Another perspective on the Tuskegee syphilis experiment. *Bulletin of the History of Medicine*, 291–316.

Lorenz, H. S., & Watkins, M. (2001). Silenced knowings, forgotten springs: Paths to healing in the wake of colonialism. *Radical Psychology, 2*(2), 1–19.

Lowe, S. M., Okubo, Y., & Reilly, M. F. (2012). A qualitative inquiry into racism, trauma, and coping: Implications for supporting victims of racism. *Professional Psychology: Research and Practice, 43*(3), 190.

Lucente Sterling, A. (2022, March 1). *How elderly Asians are coping amid rise of anti-Asian incidents.* Spectrum News NY1. https://www.ny1.com/nyc/all-boroughs/news/2022/03/01/how-elderly-asians-are-coping-amid-rise-of-anti-asian-incidents

Luo, T. (2000). "Marrying My Rapist?!": The cultural trauma among Chinese rape survivors. *Gender and Society, 14*(4), 581–597. Retrieved August 12, 2021, from http://www.jstor.org/stable/190303

Ma, P. W. W., & Lan, M. Y. (2022). Marginalized identities, family conflict, and psychological distress: The process of psychotherapy with a Chinese American adolescent. *Asian American Journal of Psychology, 13*(2), 168.

Maguire-Jack, K., Lanier, P., & Lombardi, B. (2020). Investigating racial differences in clusters of adverse childhood experiences. *American Journal of Orthopsychiatry, 90*(1), 106–114.

Maker, A. H., Shah, P. V., & Agha, Z. (2005). Child physical abuse: Prevalence, characteristics, predictors, and beliefs about parent–child violence in South Asian, Middle Eastern, East Asian, and Latina women in the United States. *Journal of Interpersonal Violence, 20*(11), 1406–1428. https://doi.org/10.1177/0886260505278713

Mar, D., & Ong, P. (2020). *COVID-19 employment disruptions to Asian Americans.* UCLA Center for Neighborhood Knowledge, the UCLA Asian American Studies Center, and Ong and Associates. http://www.aasc.ucla.edu/resources/policyreports/COVID19_Employment_CNK-AASC_072020.pdf

Marcello, R. K., Dolle, J., Tariq, A., Kaur, S., Wong, L., Curcio, J., Thachil, R., Yi, S. S., & Islam, N. (2020, November 24). Disaggregating Asian race reveals CO-

VID-19 disparities among Asian Americans at New York City's public hospital system. *medRxiv*. doi: https://doi.org/10.1101/2020.11.23.20233155

Martín-Baró, I. (1996). *Writings for a liberation psychology* (Kindle edition; A. Aron & S. Corne, Eds.). Harvard University Press.

Martz, C. D., Allen, A. M., Fuller-Rowell, T. E., Spears, E. C., Lim, S. S., Drenkard, C., Hunter, E. A., & Chae, D. H. (2019). Vicarious racism stress and disease activity: The Black women's experiences living with lupus (BeWELL) study. *Journal of Racial and Ethnic Health Disparities, 6*(5), 1044–1051.

Maton, K. I., Wimms, H. E., Grant, S. K., Wittig, M. A., Rogers, M. R., & Vasquez, M. J. (2011). Experiences and perspectives of African American, Latina/o, Asian American, and European American psychology graduate students: A national study. *Cultural Diversity & Ethnic Minority Psychology, 17*(1), 68–78. https://doi. org/10.1037/a0021668

Mehnert, A., Lehmann, C., Graefen, M., Huland, H., & Koch, U. (2010). Depression, anxiety, post–traumatic stress disorder and health–related quality of life and its association with social support in ambulatory prostate cancer patients. *European Journal of Cancer Care, 19*(6), 736–745.

Menakem, R. (2020, June 4). *On being with Krista Tippett.* https://onbeing.org/programs/resmaa-menakem-notice-the-rage-notice-the-silence/#transcript

Merrick, M. T., Ford, D. C., Ports, K. A., Guinn, A. S., Chen, J., Klevens, J., Metzler, M., Jones, C. M., Simon, T. R., Daniel, V. M., Ottley, P., & Mercy, J. A. (2019). Vital Signs: Estimated proportion of adult health problems attributable to adverse childhood experiences and implications for prevention—25 states, 2015–2017. *MMWR Morbidity and Mortality Weekly Report, 68*, 999–1005. https://doi. org/10.15585/mmwr.mm6844e1

Meston, C. M., Heiman, J. R., Trapnell, P. D., & Carlin, A. S. (1999). Ethnicity, desirable responding, and self-reports of abuse: A comparison of European- and Asian-ancestry undergraduates. *Journal of Consulting and Clinical Psychology, 67*, 139–144.

Meyer, M. (2021, May 13). *Coalition calls for hate crime probe in John Huynh murder.* Northwest Asian Weekly. http://nwasianweekly.com/2021/05/coalition-calls-for-hate-crime-probe-in-john-huynh-murder/

Meyer, O., Zane, N., & Cho, Y. I. (2011). Understanding the psychological processes of the racial match effect in Asian Americans. *Journal of Counseling Psychology, 58*(3).

Miles, J. R., & Fassinger, R. E. (2021). Creating a public psychology through a scientist-practitioner-advocate training model. *American Psychologist, 76*(8), 1232.

Miles, S. R., & Thompson, K. E. (2016). Childhood trauma and posttraumatic stress disorder in a real-world veterans affairs clinic: Examining treatment preferences and dropout. *Psychological Trauma: Theory, Research, Practice, and Policy, 8*, 464–467. http://dx.doi.org/10.1037/ tra0000132

Milkman, R., González, A., & Narro, V. (2010). *Wage theft and workplace violations in Los Angeles: The failure of employment and labor law for low-wage workers.* UCLA: Institute for Research on Labor and Employment. Retrieved from https:// escholarship.org/uc/item/5jt7n9gx

Miller, J. B., & Stiver, I. (1997). *The healing connection: How women form relationships in therapy and in life.* Beacon Press.

Millner, U. C., Maru, M., Ismail, A., & Chakrabarti, U. (2021). Decolonizing mental health *American Journal of Psychology, 12*(4), 333–345. https://doi.org/10.1037/aap0000268

Moghal, N. E., Nota, I. K., & Hobbs, C. J. (1995). A study of sexual abuse in an Asian community. *Archives of Disease in Childhood, 72*(4), 346–347. https://doi.org/10.1136/adc.72.4.346

Mott, J. M., Mondragon, S., Hundt, N. E., Beason-Smith, M., Grady, R. H., & Teng, E. J. (2014). Characteristics of U.S. veterans who begin and complete prolonged exposure and cognitive processing therapy for PTSD. *J Trauma Stress 2014, 27,* 265–73.

Murray, E. (2021, May 2). Vermonters speak out. *Burlington Free Press.*

Nadal, K. L. (2011). The racial and ethnic microaggressions scale (REMS): Construction, reliability, and validity. *Journal of Counseling Psychology, 58*(4), 470.

Nadal, K. L., Griffin, K. E., Wong, Y., Davidoff, K. C., & Davis, L. S. (2017). The injurious relationship between racial microaggressions and physical health: Implications for social work. *Journal of Ethnic & Cultural Diversity in Social Work, 26*(1–2), 6–17.

Nadal, K. L., Griffin, K. E., Wong, Y., Hamit, S., & Rasmus, M. (2014). The impact of racial microaggressions on mental health: Counseling implications for clients of color. *Journal of Counseling & Development, 92*(1), 57–66.

Nadal, K. L., Wong, Y., Griffin, K. E., Davidoff, K., & Sriken, J. (2014). The adverse impact of racial microaggressions on college students' self-esteem. *Journal of College Student Development, 55*(5), 461–474.

Naeem, F., Phiri, P., Rathod, S., & Kingdon, D. (2010). Using CBT with diverse patients: Working with South Asian Muslims. *Oxford guide to surviving as a CBT therapist, 41,* 41–56. https://doi.org/10.1093/med:psych/9780199561308.003.0002

Nagata, D. K., Kim, J. H. J., & Nguyen, T. U. (2015). Processing cultural trauma: Intergenerational effects of the Japanese American incarceration. *Journal of Social Issues,* 71(2), 356–370. https://doi.org/10.1111/josi.12115

Najarro, I. (2022, October 28). *States are mandating Asian American studies. What should the curriculum look like?* Education Week. https://www.edweek.org/teaching-learning/states-are-mandating-asian-american-studies-what-should-the-curriculum-look-like/2022/10

Najavits, L. M. (2015). The problem of dropout from "gold standard" PTSD therapies. *F1000prime reports, 7,* 43.

National Association of Social Workers. (2021). *Code of ethics of the National Association of Social Workers.* https://www.socialworkers.org/About/Ethics/Code-of-Ethics/Code-of-Ethics-English

National Center on Child Abuse and Neglect. (1999). *Child maltreatment 1997: Reports from the states to the National Child Abuse and Neglect data system.* US Government Printing Office. https://www.acf.hhs.gov/sites/default/files/documents/cb/child_maltreatment_1997.pdf

National Science Foundation, National Center for Science and Engineering Statistics (n.d.). *Survey of earned doctorates*. https://ncses.nsf.gov/pubs/nsf23300/data-tables

Neville, H. A., & Heppner, M. J. (1999). Contextualizing rape: Reviewing sequelae and proposing a culturally inclusive ecological model of sexual assault recovery. *Applied & Preventive Psychology*, *8*(1), 41–62. https://doi.org/10.1016/S0962-1849(99)80010-9

Neville, H. A., Oh, E., Spanierman, L. B., Heppner, M. J., & Clark, M. (2004). General and culturally specific factors influencing Black and White rape survivors' self-esteem. *Psychology of Women Quarterly*, *28*(1), 83–94.

Neville, H. A., Ruedas-Gracia, N., Lee, B. A., Ogunfemi, N., Maghsoodi, A. H., Mosley, D. V., LaFramboise, T. D., & Fine, M. (2021). The public psychology for liberation training model: A call to transform the discipline. *American Psychologist*, *76*(8), 1248.

Nguyen-Ngo, M. (2020, June 2). *Addressing labor exploitation: An examination of undocumented Asian Americans in the workplace.* Asian American Policy Review. Retrieved from: https://aapr.hkspublications.org/2020/06/02/addressing-labor-exploitation-an-examination-of-undocumented-asian-americans-in-the-workplace/

Nicholls, A. R., Fairs, L. R. W., Toner, J., Jones, L., Mantis, C., Barkoukis, V., Perry, J. L., Micle, A. V., Theodorou, N. C., Shakhverdieva S., Stoicescu, M., Vesic, M. V., Dikic, N., Andjelkovic, M., Grimau, E. G., Amigo, J. A., & Schomöller, A. (2021). Snitches get stitches and end up in ditches: A systematic review of the factors associated with whistleblowing intentions. *Frontiers in Psychology*, *12*. https://doi.org/10.3389/fpsyg.2021.631538

Nokes, R. G. (2009). *Massacred for gold: The Chinese in Hells Canyon*. Oregon State University Press.

Office of Minority Health (n.d.). *Mental and behavioral health—Asian Americans*. https://minorityhealth.hhs.gov/omh/browse.aspx?lvl=4&lvlid=54

Okamura, A., Heras, P., & Wong-Kerberg, L. (1995). Asian, Pacific Island, and Filipino Americans and sexual child abuse. In L. A. Fontes (Ed.), *Sexual abuse in nine North American cultures: Treatment and prevention* (pp. 67–96). Sage.

O'Meara, K., Griffin, K. A., Kuvaeva, A., Nyunt, G., & Robinson, T. N. (2017). Sense of belonging and its contributing factors in graduate education. *International Journal of Doctoral Studies*, *12*, 251–279.

Omi, Y. (2019). Corporal punishment in extracurricular sports activities (bukatsu) represents an aspect of Japanese culture. In L. Tateo (Ed.), *Educational dilemmas: A cultural psychological perspective* (pp. 139–145). Routledge.

Owen, J., Drinane, J. M., Tao, K. W., DasGupta, D. R., Zhang, Y. S. D., & Adelson, J. (2018). An experimental test of microaggression detection in psychotherapy: Therapist multicultural orientation. *Professional Psychology: Research and Practice,* *49*(1), 9–21. https://doi.org/10.1037/pro0000152

Owen, J., Tao, K. W., Imel, Z. E., Wampold, B. E., & Rodolfa, E. (2014). Addressing racial and ethnic microaggressions in therapy. *Professional Psychology: Research and Practice*, *45*(4), 283.

Palmer, A., & Parish, J. (2008). Social justice and counselling psychology: Situating the role of graduate student research, education, and training. *Canadian Journal of Counselling, 42*(4), 278–292.

Paradies, Y. (2017). Racism and health. In S. R. Quah & W. C. Cockerham (Eds.), *The international encyclopedia of public health* (2nd ed., vol. 6, pp. 249–259). Academic Press.

Parascandola, R. (2021, November 11). Asian man beaten in NYC hate crime assault. *New York Daily News.* https://www.nydailynews.com/new-york/nyc-crime/ny-asian-hate-crime-nypd-20211111-aecbpvwss5dtnpemkeg22ndlx4-story.html

Park, M., Choi, Y., Yasui, M., Hedeker, D., & Specificity, Commonality, and Generalizability in Social–Emotional Development Special Section Editors. (2021). Racial discrimination and the moderating effects of racial and ethnic socialization on the mental health of Asian American youth. *Child Development, 92*(6), 2284–2298.

Parker, K., Horowitz, J. M., Morin, R., & Lopez, M. H. (2015, June 11). *Multiracial in America: Proud, diverse, and growing in numbers.* Pew Research Center. https://www.pewresearch.org/social-trends/2015/06/11/multiracial-in-america/

Parrish, J. W., Fleckman, J. M., Prindle, J. J., Eastman, A. L., & Weil, L. E. (2020). Measuring the incidence of child maltreatment using linked data: A two-state comparison. *American Journal of Preventive Medicine, 58*(4), e133–e140.

Pereda, N., Guilera, G., Forns, F., Gómez-Benito, J. (2009). The prevalence of child sexual abuse in community and student samples: A meta-analysis. *Clinical Psychology Review, 29*(4), 328–338.

Pew Research Center (2012, February 16). *The rise of intermarriage: Executive summary.* https://www.pewresearch.org/social-trends/2012/02/16/the-rise-of-intermarriage/

Pillai, D., Yellow Horse, A., & Jeung, R. (2021). *The rising tide of violence and discrimination against Asian American and Pacific Islander women and girls.* Stop AAPI Hate and National Asian Pacific American Women's Forum. https://stopaapihate.org/wp-content/uploads/2021/05/Stop-AAPI-Hate_NAPAWF_Whitepaper.pdf

Platonova, A., & Urso, G. (2013). Asian immigration to the European Union, United States and Canada: An initial comparison. *Journal of Global Policy and Governance, 1*, 143–156. https://doi.org/10.1007/s40320-012-0018-8

Platt, M., Barton, J., & Freyd, J. J. (2009). A betrayal trauma perspective on domestic violence. In E. Stark & E. S. Buzawa (Eds.), *Violence against women in families and relationships* (vol. 1, pp. 185–207). Greenwood Press.

Platt, M. G., & Freyd, J. J. (2015). Betray my trust, shame on me: Shame, dissociation, fear, and betrayal trauma. *Psychological Trauma: Theory, Research, Practice, and Policy, 7*(4), 398.

Platt, M. G., Luoma, J. B., & Freyd, J. J. (2017). Shame and dissociation in survivors of high and low betrayal trauma. *Journal of Aggression, Maltreatment & Trauma, 26*(1), 34–49.

Proctor, S. L., Kyle, J., Lau, C., Fefer, K., & Fischetti, J. (2016, September). Racial microaggressions and school psychology students: Who gets targeted and how intern supervisors can facilitate racial justice. In *School Psychology Forum, 10*(3).

Proctor, S. L., & Truscott, S. D. (2012). Reasons for African American student attrition from school psychology programs. *Journal of School Psychology, 50*(5), 655–679. https://doi.org/10.1016/j.jsp.2012.06.002

project 1907 (2021). *Reporting centre.* Retrieved December 28, 2021, from https://www.project1907.org/reportingcentre

Pyke, K. D. (2010). What is internalized racial oppression and why don't we study it? Acknowledging racism's hidden injuries. *Sociological Perspectives, 53*, 551–572.

Rao, K., DiClemente, R. J., & Ponton, L. E. (1992). Child sexual abuse of Asians compared with other populations. *Journal of the American Academy of Child and Adolescent Psychiatry, 31*, 880–886.

Ratts, M. J., Singh, A. A., Nassar–McMillan, S., Butler, S. K., & McCullough, J. R. (2015). *Multicultural and social justice counseling competencies.* American Counseling Organization. https://www.counseling.org/docs/default-source/competencies/multicultural-and-social-justice-counseling-competencies.pdf?sfvrsn=20

Ratts, M. J., Singh, A. A., Nassar–McMillan, S., Butler, S. K., & McCullough, J. R. (2016). Multicultural and social justice counseling competencies: Guidelines for the counseling profession. *Journal of Multicultural Counseling and Development, 44*(1), 28–48.

Read, J., Mosher, L. R., & Bentall, R. P. (Eds.). (2004). *Models of madness: Psychological, social and biological approaches to schizophrenia.* Psychology Press.

Reynolds, P., & Kaplan, G. A. (1990). Social connections and risk for cancer: Prospective evidence from the Alameda County Study. *Behavioral Medicine, 16*(3), 101–110.

Roberts, S. O., Bareket-Shavit, C., Dollins, F. A., Goldie, P. D., & Mortenson, E. (2020). Racial inequality in psychological research: Trends of the past and recommendations for the future. *Perspectives on Psychological Science: A Journal of the Association for Psychological Science, 15*(6), 1295–1309. https://doi.org/10.1177/1745691620927709

Robertson, H. A., Chaudhary Nagaraj, N., & Vyas, A. N. (2016). Family violence and child sexual abuse among South Asians in the US. *Journal of Immigrant Minority Health, 18*, 921–927. https://doi.org/10.1007/s10903-015-0227-8

Robinaugh, D. J., & McNally, R. J. (2010). Autobiographical memory for shame or guilt provoking events: Association with psychological symptoms. *Behaviour Research and Therapy, 48*(7), 646–652.

Robles, T. F., & Kiecolt-Glaser, J. K. (2003). The physiology of marriage: Pathways to health. *Physiology and Behavior, 79*, 409–416.

Róisín, F. (2019, June 7). The not-so-model minority. *The Juggernaut.* https://www.thejuggernaut.com/not-so-model-minority

Rosenthal, M. N., Smidt, A. M., & Freyd, J. J. (2016). Still second class: Sexual harassment of graduate students. *Psychology of Women Quarterly, 40*(3), 364–377.

Rothenberg, A. (1987). Empathy as a creative process in treatment. *International Review of Psycho-Analysis, 14*, 445–463.

Rummell, C. M. (2015). An exploratory study of psychology graduate student workload, health, and program satisfaction. *Professional Psychology: Research and Practice, 46*(6), 391–399. https://doi.org/10.1037/pro0000056

Sackett, C. R., & Jenkins, A. M. (2019). Utilizing relational cultural theory in addressing sexism in the counseling relationship. *Journal of Creativity in Mental Health*, *14*(4), 492–498.

Sacks, V., & Murphey, D. (2018). *The prevalence of adverse childhood experiences, nationally, by state, and by race or ethnicity*. Child Trends. https://www.childtrends.org/publications/prevalence-adverse-childhood-experiences-nationally-state-race-ethnicity.

Salter, M. D. (1940). *An evaluation of adjustment based upon the concept of security: Child development series*. University of Toronto Press.

Scheff, T. J. (2001). Shame and community: Social components in depression. *Psychiatry: Interpersonal and Biological Processes*, *64*(3), 212–224.

Schneider, M., Baker, S., & Stermac, L. (2002). Sexual harassment experiences of psychologists and psychological associates during their graduate school training. *Canadian Journal of Human Sexuality*, *11*.

Schoen, C., Davis, K., DesRoches, C., & Shekhdar, A. (1998). *The health of adolescent boys: Commonwealth fund survey findings*. The Commonwealth Fund.

Schore, A. N. (1994). *Affect regulation and the origin of the self: The neurobiology of emotional development*. Erlbaum.

Schore, A. N. (1998). Early shame experiences and infant brain development. In P. Gilbert & B. Andrews (Eds.), *Shame: interpersonal behavior, psychopathology, and culture* (pp. 57–77). Oxford University Press.

Schore, A. N. (2000). Attachment and the regulation of the right brain. *Attachment & Human Development*, *2*(1), 23–47.

Schweitzer, R., Melville, F., Steel, Z., & Lacherez, P. (2006). Trauma, post-migration living difficulties, and social support as predictors of psychological adjustment in resettled Sudanese refugees. *Australian & New Zealand Journal of Psychiatry*, *40*(2), 179–187.

Semrud-Clikeman, M., & Hynd, G. W. (1990). Right hemisphere dysfunction in nonverbal learning disabilities: Social, academic, and adaptive functioning in adults and children. *Psychological Bulletin*, *107*, 196–209.

Sen, A. K. (1982). *Poverty and famines: An essay on entitlements and deprivation*. Clarendon Press.

Shah, S., & Tewari, N. (2019). Cognitive behavior therapy with South Asian Americans. In G. Y. Iwamasa & P. A. Hays (Eds.), *Culturally responsive cognitive behavior therapy: Practice and supervision* (pp. 161–182). American Psychological Association. https://doi.org/10.1037/0000119-007

Shedler, J. (2020). Where is the evidence for "evidence-based" therapy? In M. Leuzinger-Bohleber, M. Solms, and S. E. Arnold (Eds.), *Outcome research and the future of psychoanalysis* (pp. 44–56). Routledge.

Shon, S. P., & Ja, D. Y. (1982). Asian families. *Ethnicity and Family Therapy*, *208*, 229.

Shyong, F. (2021, October 24). History forgot the 1871 Los Angeles Chinese massacre, but we've all been shaped by its violence. *Los Angeles Times*. https://www.latimes.com/california/story/2021-10-24/150th-anniversary-los-angeles-chinese-massacre

Siddiqui, K. (2017). The Bolshevik Revolution and the collapse of the colonial system in India. *International Critical Thought, 7*(3), 418–437. Routledge Taylor & Francis. doi.org/10.1080/21598282.2017.1355743.

Siddiqui, K. (2020, July 30). *The political economy of famines during the British rule in India: A critical analysis.* The World Financial Review. https://worldfinancialreview.com/the-political-economy-of-famines-during-the-british-rule-in-india-a-critical-analysis/

Sieben, A., Lust, K., Crose, A., Renner, L. M., & Nguyen, R. H. N. (2019a). Race and sex differences in adverse childhood experiences among Asian/Pacific Islander college students. *Journal of American College Health, 69*(4), 353–360. doi: 10.1080/07448481.2019.1677671

Sieben, A., Renner, L. M., Lust, K., Vang, W., & Nguyen, R. H. N. (2019b). Adverse childhood experiences among Asian/Pacific Islander sexual minority college students. *Journal of Family Violence, 35*, 297–303. https://doi.org/10.1007/s10896-019-00095-7

Sieff, D. F. (2014). *Understanding and healing emotional trauma: Conversations with pioneering clinicians and researchers.* Routledge.

Siegel, D. J. (2006). An interpersonal neurobiology approach to psychotherapy: Awareness, mirror neurons, and neural plasticity in the development of well-being. *Psychiatric Annals, 36*(4), 248–256.

Singh, A. A., Appling, B., & Trepal, H. (2020). Using the multicultural and social justice counseling competencies to decolonize counseling practice: The important roles of theory, power, and action. *Journal of Counseling & Development, 98*(3), 261–271. https://doi.org/10.1002/jcad.12321

Slack, K. S., Font, S. A., & Jones, J. (2017). The complex interplay of adverse childhood experiences, race, and income. *Health & Social Work, 42*(1), e24–e31.

Slay, K. E., Reyes, K. A., & Posselt, J. R. (2019). Bait and switch: Representation, climate, and tensions of diversity work in graduate education. *The Review of Higher Education, 42*(5), 255–286.

Slopen, N., Shonkoff, J. P., Albert, M. A., Yoshikawa, H., Jacobs, A., Stoltz, R., & Williams, D. R. (2016). Racial disparities in child adversity in the U.S.: Interactions with family immigration history and income. *American Journal of Preventive Medicine, 50*(1), 47–56. https://doi.org/10.1016/j.amepre.2015.06.013

Smidt, A. M., Adams-Clark, A. A., & Freyd, J. J. (2023). Institutional courage buffers against institutional betrayal, protects employee health, and fosters organizational commitment following workplace sexual harassment. *PloS One, 18*(1), e0278830. https://doi.org/10.1371/journal.pone.0278830

Smith, C. P., & Freyd, J. J. (2013). Dangerous safe havens: Institutional betrayal exacerbates sexual trauma. *Journal of Traumatic Stress, 26*, 119–124.

Smith, C. P., & Freyd, J. J. (2017). Insult, then injury: Interpersonal and institutional betrayal linked to health and association. *Journal of Aggression, Maltreatment, & Trauma, 26*, 1117–1131. doi: 10.1080/10926771.2017.1322654

Spencer, M., Chen, J., Gee, G., Fabian, C., & Takeuchi, D. (2010). Discrimination and mental health-related service use in a national study of Asian Americans. *American Journal of Public Health, 100*(12), 2410–2417.

Stadter, M., & Jun, G. (2020). Shame East and West: Similarities, differences, culture, and self. *Psychoanalysis and Psychotherapy in China, 3*(1), 1–21.

Statistics Canada (2019). *Family matters: Adults living with their parents.* https://www150.statcan.gc.ca/n1/daily-quotidien/190215/dq190215a-eng.htm

Steele, C. (2018). *Stereotype threat and African-American student achievement.* Routledge.

Steele, C. M., & Aronson, J. (1995). Stereotype threat and the intellectual test performance of African Americans. *Journal of Personality and Social Psychology, 69*(5), 797.

Steenkamp, M. M., Litz, B. T., & Marmar, C. R. (2020). First-line psychotherapies for military-related PTSD. *JAMA, 323*(7), 656–657.

Steenkamp, M. M., Litz, B. T., Hoge, C. W., & Marmar, C. R. (2015). Psychotherapy for military-related PTSD: A review of randomized clinical trials. *JAMA, 314*(5), 489–500.

Stiver, I. P., Rosen, W., Surrey, J., & Miller, J. B. (2008). Creative moments in relational-cultural therapy. *Women & Therapy, 31*(2–4), 7–29.

Stoltenborgh, M., van IJzendoorn, M. H., Euser, E. M., & Bakermans-Kranenburg, M. J. (2011). A global perspective on child sexual abuse: Meta-analysis of prevalence around the world. *Child Maltreatment, 16*(2), 79–101.

Syropoulos, S., Wu, D. J., Burrows, B., & Mercado, E. (2021). Psychology doctoral program experiences and student well-being, mental health, and optimism during the COVID-19 pandemic. *Frontiers in Psychology,* 4035.

Sue, D. W. (2015). *Race talk and the conspiracy of silence: Understanding and facilitating difficult dialogues on race.* John Wiley & Sons, Inc.

Sue, D. W., Arredondo, P., & McDavis, R. J. (1992). Multicultural counseling competencies and standards: A call to the profession. *Journal of Counseling & Development, 70*(4), 477–486.

Sue, D. W., Bucceri, J., Lin, A. I., Nadal, K. L., & Torino, G. C. (2007). Racial microaggressions and the Asian American experience. *Cultural Diversity and Ethnic Minority Psychology, 13*(1), 72.

Sue, D. W., Capodilupo, C. M., Nadal, K. L., & Torino, G. C. (2008). Racial microaggressions and the power to define reality. *American Psychologist, 63*(4), 277–279. https://doi.org/10.1037/0003-066X.63.4.277

Sue, D. W., Capodilupo, C. M., Torino, G. C., Bucceri, J. M., Holder, A. M., Nadal, K. L., & Esquilin, M. (2007). Racial microaggressions in everyday life: Implications for clinical practice. *American Psychologist, 62*(4), 271.

Sue, D. W., & Sue, D. (1990). *Counseling the culturally different: Theory and practice.* Wiley.

Sue, S., & Morishima, J. K. (1982). *The mental health of Asian Americans.* Jossey-Bass.

Sue, S., Sue, D. W., Sue, L., & Takeuchi, D. T. (1995). Psychopathology among Asian Americans: A model minority? *Cultural Diversity and Mental Health, 1*(1), 39.

Sznycer, D., Tooby, J., Cosmides, L., Porat, R., Shalvi, S., & Halperin, E. (2016). Shame closely tracks the threat of devaluation by others, even across cultures. *Proceedings of the National Academy of Sciences, 113*(10), 2625–2630.

Tang, S. S. S. (2009). *Social context in traumatic stress: Gender, ethnicity, and betrayal.* University of Oregon.

Tang, S. S., & Freyd, J. J. (2012). Betrayal trauma and gender differences in post-traumatic stress. *Psychological Trauma: Theory, Research, Practice, and Policy, 4*, 469–478.

Tang, T., & Fingerhut, H. (2021, May 26). *AP-NORC poll: More Americans believe anti-Asian hate rising.* AP News. https://apnews.com/article/donald-trump-el-paso-texas-mass-shooting-racial-injustice-health-coronavirus-pandemic-5e97feb8c-498cbf80718a62d164f8285

Tantillo, M., & Sanftner, J. L. (2010). Measuring perceived mutuality in women with eating disorders: The development of the connection-disconnection scale. *Journal of Nursing Measurement, 18*(2), 100–119.

Taylor, S. E., Welch, W. T., Kim, H. S., & Sherman, D. K. (2007). Cultural differences in the impact of social support on psychological and biological stress responses. *Psychological Science, 18*(9), 831–837. https://doi.org/10.1111/j.1467-9280.2007.01987.x

Teo, T. (2008). From speculation to epistemological violence in psychology: A Critical-hermeneutic reconstruction. *Theory & Psychology, 18*(1), 47–67. https://doi.org/10.1177/0959354307086922

Teo, T. (2010). What is epistemological violence in the empirical social sciences? *Social and Personality Psychology Compass, 4*(5), 295–303.

Thakore-Dunlap, U., & Van Velsor, P. (2014). Group counseling with South Asian immigrant high school girls: Reflections and commentary of a group facilitator. *Professional Counselor, 4*(5), 505–518.

Thalmayer, A. G., Toscanelli, C., & Arnett, J. J. (2021). The neglected 95% revisited: Is American psychology becoming less American? *American Psychologist, 76*(1), 116–129. https://doi.org/10.1037/amp0000622

Thoits, P. A. (2011). Mechanisms linking social ties and support to physical and mental health. *Journal of Health and Social Behavior, 52*(2), 145–161.

Todd, D. (2016, May 25). South Asian grandparents are eight times more likely to live with grandchildren. *Vancouver Sun.* https://vancouversun.com/opinion/columnists/south-asian-grandparents-eight-times-more-likely-to-live-with-grandchildren

Torres Rivera, E. (2020). Concepts of liberation psychology. In L. Comas-Díaz & E. Torres Rivera (Eds.), *Liberation psychology: Theory, method, practice, and social justice* (pp. 41–51). American Psychological Association. https://doi.org/10.1037/0000198-003

Trent, F., Dwiwardani, C., & Page, C. (2020). Factors impacting the retention of students of color in graduate programs: A qualitative study. *Training and Education in Professional Psychology, 15*(3), 219–229. https://doi.org/10.1037/tep0000319

Two years and thousands of voices: What community-generated data tells us about anti-AAPI hate (National Report). (2022). Stop AAPI Hate. https://stopaapihate.org/wp-content/uploads/2022/07/Stop-AAPI-Hate-Year-2-Report.pdf

Umberson, D., & Montez, J. K. (2010). Social relationships and health: A flashpoint for health policy. *Journal of Health and Social Behavior, 51*(Suppl), S54–S66. https://doi.org/10.1177/0022146510383501

Unconscious bias. (n.d.). Elsevier. Retrieved April 27, 2022, from https://www.else-vier.com/open-science/science-and-society/unconscious-bias

US Census Bureau, American Community Survey (2019). ACS Demographic and Housing Estimates (DP05). https://data.census.gov/cedsci/table?q=Race%20 and%20Ethnicity&t=Race%20and%20Ethnicity&tid=ACSDP1Y2019. DP05&hidePreview=false

US Department of Health & Human Services, Administration for Children and Fami-lies, Administration on Children, Youth and Families, Children's Bureau (2021). *Child maltreatment 2019.* https://www.acf.hhs.gov/cb/research-data-technology/ statistics-research/child-maltreatment

US Department of State—Bureau of Consular Affairs (n.d). *Adoption statistics*. Re-trieved 2021 from https://travel.state.gov/content/travel/en/Intercountry-Adoption/ adopt_ref/adoption-statistics-esri.html?wcmmode=disabled

Uyematsu, A. (1971). The emergence of yellow power in America. In A. Tachiki (Ed.), *Roots: An Asian American reader* (pp. 9–13). University of California Press.

Vaillant, G. E. (2012). *Triumphs of experience*. Harvard University Press.

Vaughan R. (2017). Oversampling in health surveys: Why, when, and how? *American Journal of Public Health*, *107*(8), 1214–1215. https://doi.org/10.2105/ AJPH.2017.303895

Venkatramen, S. (2021, December 9). *N.Y. enacts "groundbreaking" law to change how Asian American populations are counted.* NBC News. https://www.nbc-news.com/news/asian-america/new-york-state-disaggregate-data-asian-american-groups-rcna10237

Walker, M., & Rosen, W. B. (Eds.). (2004). *How connections heal: Stories from relational-cultural therapy*. Guilford Press.

Wampold, B. E., & Imel, Z. E. (2015). *The great psychotherapy debate: The evidence for what makes psychotherapy work*. Routledge.

Wan, X. (2020). Chinese students wary of studying in the United States. *Interna-tional Higher Education*, (101), 26–27. https://www.internationalhighereducation. net/api-v1/article/!/action/getPdfOfArticle/articleID/2886/productID/29/filename/ article-id-2886.pdf

Wang, S. W., & Lau, A. S. (2018). Ethnicity moderates the benefits of perceived sup-port and emotional expressivity on stress reactivity for Asian Americans and Euro Americans. *Cultural Diversity and Ethnic Minority Psychology*, *24*(3), 363.

Watkins, M. & Shulman, H. (2008). *Toward psychologies of liberation.* Palgrave Macmillan.

Weinhardt, L. S., Xie, H., Wesp, L. M., Murray, J. R., Apchemengich, I., Kioko, D., Weinhardt, C. B., & Cook-Daniels, L. (2019). The role of family, friends, and significant other support in well-being among transgender and non-binary youth. *Journal of GLBT Family Studies*, *15*(4), 311–325.

Westerman, A. (2018, June 25). Why international adoption cases in the U.S. have plummeted. *NPR*. https://www.npr.org/2018/06/25/623114766/why-international-adoption-cases-in-the-u-s-have-plummeted

Williams, D., & Williams-Morris, R. (2000). Racism and mental health: The African American experience. *Ethnicity and Health*, *5*(3–4), 243–268.

Wong, D. (1987). Preventing child sexual assault among Southeast Asian refugee families. *Children Today*, *16*(6), 18–22.

Wu, C., Qian, Y., & Wilkes, R. (2021). Anti-Asian discrimination and the Asian–White mental health gap during COVID-19. *Ethnic and Racial Studies*, *44*(5), 819–835.

Wyatt, G. E., & Peters, S. D. (1986). Methodological considerations in research on the prevalence of child sexual abuse, *Child Abuse & Neglect*, *10*(2), 241–251, https://doi.org/10.1016/0145-2134(86)90085-2

Wyatt, R. C. (n.d.). *Kenneth V. Hardy on multiculturalism and psychotherapy.* Psychotherapy. Retrieved January 4, 2023, from https://www.psychotherapy.net/interview/kenneth-hardy

Xiong, M. (2014). *Manichan Xiong.* University of Minnesota, Immigration History Research Center. https://umedia.lib.umn.edu/item/p16022coll554:13?facets%5Bcollection_name_s%5D%5B%5D=Immigrant+Stories&page=3&rows=100

Yakushko, O. (2019). Eugenics and its evolution in the history of western psychology: A critical archival review. *Psychotherapy and Politics International*, *17*(2), e1495.

Yamazaki-Jones, J. (2023). *Anti-Asian American racial microaggressions in psychology graduate programs: Mental health and the role of internalized racialism* [Unpublished doctoral dissertation]. Wright Institute Graduate School of Psychology.

Yan, B. W., Hwang, A. L., Ng, F., Chu, J. N., Tsoh, J. Y., & Nguyen, T. T. (2021). Death toll of COVID-19 on Asian Americans: Disparities revealed. *Journal of General Internal Medicine*, 1–5. Advance online publication. https://doi.org/10.1007/s11606-021-07003-0

Yang, C. C., Tsai, J. Y., & Pan, S. (2020). Discrimination and well-being among Asians / Asian Americans during COVID-19: The role of social media. *Cyberpsychology, Behavior, and Social Networking*, *23*(12), 865–870.

Yee, A. (2021, March 2). It's a myth that Asian Americans are doing well during the pandemic. *Scientific American.* https://www.scientificamerican.com/article/its-a-myth-that-asian-americans-are-doing-well-in-the-pandemic/

Yeh, C., & Hwang, M. (1999). The sociocultural context of Asian Pacific American ethnic identity and self: Implications for counseling. In D. S. Sandhu (Ed.), *Asian and Pacific Islander Americans: Issues and concerns for counseling and psychotherapy.* Nova Science Publishers.

Yi, V., Mac, J., Na, V. S., Venturanza, R. J., Museus, S. D., Buenavista, T. L., & Pendakur, S. L. (2020). Toward an anti-imperialistic critical race analysis of the model minority myth. *Review of Educational Research*, *90*(4), 542–579.

Yi, V., & Museus, S. D. (2015). Model minority myth. In *The Wiley Blackwell encyclopedia of race, ethnicity, and nationalism* (pp. 1–2). John Wiley & Sons.

Yip, T., Chung, K., & Chae, D. H. (2022). Vicarious racism, ethnic/racial identity, and sleep among Asian Americans. *Cultural Diversity and Ethnic Minority Psychology.* doi: 10.1037/cdp0000534

Yu, Y. (2021, May 14). *How inclusive is "AAPI"? Pacific Islanders debate the label.* Today. https://www.today.com/news/how-inclusive-aapi-pacific-islanders-debate-label-t218371?fbclid=IwAR3I3vnGBh_4L4ONi9vmCbUN2o0A6L2a0VfVUbmdrSmV7XFXfwf9sjv_s48

Yuen, N. Y., Nahulu, L. B., Hishinuma, E. S., & Miyamoto, R. H. (2000). Cultural identification and attempted suicide in Native Hawaiian adolescents. *Journal of the American Academy of Child & Adolescent Psychiatry*, 39(3), 360–367.

Yusin, J. (2017). *The future life of trauma: Partitions, borders, repetition*. Fordham University Press.

Zane, N., & Yeh, M. (2002). The use of culturally-based variables in assessment: Studies on loss of face. In Kurasaki, K. S., Okazaki, S., & Sue, S. (Eds.), *Asian American mental health: Assessment theories and methods* (pp. 123–138). Kluwer Academic/Plenum.

Zesch, S. (2012). *The Chinatown war: Chinese Los Angeles and the massacre of 1871* (Kindle ed.). Oxford University Press.

Zhai, F., & Gao, Q. (2009). Child maltreatment among Asian Americans: Characteristics and explanatory framework. *Child Maltreatment*, *14*(2), 207–224. https://doi.org/10.1177/1077559508326286

Zou, L. X., & Dickter, C. L. (2013). Perceptions of racial confrontation: The role of color blindness and comment ambiguity. *Cultural Diversity and Ethnic Minority Psychology*, *19*(1), 92.

Index

About the Author

For more than two decades, **Dr. Shin Shin Tang** has provided psychotherapy to a wide range of Asian and Asian American communities, including war refugees, adoptees, veterans, international students, immigrants, and subsequent generations. She has also conducted national and international research focusing on the intersection of trauma, gender, and culture. A former engineering major at UC Berkeley, Dr. Tang earned her PhD in clinical psychology from the University of Oregon, where she also served as adjunct faculty. She maintains a private practice in Eugene, Oregon, the traditional homeland of the Kalapuya people. Her website shinshintang.com hosts resources for therapy with Asians and Asian Americans.

www.ingramcontent.com/pod-product-compliance
Lightning Source LLC
Chambersburg PA
CBHW052004270326
41929CB00015B/2788